GOD LOVES

GOD LOVES

JESUS CHRIST ENTERS THE WORLD

Ave Maria Press AVE Notre Dame, Indiana

Textbook Writers
Michael Amodei
Michael Pennock

Educational Consultant
Sara Burmeister, PhD
Assistant Clinical Professor
College of Education
Marquette University

Sacred art is true and beautiful when its form corresponds to its particular vocation: evoking and glorifying, in faith and adoration, the transcendent mystery of God—the surpassing invisible beauty of truth and love visible in Christ, who "reflects the glory of God and bears the very stamp of his nature," in whom "the whole fullness of deity dwells bodily." This spiritual beauty of God is reflected in the most holy Virgin Mother of God, the angels, and saints. Genuine sacred art draws man to adoration, to prayer, and to the love of God, Creator and Savior, the Holy One and Sanctifier.

Catechism of the Catholic Church, 2502

We will begin each chapter with a short study and reflection on a piece of sacred art in order to visually portray an important aspect of our faith and to pass on this wonderful tradition of our Catholic faith.

CONTENTS

Jesus Is the Way, the Truth, and the Life

Madonna and Child

➤*Duccio di Buoninsegna*

In comparison with large-scale frescoes and other altarpieces of the day, the relatively small eight-by-eleven-inch painting *Madonna and Child* evokes even by its size an intimate look shared between the Infant Christ and his mother.

Because of its compact size, *Madonna and Child* was likely intended to be a source of prayerful meditation when placed in a church. The burn marks at the bottom of the painting are from candles placed under it. Painted by Duccio di Buoninsegna (ca. 1255–1260), an important Italian artist from Siena, the work reflects the influence of the medieval period. Yet it also gives a glimpse of how Duccio himself influenced the Renaissance, which was to come about a century after the completion of this painting.

The humanism present reveals a hint of the Renaissance; note the infant pulling the veil back from his mother's face in order to get a close and loving glimpse of her. On the other hand, Mary's expression is one of sadness as she knows what is ahead for her Son. The "fence" at the bottom of the painting is intended to draw the eyes upward to give full attention to the mother and child. The sharing of detailed human expressions, and even the crevices and folds of Mary's veil, are meant to communicate the mystery of God becoming man and participating in our world.

Duccio's *Madonna and Child* is now on display at the Metropolitan Museum of Art in New York. After passing through private ownership for most of the nineteenth and twentieth centuries, the painting was acquired by the museum in 2004 at an estimated cost of $45 million. The high price is due in part to the rarity of Duccio's works; there are only thirteen known surviving paintings by the artist in the world.

If you would like to learn more about when and where Madonna and Child *was created, see Chapter 1 Review, Chapter Project 1.*

How is Jesus both true God and true man?

Chapter Overview

Introduction

God Reveals Himself to Us

Section 1

How Is Jesus True God?

Section 2

How Is Jesus True Man?

Section 3

Historical Evidence and Beliefs about Jesus from Outside of Christianity

Section 4

The Truth of Christ Is Preserved in the Church

GOD REVEALS HIMSELF TO US

No matter the hectic nature of your life—maintaining a GPA, participating in extracurriculars, working a part-time job, having a social life, living in a family—you are bound to sometimes look way out into your future and ask yourself "the big questions": "Why am I here?" "What is the purpose of life?" "What happens after I die?" Asking these questions is not out of the normal. There is no escaping that you are hardwired for something more than any of your current tasks and goals.

The perennial big questions have been asked by people for all time. Neither is this by accident. You were, indeed, made for *much, much more.* You instinctively know that you are unique among all other people. Scientifically, it is a factual statement to say that no one else exists or has existed with your exact DNA. Your life didn't come about by chance. There is a Creator who designed you and brought you into existence. The Almighty God who made you understandably wants you, his creation, to be connected with him. Think of the bond parents want with their children. God desires this connection on an even deeper level, a level called *communion.* The *Catechism of the Catholic Church* puts it this way: "The desire for God is written in the human heart, because [you have been] created by God and for God" (27).

Sometimes these big questions come to the forefront when you are disappointed by something or someone. Or you may even feel pensive in this way after successfully reaching a goal that you worked very hard to achieve. After a bit of jubilation, you may have thought to yourself, "Is that *it*?" Even people who achieve the highest levels of success in business, athletics, popular stardom—whatever—usually end up asking themselves that exact same question: "Is that *it*?" Typically, though, most of us brush off the thought and move on to the next goal. However, it *is* worth your time to give the big questions of life some additional consideration. This course will provide information and resources to help you examine in greater detail someone Catholics profess to be the Incarnate Son of God who came to the earth to provide answers. That person is Jesus Christ. The Apostle Thomas asked Jesus a "big question" at the Last Supper: "How can we know the way?" Jesus replied, "I am the way and the truth and the life" (Jn 14:5, 6).

Waiting for the Messiah

Through human reason, people from all time have formed answers to questions about life, death, eternity, and God himself. Human reason allows us the capacity for understanding *some* of life's mystery. For example, humans know instinctively that killing an innocent person is wrong. Human reason is not enough to understand the deepest and complete designs of God, however. God himself must reveal himself and the depths of the plans he has for human beings. God did so through the course of *salvation history*, the name for the account of God's saving activity and intervention on humanity's behalf. The events of salvation history are told in Sacred Scripture, in both the Old Testament and the New Testament.

God's Revelation progressed in response to the **Original Sin** of the first humans, named Adam and Eve, who rejected a life of communion with God.∞ After their fall, he chose a specific ethnic people to be his own and began to reveal himself to them over centuries. Through a series of covenants

∞ Note

Redemption in Christ, which will be covered in more depth throughout this text, includes forgiveness of Original Sin and all personal sins in the Sacrament of Baptism. However, the other effects of Original Sin, including the struggle with concupiscence (inclinations to sin), remain and call people to maintain a constant spiritual battle with evil (see *CCC*, 409).

Original Sin Refers to the personal sin of the first two people, called Adam and Eve, which, in an analogous way, describes the fallen state of human nature into which all generations are born. Adam and Eve transmitted Original Sin to their descendants. Jesus came to save the world from Original Sin and all personal sin.

The Last Supper.

(see accompanying infographic) with the Israelites (later called the Jews), God offered human beings a new chance not only to know him but to know him better. Within the Sinai Covenant with Moses, for example, God provided a Law to help them better understand how they should live moral lives. This was something other nations did not possess. Ultimately, God offered the promise of **redemption**, which many Israelites understood would come from a chosen prophet, king, or messiah.

The New Testament period of the early first century AD was high in messianic expectations. Most Jews believed that God would send his Chosen One, the Messiah, very soon. The Hebrew word *masiah* translates to the Greek word *Christos* (Christ), which means "anointed one." At first, the title messiah applied to the king of Israel (i.e., King David and his successors). However, David's successors were mostly weak and corrupt.

Even when the monarchy era ended for the Jews, the belief in God's promise to provide a messiah never died among them. By the time of Jesus, many Jews increasingly believed that a messiah would usher in God's Kingdom or reign. Various Jewish sects in Jesus's day (e.g., the Sadducees, Pharisees, Zealots, and Essenes) had different expectations about who or what kind of person the Messiah would be. Most Jews expected a political or military leader

---

redemption The name for Christ's sacrificial Death on the Cross that paid the price to free us from the slavery of sin.

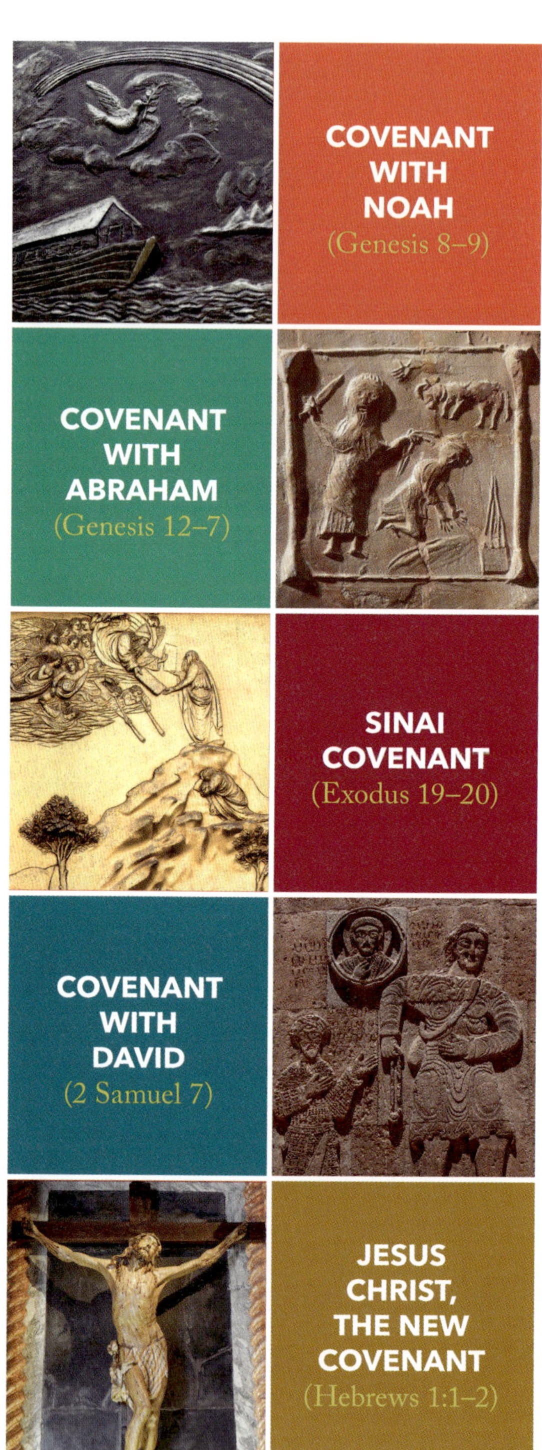

like King David who would lead them to reestablish a strong, independent nation of Israel and help usher in God's Kingdom on earth. Some Jews (possibly including John the Baptist) fully expected the coming of the Messiah to be accomplished in a dramatic, *apocalyptic* event, which would point to the Messiah's identity and the glorious establishment of God's Kingdom.

The Uniqueness of Jesus

What none of the Jews or anyone else of the first century could have imagined was that the Messiah would be a God/Man. Jesus is unique in that in his one Divine Person he brings together the human and divine natures. This is called the *hypostatic union*.∞ Jesus is not "part man, part God." He is not a mixture of the two. Nor is he sometimes God, sometimes man, as if he could turn one or the other on and off as with a light switch. **Jesus became truly man while remaining truly God.** This truth about Jesus, the Messiah, means that he is *most unique* in all human history; the Incarnation—that is, the coming of God in human form to this planet—happened only once. As Pope John Paul II wrote in *Crossing the Threshold of Hope*, "If he were only a wise man like Socrates, if he were a 'prophet' like Muhammad, if he were an 'enlightened' like Buddha, without any doubt he would not be what he is. He is the one mediator between God and humanity. He is mediator because he is both God and man."[1]

Questions about the relationship between Jesus Christ's humanity and divinity are the focus of *Christology* and the subject of this course. All the Gospels address Christological questions, always with the purpose of helping us to know more about Jesus and understand that he is the Son of God. For example, the prologue of John's Gospel (1:1–18) stresses very strongly Jesus's heavenly origins, his fundamental identity as the Son of God, and his preexistence as the Word of God. While the synoptic Gospels also share several examples of Jesus's heavenly origins, their starting point is the concrete memories of Jesus of Nazareth and his impact on people. They then move on to develop his story as an ascent to heavenly glory through his Passion, Death, Resurrection, and Ascension.

All of God's Revelation is contained in the **Deposit of Faith**, which is the body of truths of Catholicism. The Deposit of Faith is contained in Sacred Scripture *and* Sacred Tradition. The study of Christ in this text will focus on the teachings of both Sacred Scripture and Sacred Tradition, which is the Church's doctrine, life, and worship as preserved by the Magisterium and passed on to every generation. Christ is the completion of God's Revelation and of salvation history. This includes teachings about Christ studied and taught

> **∞ Note**
>
> *Hypostatic* comes from a Greek term that means "which lies beneath as basis or foundation." The term was used by Greek philosophers to distinguish what can be seen on the surface from the reality that lies below.

Deposit of Faith The body of saving truths and core beliefs of Catholicism that are contained in Sacred Scripture and Sacred Tradition and are faithfully preserved and handed on by the Magisterium. The Deposit of Faith contains the fullness of God's Revelation.

by the Church.∞ The Church, guided by the Holy Spirit, is the protector of Sacred Tradition. It is the Church who teaches about Christ and with Christ's own authority.

> **∞ Note**
>
> The Second Vatican Council teaches, "The most intimate truth which this revelation gives us about God and the salvation of man shines forth in Christ, who is himself both the mediator and the fullness of all revelation" (*Dei Verbum*, 2).

SECTION Assessment

Comprehension

1. How did Jesus answer the Apostle Thomas's question, "How can we know the way?"

2. Name the major Old Testament covenants God made with the Jewish people.

3. What was a common Jewish expectation of a messiah in Jesus's time?

Vocabulary

4. What are two parts of the *Deposit of Faith*?

Reflection

5. What is a "big question" you have often asked yourself? What kind of answer did you formulate?

HOW IS JESUS TRUE GOD?

"Is Jesus of Nazareth God?" was one of the most pressing questions faced by the first disciples. Imagine being raised a faithful Jew and having to explain to your parents and family members that you have come to believe that an itinerant preacher, the son of a carpenter from an out-of-the-way village, is God in the flesh.

John's Gospel, the final Gospel written, provides a source to help answer the question of Jesus's divinity. One way that John's Gospel emphasizes the divinity of Jesus is to show him always present with the Father and in control of all things, including creation. In fact, this focus on Jesus's divinity is present in the famous prologue at the very beginning of John's Gospel:

> In the beginning was the Word,
> and the Word was with God,
> and the Word was God.
> He was in the beginning with God.
> All things came to be through him,
> and without him nothing came to be.
> What came to be through him was life,
> and this life was the light of the human race;
> the light shines in the darkness,
> and the darkness has not overcome it. . . .
> And the Word became flesh
> and made his dwelling among us,
> and we saw his glory,
> the glory as of the Father's only Son,
> full of grace and truth. (Jn 1:1–5, 14)

John used the expression "the Word became flesh" to state emphatically that God assumed human nature and became man. John may have done so to counteract a first-century heresy known as **Docetism** (see the subsection "Jesus's Humanity Is Confirmed" in Chapter 1, Section 4). Docetists did not believe that God would demean himself by taking on all the weakness of humanity. To Docetists, Jesus *seemed* to be a man or *seemed* to take on the appearance of a man but not the reality of a man—that is, his body was an illusion. The presence of this heresy indicates that, for many, it was difficult to comprehend that God the Son assumed a human nature with a human body without losing his divine nature.

The Gospels provide other evidence of Jesus's divinity. For example, Jesus asked his disciples who they and others believed him to be: "Who do people say that I am?" (Mk 8:27). The disciples replied with various answers, saying that he was John the Baptist, Elijah, or other prophets. **When Jesus directly asked the disciples, "But who do you say that I am?" Peter answered correctly, "You are the Messiah" (v. 29), but was then chastised by Jesus for contradicting what being the Messiah really entailed.** The next time Jesus asked the disciples for reactions to his explanation of his identity, "they did not understand the saying, and they were afraid to question him" (Mk 9:32). When Jesus was charged with blasphemy and questioned by the Jewish court as to whether he was "the Messiah, the son of the Blessed One" (Mk 14:61), he responded "I am," indicating the traditional Jewish name, YHWH, for God.

Interestingly, some people who were not followers of Jesus could also recognize his divinity. These were people who were possessed by demons. In Luke's Gospel, a man in a synagogue plagued with an evil spirit shrieked, "Ha! What have you to do with us, Jesus of Nazareth? Have you come to destroy us? I know who you are—the Holy One of God!" (Lk 4:34). Jesus told him to "Be quiet!" Then the man was healed. The demon threw the man to the ground and "came out of him without doing him any harm" (v. 35). Other examples of demons recognizing the divinity of Jesus are recorded in Mark 1:21–28 and Luke 4:31–37; 8:26–39. Demons identified who Jesus was by perceiving his holiness, which was a threat to the evil of Satan. As the holy

---

Docetism A first-century heresy that taught that Jesus only "seemed" to be human. Docetism comes from a Greek word meaning "to seem."

Son of God, Jesus came to save humankind from all that is not good, right, and just—that is, all evil—even Satan, the father of evil.

After the apostolic era, the Church addressed heresies about Jesus that claimed just the opposite of Docetism. Rather than denying his humanity, other heresies denied Jesus's divinity. A priest from Alexandria, Arius (AD 250–336), held that Christ was God's greatest creature, who was made before time but a creature nonetheless. He taught that Christ did not take on human flesh, arguing that if he *had* taken on human flesh, he could not be God. He also falsely taught that if Christ was God, there would be two gods. **Arianism** had grave consequences for the Church's teaching on salvation. The Church responded to Arianism and other false teachings at gatherings, or councils, of bishops and church leaders (see the subsection "Jesus's Divinity Is Confirmed" in Chapter 1, Section 4), clarifying the Church's belief that Jesus Christ is both truly man and truly God.

Ethiopian Christians annually celebrate the Baptism of Jesus at the Timkat Festival. Timkat *is the Ethiopian word for Baptism.*

Arianism A heresy common in certain times and places during the early Church that denied that Jesus was truly God. It is named after Arius (AD 250–336), a priest and popular preacher from Alexandria, Egypt.

Jesus Fulfilled Old Testament Prophecies

The Old Testament contains many prophecies about the coming Messiah. A careful reading of the Gospels makes a clear case that Jesus fulfilled all of these prophecies concerning God's Anointed One. These include the prophecies that declared:

- He would be born of the tribe of Judah (Gn 49:10).

- He would be of the House of David (Is 11:1–2).

- He would be born in Bethlehem (Mi 5:1).

- He would be born of a virgin (Is 7:14).

- He would be worshipped by kings from afar (Ps 72:10).

- His Death and the manner of his suffering were also foretold:

- He would be betrayed (Ps 41:10).

- He would be sold for thirty pieces of silver (Zec 11:12–13).

- He would suffer for the sins of humankind (Is 50:6).

- He would be led like a lamb to slaughter (Is 53:7).

- He would have his hands and feet pierced (Ps 22:17).

Jesus himself also made prophecies that were fulfilled. For example, he predicted that he would be condemned to death by the religious authorities, mocked by Gentiles, betrayed by one of his Apostles, and denied three times by Peter. He also predicted the destruction of the Temple, an event that occurred during the First Jewish Revolt (AD 66–70).

The fulfillment of the Old Testament prophecies and Jesus's own prophecies does indeed offer evidence that he truly is the Son of God, sent by the Father, to be the Savior of the world. As Jesus said when predicting his betrayal by Judas, "From now on I am telling you before it happens, so that when it happens you may believe that I AM" (Jn 13:19).

Jesus Performed Miracles

Another clear sign of Jesus's divinity is this: Anyone who has the power demonstrated by Jesus's miracles—the power over nature, sickness and death, Satan, and sin itself—must be God. The greatest sign of all was the Resurrection of Jesus from the dead. All four Gospels cite miracles of Jesus. By definition, the miracles are "extraordinary and observable events that cannot be explained by human abilities or known natural forces." Miracles can only be explained by divine intervention. That is why the miracles of Jesus point to who he really is.

The miracles worked by Jesus attest that he came from the Father. They invite belief in him. To those who turn to him in faith, he grants what they ask. So miracles strengthen faith in the One who does his Father's works; they bear witness that he is the Son of God (see *CCC*, 548).

The number and variety of miracles Jesus performed were great (see Mark 1:32–34). There were physical healings, nature miracles (e.g., Jesus's walking on water), exorcisms (expulsion of evil spirits), and the raisings of people from the dead. In one dramatic example, Jesus raised his friend Lazarus, whose body had already been decaying in the tomb for several days when

Christ Walking on the Water *(1840?) by Aleksandr Ivanov.*

Jesus brought him back to life (see John 11:1–44).

The synoptic Gospels use the Greek word *dynamis*, which means "act of power," to describe Jesus's miracles. John's Gospel uses two Greek words, *ergon* (work) and *semeion* (sign), to indicate miracles. Jesus's "works and signs" reveal his glory, purpose, identity, and relationship to God the Father. His miracles were both *power*ful and *sign*ificant.

The vast majority of people who witnessed Jesus's miracles knew something spectacular was happening. They saw these miracles with their own eyes or were blessed to be healed themselves. Yet many other people doubted or misinterpreted the miracles. Some called Jesus a prophet. Others said he committed evil, as when he healed the man born blind on the Sabbath (see John 9:1–41). Some of his opponents said that the power of Jesus was emanating from Satan.

"[Jesus] cried out in a loud voice, 'Lazarus, come out!' The dead man came out, tied hand and foot with burial bands, and his face was wrapped in a cloth. So Jesus said to them, 'Untie him and let him go'" (Jn 11:43–44).

Jesus offered an explanation for why he performed miracles: "These works that I perform testify on my behalf that the Father has sent me" (Jn 5:36). His miracles were intended to help those who witnessed them to conclude that he is the Son of God.

Jesus Forgave Sins

Jesus also demonstrated his divine nature by forgiving people's sins. For example, note that the forgiveness of sins accompanied the healing of the paralytic (see Mark 2:1–12; Matthew 9:1–8; Luke 5:17–26). The connection between the forgiveness of sins and the cure of the paralytic was based on a common

Jewish belief of Jesus's time that illness and physical disabilities were the result of a person's own sin or the sin of his ancestors (see Exodus 20:5).

The healing and forgiving of the paralytic showed that Jesus had the power to heal both the inner brokenness of human beings—their sins—and their bodily ailments. This connection between physical healing and forgiveness of sins helped to establish Jesus's divinity. However, some scribes who heard Jesus forgive the man's sin accused him of blasphemy. This was a charge that Jesus would ultimately be convicted of by the Sanhedrin, the Jewish high court. During that trial, Joseph Caiaphas, the high priest, shouted to Jesus,

> "I order you to tell us under oath before the living God whether you are the Messiah, the Son of God." Jesus said to him in reply, "You have said so. But I tell you: From now on you will see 'the Son of Man seated at the right hand of the Power' and 'coming on the clouds of heaven.'" Then the high priest tore his robes and said, "He has blasphemed! What further need have we of witnesses? You have now heard the blasphemy; what is your opinion?" They said in reply, "He deserves to die!" (Mt 26:63–66)

"Which is easier, to say to the paralytic, 'Your sins are forgiven,' or to say, 'Rise, pick up your mat and walk'?" (Mk 2:9).

Jewish authorities sentenced Jesus for claiming to be something that no ordinary man could claim to be. For them, the claims of Jesus were an outrage, punishable by death under Mosaic Law. Notice that Jesus never said they were mistaken in their accusation.

Greatest Evidence: The Resurrection

While Jesus's "deeds, miracles, and words all revealed that 'in him the whole fullness of deity dwells bodily'" (*CCC*, 515, quoting Colossians 2:9), the most powerful evidence for Christ's divinity is provided by his Resurrection. As the *Catechism of the Catholic Church* teaches, "The Resurrection of the crucified one shows that he was truly 'I AM,' the Son of God and God himself" (653).

The Resurrection is a historical event involving the whole of Jesus's humanity (see the feature in Section 1, "Historical Arguments for the Resurrection of Jesus"). **The Father raised Jesus from the dead by the power of the Holy Spirit.** "After his Resurrection, Jesus's divine sonship becomes manifest in the power of his glorified humanity" (*CCC*, 445). During the forty days he was on earth after the Resurrection, Jesus's glory remained partially hidden "under the appearance of ordinary humanity" (*CCC*, 659). St. Paul wrote to the Corinthians:

> For I handed on to you as of first importance what I also received: that Christ died for our sins in accordance with the scriptures; that he was buried; that he was raised on the third day in accordance with the scriptures; that he appeared to Cephas, then to the Twelve. After that, he appeared to more than five hundred brothers at once, most of whom are still living, though some have fallen asleep. (1 Cor 15:3–6)

While Jesus historically rose from the dead within this world, the power by which he was resurrected was not an earthly or human power. The Father raised him from the dead by the power of the Holy Spirit. Once Jesus had risen in glory, the disciples could see and touch him and he could eat and speak as a human, yet he was no longer subservient to the laws of the created world. His risen body also showed the marks of his Passion. And yet, his Resurrection was not merely resuscitation or a return to earthly life (like the miracle of Lazarus); instead, his body was filled with the power of the Holy Spirit and thus transformed. This real body possessed the new properties of a

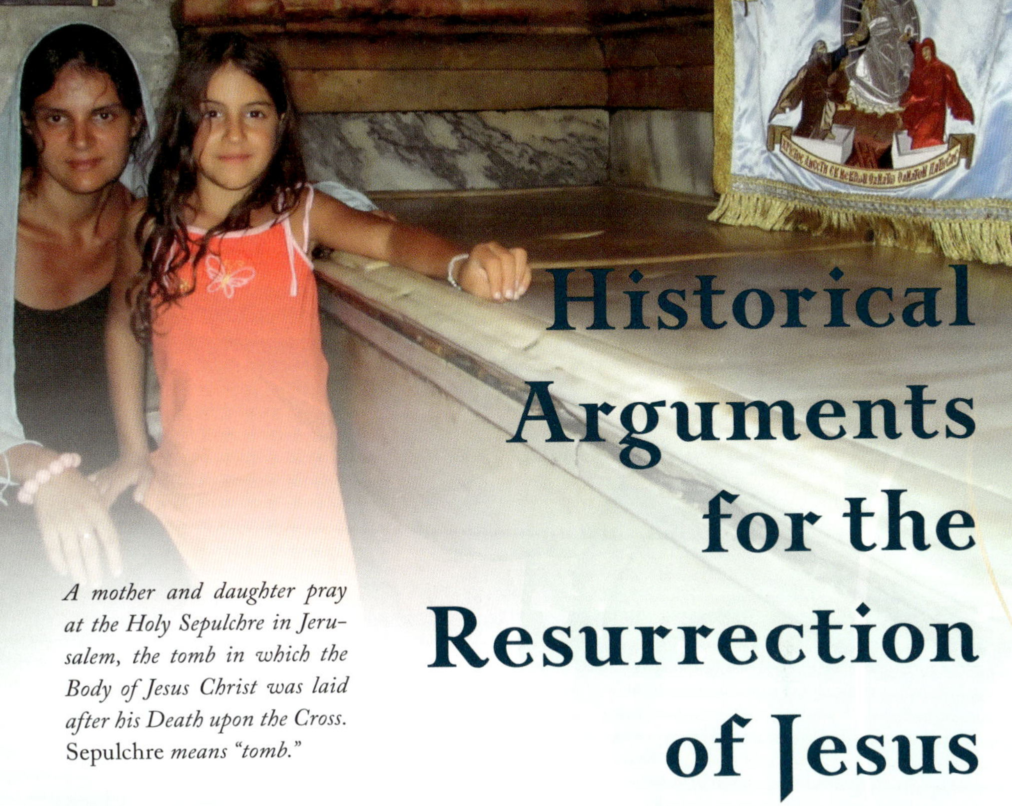

A mother and daughter pray at the Holy Sepulchre in Jerusalem, the tomb in which the Body of Jesus Christ was laid after his Death upon the Cross. Sepulchre means "tomb."

Historical Arguments for the Resurrection of Jesus

Focus Question: How is Jesus both true God and true man?

There is a great deal of historical evidence to prove that Jesus was a preacher who attracted many followers in the early first century AD in and around Galilee. His hometown was Nazareth, the home of his foster father, Joseph. There are many non-Christian sources that support the fact that Jesus was a historical person. (See Chapter 1, Section 3, "Historical Evidence and Beliefs about Jesus from Outside of Christianity.")

The argument that the Resurrection of Jesus was a historical event has one key piece of evidence missing: no other person witnessed his human body, crucified by the Romans on a cross (again plenty of historical evidence for the Crucifixion), either literally rising upward or disappearing in a flash from a tomb. Rather, the first source of evidence is that some of his women followers came to the tomb on the morning of the third day and saw it empty. The Gospels report they spoke to angels, a gardener, and Jesus himself in the various accounts. Though as his disciples they themselves were in danger from the Roman authorities, they boldly reported this news to the Apostles. What would be the benefit for them to create such a tale? That is one question to reflect on as we look for historical evidence of the Resurrection. Through several philosophical arguments, Catholics over the years have offered other step-by-step responses to arguments against the Resurrection as a historical event. Five such arguments and their responses[2] are briefly named below:

> **The disciples made up the story of Jesus's Resurrection.**

As mentioned, why would the disciples fabricate this account? Basically, they were cowards as evidenced by their lack of appearance near Jesus's trial or at Golgotha where he was crucified. They had everything to lose and nothing to gain by sharing this story.

> **Jesus died, but the Apostles and other disciples were deceived in some way. Maybe those who had encountered people at the tomb hallucinated. Maybe the Apostles themselves hallucinated Jesus's appearance to them in the forty days after his Crucifixion.**

Hallucinations do not last for forty days! To accept this argument, we would have to believe that hundreds of ordinary people with plenty of common sense all hallucinated.

> **The Resurrection of Jesus was a myth that the Apostles concocted to explain Jesus's message after he had died.**

The problem with this argument is that the Resurrection accounts were written down within thirty to sixty years after Jesus's life. Each of these accounts includes the names of real historical people that others would either know or know of. Also, the Resurrection accounts do not read like a myth. There are no fantastical symbols or magical characters. The accounts read as history. Even more evidence from Scripture comes from St. Paul's First Letter to the Corinthians (written approximately fifteen years after the earthly life of Jesus). In it he wrote a very precise and detailed account of appearances of the Risen Jesus: "[H]e appeared to Cephas, then to the Twelve. After that, he appeared to more than five hundred brothers at once, most of whom are still living, though some have fallen asleep. After that he appeared to James, then to all the apostles. Last of all, as to one born abnormally, he appeared to me" (1 Cor 15:5–8).

> **The Apostles stole Jesus's body in order to make up tales about the Resurrection (for some unknown reason).**

After Christ died on the Cross, the high priest asked Pontius Pilate to secure the burial site. Pilate authorized the use of a four-man guard. It is inconceivable that the disciples could have come to the tomb and moved the heavy stone while all four guards were sleeping at the same time.

> **Jesus didn't really die on the Cross. Maybe he just went into a coma or fainted.**

This argument would mean that Jesus survived a brutal scourging, being nailed to the Cross, and being stabbed in the side. Even if that were possible, he would then, in this injured state, have had to push the stone away from the cave by himself. Also, when Mary Magdalene and the disciples encountered a man they understood to be Jesus outside of the tomb, they conversed with him in a normal fashion. If he was badly injured and left for dead, it seems likely that Mary and the disciples would have gone to get medical help.

The most assured evidence of the Resurrection of Jesus comes from the Gospels themselves. Be careful not to dismiss the historical aspect of the writing because these accounts were authored by Jesus's disciples. One scholar refers to three markers that we can use to test whether the Resurrection accounts in the Gospels can be taken literally: (1) They have a history of being composed following an oral telling of the accounts; (2) they are set in a specific historical time and place; (3) they are written to convey historically accurate information, not as a homily to build up the faith of those who already believed.[3]

Comprehension

1. Why did the disciples have nothing to gain by making up a story about Christ's Resurrection?
2. How would it have been virtually impossible for the disciples to have stolen Jesus's body from the tomb?
3. Counter the argument that Jesus might not have been dead and removed the stone himself.

Reflection

Which argument against Jesus's Resurrection is least convincing to you? Which argument is most convincing? Explain.

glorious body, "not limited by space and time but able to be present how and when he wills; for Christ's humanity can no longer be confined to earth, and belongs henceforth only to the Father's divine realm" (*CCC*, 645).

The significance of Christ's Resurrection cannot be overstated. It is the confirmation of Jesus's divinity and of his words and teachings, along with promises of the Old Testament. Jesus said, "When you lift up the Son of Man, then you will realize that I AM" (Jn 8:28). Indeed, "all truths, even those most inaccessible to human reason, find their justification if Christ by his Resurrection has given the definitive proof of his divine authority, which he had promised" (*CCC*, 651). Furthermore, Christ's Resurrection is a promise of our own resurrection:

> But now Christ has been raised from the dead, the firstfruits of those who have fallen asleep. For since death came through a human being, the resurrection of the dead came also through a human being. For just as in Adam all die, so too in Christ shall all be brought to life. (1 Cor 15:20–22)

SECTION Assessment

Comprehension

1. Name two Old Testament prophecies Jesus fulfilled.

2. What are two Old Testament passages that predict the type of suffering Jesus would experience?

3. Name one prophecy Jesus made about himself that was fulfilled.

4. What was Jesus's explanation for why he performed miracles?

5. Why is Jesus's response to the charge of blasphemy against him in itself a sign of his divinity?

6. What is the greatest evidence of Jesus's divinity?

Vocabulary

7. Define *Docetism*.

Reflection

8. Write at least one statement countering or casting doubt on each of the five arguments against the historical nature of Jesus's Resurrection.

HOW IS JESUS TRUE MAN?

In philosophy, the term *nature* refers to what something is. For example, trees possess the nature of being trees, elephants share the same nature as other elephants, and human beings share the same human nature as one another. Also, the Father, the Son, and the Holy Spirit share the same divine nature as the one God.

At the Incarnation, human nature was assumed or taken on by Christ, the Second Divine Person of the Blessed Trinity. It was not absorbed by him. "What he was, he remained and what he was not, he assumed," proclaims an ancient Church liturgy. This means that Jesus, the Son of God, did not redefine human nature when he became human. He didn't become a "different kind of human." Nor was human nature absorbed by his divine nature. Instead, Jesus assumed human nature and everything that goes with it—emotions, pain, work, sickness, and even death. Everything that belongs to Christ's human nature belongs to the Divine Person of the Son of God who assumed it.

In becoming fully human, Christ raised all people to a dignity that is beyond compare. He united himself with each individual. As the Second Vatican Council taught: "[He] worked with human hands; he thought with a human mind. He acted with a human will, and with a human heart he loved. Born of the Virgin Mary, he has truly been made one of us, like us in all things except sin" (*Gaudium et Spes*, 22, quoted in *CCC*, 470). **Christ indeed is like us in all things but sin. Christ had human knowledge of everything relating to God, including the private thoughts of other people. Christ knew of God's eternal plan for salvation.** In the words of seventh-century theologian St. Maximus the Confessor, "The human nature of God's Son, not by itself but by its union with the Word, knew and showed forth in itself everything that pertains to God" (quoted in *CCC*, 473).

We can learn more about what it means to be a human by knowing Christ. Since all human beings—the billions who are alive now—possess a human nature, each person, although different, possesses two qualities that make him or her a human being. These two qualities are a human body and a human soul. The soul is "the spiritual principle of human beings" (*CCC*, Glossary). The soul and body together form one human nature. To be a human, then, means having a body and an immortal soul. Jesus, the Second Divine Person of the Blessed Trinity, assumed these qualities too.

Vitruvian Man, drawn by Leonardo da Vinci in the fifteenth century, was inspired by the writings of the ancient Roman artist Vitruvius. It is meant to depict da Vinci's conception of the ideal human body. It is rarely on public display because of the drawing's sensitivity to light. It was borrowed by the Louvre in 2019 for an exhibit to mark the five hundredth anniversary of da Vinci's death.

Jesus: Human in Both Body and Soul

As the Second Divine Person of the Blessed Trinity, Jesus possessed a divine nature. His Divine Person assumed a human nature at the time of the Incarnation. This means that Jesus took on a human body and a human soul, the two qualities that make up a human being. Except for being free from Original Sin as well as from all personal sin, Jesus's human body was like ours:

- He was hungry—for example, when he fasted in the desert (Mt 4:2).

- He was thirsty—for example, when he met and talked with the Samaritan woman at the well (Jn 4:6–29) and when he hung on the Cross (Jn 19:29).

- He was tired. He said, "Foxes have dens and birds of the sky have nests, but the Son of Man has nowhere to rest his head" (Lk 9:58).

All human bodies are corruptible. From the moment you are born, your body is at once growing to full maturity and also beginning a process that culminates in its death. Jesus suffered death. In fact, Jesus endured one of the cruelest forms of capital punishment. The actual cause of his Death could have been asphyxiation, brought about when he could no longer raise his chest to inhale and fill his lungs as he hung on the Cross. Jesus's suffering and Death bore a new understanding of what happens to

A painting by J. Lepesov, titled Aral Sea Pieta, *of Mary holding her Son. The Aral Sea is a dried-up lake between Kazakhstan and Uzbekistan.*

the human body after it dies. Understanding Jesus's suffering and Death is connected explicitly to his Paschal Mystery (see the subsection "What Did Jesus Teach about Suffering?" in Chapter 2, Section 2).

Regarding Jesus's human soul, you will recall the mention of several heresies concerning Jesus's human and divine nature that arose in the early Church. A related heresy erupted in the fourth century. Apollinaris the Younger, the bishop of Laodicea, taught that, though Jesus had a human body, he had no human soul. This heresy is known as *Apollinarianism.*

Though the doctrine of hypostatic union had not been formally defined in the fourth century, Pope Damasus I responded to Apollinarianism at the Council of Rome in 382, stating that Jesus did have a human soul that "is endowed with a true human knowledge" (*CCC*, 472). This is why, in fact, Jesus was able to grow in "wisdom and age and favor before God and man" (Lk 2:52). At the Third Council of Constantinople in 681, the Church formally taught against Apollinarianism and declared that Christ possesses two wills and two natural ways of operating, a divine nature and a human nature. The council taught that Christ's human will "does not resist or oppose but rather submits to his divine and almighty will."

Other references in the Gospels help to explain the mysterious union of Jesus's divine and human natures in one Divine Person. For example, consider the story of a woman suffering from a hemorrhage who pushed through a swarming crowd and touched the tassel on Jesus's cloak. Immediately her bleeding stopped (see Luke 8:43–48). Jesus asked Peter and his other disciples, "Who touched me?" Peter recognized the futility of answering Jesus. There were so many people "pushing and pressing" against Jesus. But Jesus persisted: "Someone has touched me; for I know that power has gone out from me" (Lk 8:46). By asking this question, Jesus showed that he was completely aware of the woman who had faith. He was completely aware that she was healed.

Jesus's question provides a remarkable glimpse into the interplay between his human nature and divine nature. The **Church Fathers** called miracles "Theandric actions"—that is, divine deeds done humanly. In this case, through the woman touching the humanity of Jesus, she was healed by his divine power or that of the Holy Spirit. This incident teaches that Jesus hears and answers prayers, whether expressed to him in words or in silence as this woman had prayed. Also, this miracle teaches that Jesus did not do some deeds as a man and some deeds as God. Everything that the Son of God did as a man was done humanly because that is the manner in which he existed—as a man.

Jesus interacted with people in a most loving, caring, and compassionate human way. In union with the Word, the Son of God had immediate knowledge of the Father and of the secret thoughts of people. He was always aware of "God's big picture," the eternal plan of salvation that he came to reveal. The early Church condemned those who denied that Jesus had a human body (Gnostics) and those who denied that Jesus had a human soul (Apollinarius). Jesus, the Second Divine Person of the Blessed Trinity, was fully human and therefore possessed a human body, a human intellect, a human will, and a human soul just as we do.

Church Fathers Bishops, theologians, teachers, and scholars whose writings have greatly contributed to Church doctrine and practice. In both the Western Church and the Eastern Church, four Fathers are most prominent. In the Western Church, they are St. Ambrose (AD 340-397), St. Jerome (AD 347-420), St. Augustine (AD 354-430), and St. Gregory the Great (AD 540-604). In the Eastern Church, they are St. Basil (ca. AD 329-379), St. Athanasius (ca. AD 296-373), St. Gregory of Nazianzus (AD 329-ca. 398), and St. John Chrysostom (AD 347-407).

Jesus Understands Our Human Experience

As far as Jesus's human nature was concerned, he matured like anyone else. He gained knowledge as any other human. Jesus gained three kinds of knowledge by way of his human nature:

1. The knowledge of God by virtue of hypostatic union. This type of knowledge did not increase throughout Jesus's human life. He always possessed it at the same ultimate degree.

2. Infused knowledge, that is, the type of knowledge that could read the thoughts and hearts of other people. Jesus knew everything. Again, this type of knowledge did not grow; he always possessed it.

3. Acquired knowledge, that is, the type of knowledge Jesus gained through his human experience and reflection. This type of knowledge increased as Jesus's life went on.

As true man, Jesus is able to understand our human experience because he lived a human life as fully as we do. His human experience is similar to ours physically, mentally, and emotionally. For example, Jesus felt and acted on many common emotions:

Jesus wept.

Jesus showed his grief at the death of his friend Lazarus (see John 11:35). He also wept over the holy city of Jerusalem, which he knew would not accept him as the Messiah and would face destruction (see Luke 19:41–44).

Jesus was joyful.

Jesus participated in many joyful occasions, such as the wedding feast at Cana (see John 2:2–11) and the meal with the repentant Zacchaeus (see Luke 19:1–10). Jesus also rejoiced when his seventy-two disciples came back from their mission (see Luke 10:21). Jesus so enjoyed himself on some occasions that his opponents mischaracterized his festive attitude by labeling him "a glutton and a drunkard" (Lk 7:34).

Jesus was angry.

Don't forget that, as an emotion or passion, anger is neither good nor evil in itself. It's what you do with anger that makes it good or bad. An example of a good angry response is if you see an innocent person being harmed. Anger can spur you to action. The Gospels describe examples of Jesus's anger. For example, he was angry when those in opposition to him questioned him about performing a healing miracle on the Sabbath (see Mark 3:5). He angrily cleared the money-changers out of the Temple because they were disrespecting a place of worship (see John 2:13–17). He was angry with Peter for suggesting that Jesus should not follow the way of the Cross (see Mark 8:33).

Jesus was distressed.

Certainly, approaching his arrest, trial, and Crucifixion, Jesus was worried, sorrowful, and distressed. At the Last Supper, he was deeply troubled that one of his disciples would betray him (see John 13:21). In the Garden of Gethsemane, Jesus told his Apostles, "My soul is sorrowful even to death" (Mt 26:38). Jesus genuinely feared his Death, yet he put his trust in the Father: "My Father, if it is possible, let this cup pass from me; yet, not as I will, but as you will" (Mt 26:39).

Jesus also gained wisdom through lived experience, which is related to acquired knowledge. From the first instance of his human existence, Jesus, like his mother, was full of grace, because he was true God by the hypostatic union.

SECTION Assessment

Comprehension

1. In what way did the Second Divine Person of the Blessed Trinity assume human nature?

2. What were exceptions to Jesus's sharing in human nature?

3. What did the Third Council of Constantinople teach to counteract the heresy of Apollinarianism?

4. How does Jesus's healing of the woman with the hemorrhage provide a glimpse of the interplay between Jesus's human nature and divine nature?

5. Explain the difference between Jesus's knowledge possessed by virtue of the hypostatic union, infused knowledge, and acquired knowledge.

Reflection

6. Which example of Jesus's expression of human emotion surprises you the most? Why?

HISTORICAL EVIDENCE AND BELIEFS ABOUT JESUS FROM OUTSIDE OF CHRISTIANITY

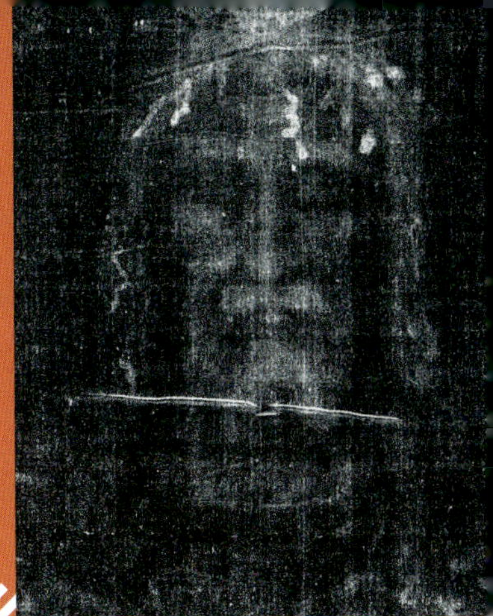

Recall the famous conversation that Jesus had with Thomas after allowing the Apostle to probe his wounds as proof that it was actually him, raised from the dead. Thomas exchanged his earlier unbelief for faith. "My Lord and my God!" he exclaimed. Jesus responded with words intended for generations that would follow, including our own: "Have you come to believe because you have seen me? Blessed are those who have not seen and have believed" (Jn 20:28–29).

Was Jesus a true man? There is no reason for even nonbelievers to doubt that Jesus of Nazareth existed. This fact can be easily shown through the historical record, the subject of this section. Within the Gospels and other writings of the New Testament, there are several historical references to people, dates, and events that can be verified by sources outside of Sacred Scripture. Likewise, there are numerous non-Christian references to Jesus and early Christianity that date from the second century and beyond.

Although these non-Christian sources do not provide detailed biographical information about Jesus, they strongly support the fact that a man named Jesus, and particularly followers of Jesus, did exist during the time suggested by New Testament writings and reports of early Christian writers. These non-Christian sources do not affirm Jesus's divinity, and at certain times they attempt to contradict it. Nevertheless, these ancient Roman, Jewish, and Greek writers made fascinating and interesting statements about Jesus and his followers that can benefit people today who first question if a man named Jesus lived on earth. It is ironic that Christians today can use statements made by non-Christians to prove to nonbelievers that there was a historical person, Jesus of Nazareth, who lived in the first century in Palestine. It is fortunate that these sources are available to us. Because of disasters like fire and plundering and the natural passing of time, only a fraction of what was written down in the ancient world has survived. Yet, while we don't have all the early documentation, we do possess enough to prove the existence of Jesus and his followers.

Roman Historians

Tacitus (ca. AD 56–117)

Cornelius Tacitus was a Roman senator and the greatest Roman historian of his time. His two most important works were *Histories*, which covered the years AD 69 to 96, and *Annals*, an unfinished work that chronicled the reigns of four Roman emperors: Tiberius, Caligula, Claudius, and Nero.

It is in *Annals* (ca. AD 115) that Tacitus mentions Jesus Christ. Writing of the Great Fire that broke out in Rome in AD 64 during the reign of Emperor Nero, Tacitus recounts that Nero blamed the fire on Christians as an excuse to persecute them:

> To suppress this rumor [that he had started the fire], Nero fabricated scapegoats—and punished with every refinement the notoriously depraved Christians (as they were popularly called). Their originator, Christ, had been executed in Tiberius's reign by the governor of Judea, Pontius Pilate. But in spite of this temporary setback the deadly superstition had broken out afresh, not only in Judea (where the mischief had started) but even in Rome. All degraded and shameful practices collect and flourish in the capital. (*Annals*, 15.44)

This account verifies that the public ministry of Jesus took place during the reign of Emperor Tiberius. Luke's Gospel also mentions this important detail (see Luke 3:12). Tacitus likely used Roman records to chronicle history. He is the only Roman historian to mention Pontius Pilate, although two Jewish writers—Josephus and Philo—tell of Pilate's harsh rule in Judea.

Reading the passage from *Annals*, it is not hard to see the contempt that Tacitus had for Christianity. He described it as a "degrading and shameful" superstition that had made its way to Rome. He certainly was no Christian, but neither did he deny the existence of Jesus Christ. Also in *Annals*, he reported how some Christians were arrested, mocked, covered in the skins of animals, and then put before bloodthirsty dogs. Others were crucified. He also wrote that Nero soaked the corpses of Christians with oil and burned them as torches.

Suetonius (ca. AD 70–140)

Gaius Suetonius Tranquillus was a Roman biographer and writer. Though his writings do not reveal much information about Jesus, he does verify that Christians were upsetting Roman authorities just two decades after the Death and Resurrection of Christ. In fact, one of the details he wrote about was an incident in which Jews and Christians were removed from Rome during the reign of Emperor Claudius (41–54). In his *Lives of the Caesars* (ca. 112), he wrote, "He expelled the Jews from Rome on account of the riots in which they were constantly indulging, at the instigation of Chrestus" (24).

There are some errors in this account. Suetonius assumed that Jesus (whom he misnamed "Chrestus") was there and responsible for the incident. What was more likely the case is that when the first Christians went to Rome to preach in the Jewish synagogues about Jesus as the Messiah, they were met with violent resistance by some Jews. Claudius apparently believed that Christians and Jews were members of the same religious sect. Therefore, he banished them all after their public infighting. Interestingly, this incident is also referred to in the Acts of the Apostles (see Acts 18:2).

Pliny the Younger (ca. AD 61–113)

Gaius Plinius Caecilius Secundus was the nephew and adopted son of the Roman writer Pliny the Elder. Known as Pliny the Younger, Secundus was a Roman senator. He is most noted for his books of letters, many of which are literary masterpieces. His references to Christ and Christians occur in his last volume of letters, including his own correspondence with Emperor Trajan when Trajan was the governor of Bithynia (modern Turkey) in AD 111–113. These letters are the largest collection of administrative correspondence from Roman times.

In Letter 96, Pliny wrote to Emperor Trajan asking how to deal with Christians who would not submit to Roman law and beliefs. In this letter, he gives the impression that Christians were foolish zealots, though he admits they were people who lived morally. Pliny was concerned about what he called a "superstition" because it challenged the Roman practice of worshipping the emperor. Note a following key part of Pliny's letter to Trajan:

> They asserted that this was the sum and substance of their error; namely that they were in the habit of meeting before dawn on a stated day and singing alternately a hymn to Christ as to a god, and then they bound themselves by an oath, not to the commission of any wicked deed, but that they would abstain from theft and robbery and adultery, that they would not break their word, and that they would not withhold a deposit to meet together again for a meal, which however was of the ordinary kind and quite harmless. (Epp. X. 96/97: Lightfoot's translation)

This passage is filled with important historical data. It tells that Christians met together to worship, to sing hymns to Christ, to recite a creed, to promise to live morally, and to worship Christ as God. Nonetheless, the Romans thought the Christians to be worthy of death. Trajan wrote back, reassuring Pliny that he had done well in dealing with Bithynian Christians. The emperor confirmed that any Christians who came to Pliny's attention should be punished, but also said that Pliny should not go looking for them.

A Jewish Historian

Josephus (ca. AD 37–101)

Born Joseph ben Matthias in AD 37, Josephus was commander of the Jewish forces in Galilee during the First Jewish Revolt (AD 66–70). Josephus was captured by the Romans, but he became a confidant and friend of a Roman commander, Vespasian, who became Roman emperor in AD 68. Josephus's life was spared because of this friendship, and he became a Roman citizen.

Josephus wrote *The Jewish Wars* and a twenty-volume history of the Jews, *Jewish Antiquities*. These two works are major sources of historical information on the Jews and life in Palestine under Roman rule. In *Jewish Antiquities*, Josephus writes of John the Baptist, calling him "a good man" (18). In book 20 of the series, he notes that Annas the Younger—the son of the Jewish high priest mentioned in John 18:12–24—put to death James the Just in AD 62. He refers to James as the "brother of Jesus who is called Christ."

Most noteworthy of Josephus's writings for our current study is his account of the rule of Pontius Pilate. Though it is credited to Josephus, note that some passages sound as if they were written by a Christian believer:

> Now about this time lived Jesus, a wise man, if indeed he should be called a man. He was a doer of wonderful works, a teacher of men who receive truth with pleasure, and won over many Jews and Greeks. He was the Christ. And when Pilate, at the information of the leading men among us sentenced him to the cross, those who loved him at the start did not cease to do so, for he appeared to them alive again on the third day as had been foretold—both this and ten thousand other wonderful things concerning him—by the divine prophets. Nor is the tribe of Christians, so named after him, extinct to this day. (*Jewish Antiquities*, 18)

Did you notice the parts that sound like faith statements (e.g., "he was a doer of wonderful works" and "he was the Christ")? Church Father Origen was adamant that Josephus never accepted Christianity. One theory is that a Christian copyist added certain passages to Josephus's writings to support Christian beliefs.

Regardless, it is clear that this Jewish historian, a nonbeliever in Christ, did not question the historical existence of Jesus or that Jesus was put to death at Pilate's order sometime between AD 26 and 36. Further, Josephus states that the followers of Jesus were very much present at the end of the first century.

Greek Historians and Writers

Thallus (wrote ca. AD 55)

Thallus was a Greek historian. Many of his writings detailing the history of the eastern Mediterranean from the period of the fall of Troy in the twelfth century BC to around AD 50 have not survived. However, a portion of his writings were quoted in historical documents of a third-century writer whose work was, in turn, preserved by a Byzantine historian (ca. 800).

The quotation from Thallus in the Byzantine source concerns the earthquake and darkness that descended on the land when Jesus died (see Matthew 27:45 and Luke 23:44–45). Thallus wrote that the darkness was caused by a natural eclipse of the sun. It appears he was attempting to refute the miraculous aspect of what occurred, but his testimony instead strengthens the fact that Jesus often accompanied his words with "mighty deeds, wonders, and signs" (Acts 2:22). What is interesting is that Thallus wrote about this incident at least fifteen years before the first Gospels were recorded. This would make Thallus the first known ancient writer to record elements surrounding Christ and Christianity.

This is a partial eclipse of the sun, a fairly regular occurrence. On April 8, 2024, a rare total solar eclipse occurred over most of North America.

Mara bar Serapion (wrote ca. AD 73)

Mara bar (*bar* is Aramaic for "son of") Serapion was a Greek philosopher. In a letter recovered in the seventh century, written in Syriac and addressed to his son, bar Serapion wrote about tyrants who made the mistake of killing their wise thinkers or rulers. Scholars believe that the "wise King" referred to in this passage is Jesus:

> What advantage did the Athenians gain from putting Socrates to death? Famine and plague came upon them as a judgment for their crime. What advantage did the men of Samos gain from burning Pythagoras? In a moment their land was covered with sand. What advantage did the Jews gain from executing their wise King? It was just after that their Kingdom was abolished. God justly avenged these three wise men: the Athenians died of hunger; the Samians were overwhelmed by the sea; the Jews, ruined and driven from their land, lived in complete dispersion. But Socrates did not die for good; he lived on in the teaching of Plato. Pythagoras did not die for good; he lived on in the statue of Hera. Nor did the wise King die for good; he lived on in the teaching that he had given.

Syriac writing is in cursive and written from right to left.

This text can be cited as secular historical evidence for Christ's Death. Mara bar Serapion thought that there was a link between the Death of the "wise King" and the destruction of the Jewish nation by the Romans. Jesus, the wise and just king, did predict such destruction (see Matthew 24:1–2). This passage was likely what bar Serapion was commenting on.

There are inaccuracies in his text, however. Bar Serapion unfairly implicates Jews collectively in the execution of Jesus. The events surrounding Jesus's trial were much more complex. Only God knows the personal sin of the participants (e.g., Judas, the Sanhedrin, Pilate). "Hence we cannot lay responsibility for the trial on the Jews in Jerusalem as a whole, despite the outcry of a manipulated crowd and the global reproaches contained in the apostles' calls to conversion after Pentecost" (*CCC*, 597). Bar Serapion further mentioned that the teaching of the wise King lived on through the teachings he left his followers.

Lucian of Samosata (wrote ca. AD 115–200)

Lucian was a Greek satirist. In one of his works, he mocked the Christian faith, including the belief in the Resurrection. He said Christians follow the teaching of "that one"—further describing "that one" as their founder and lawgiver who was crucified.

Celsus (wrote ca. AD 175)

Celsus was a late-second-century Greek philosopher who wrote a vicious attack on Christianity around AD 175. The writings of Celsus were preserved by Origen, whose work, *Against Celsus*, preserves some of the false charges Celsus made against Jesus. For example, Celsus claimed that Jesus was illegitimate and that his father was a Roman soldier named Panthera. Further, he claimed that Jesus went to Egypt to learn sorcery. Origen thoroughly and systematically refuted these false claims. It is clear that Celsus hated Christianity and hated Jesus Christ. However, he never denied the existence of Jesus Christ.

Besides the references of these Roman, Jewish, and Greek historians, philosophers, and writers, there is also a reference to Jesus in the Babylonian Talmud, a commentary on Jewish law written in the third century. One passage mentions a certain Yeshu (Jesus) who practiced magic and led Israel away from true Jewish worship. It also reports that this man had disciples and that he was "hanged on the eve of Passover."

SECTION Assessment

Comprehension

1. Why might Suetonius have connected Christians with the Jews who were removed from Rome during the reign of Emperor Claudius?

2. How did Pliny the Younger describe Christians?

3. Even if Christian faith statements were later added to Josephus's account in *Jewish Antiquities*, what value does it nevertheless hold as an independent historical source?

4. What incident common to the Gospels did Thallus write about at least fifteen years before the Gospels were recorded?

5. What title is it believed that Mara bar Serapion used to describe Jesus?

6. Where were the writings of Celsus preserved?

Reflection

7. Give some reasons why it is important for Christians that non-Christian sources validate that Jesus really existed.

8. Which of the historical resources from this section seem to be most important? Why?

9. In the ancient world, some Roman emperors required people to worship them. What are some of the false gods people worship today? How are people enticed to do so?

THE TRUTH OF CHRIST IS PRESERVED IN THE CHURCH

Every major religion founded before, during, and after the time of Jesus considers Jesus to be an important figure, and some of these religions acknowledge elements of his divine nature. For example, Hinduism, a religion dating back to about twelve centuries before Christ and based in India, holds that Jesus existed and was a wise teacher and holy man. Some Hindus acknowledge the divinity of Christ but not his unique divinity. Many Buddhists (including the fourteenth Dalai Lama, Tenzin Gyatso) recognize Jesus as a *bodhisattva*—that is, one who dedicates their life sacrificially for the betterment of others. Islam, a religion founded by Muhammad in the seventh century, reveres Jesus as a prophet.

Collectively, these non-Christian historians and religions do not reveal much about the life of Jesus, but they all recognize that Jesus really did exist. It would have been absurd for any ancient historian or faith leader to make any other assertion. Also, it would be highly unlikely for a movement—Christianity—to carry the name of a man who never existed and that other religions cited in their own writings. It would be even more difficult to deny that the Apostles all preached, under the risk of arrest and death, that Christ rose from the dead and that he was the Son of God.

During the first five centuries, the Church answered several questions about Jesus's identity. **Early Church Fathers helped to clarify teaching regarding the question "Who is Jesus Christ?"** The Church Fathers and bishops, gathered at ecumenical councils, issued dogmatic teachings about the Catholic faith. They promulgated the Nicene Creed, which Catholics recite at Sunday Mass.

Jesus's Humanity Is Confirmed

The first set of false teachings about Jesus concerned whether or not he was truly man. Recall from Chapter 1, Section 1 that a heresy known as Docetism held that Jesus only *seemed* to be a man. Docetists denied the humanity of Jesus. The Docetist heresy was a form of *Gnosticism*, a heresy that falsely held that Jesus shared "secret knowledge" with just a few close friends. Besides denying the true humanity of Jesus and his Resurrection, Gnostics also denied the validity of Sacred Scripture and the authority of bishops to rule the Church.

St. Irenaeus

St. Irenaeus, the bishop of Lyons, answered the false teachings of Gnosticism in his major work, *Against Heresies* (ca. AD 180). Irenaeus drew heavily on the Gospel of John and, in fact, can trace a connection directly to the Apostle. St. Irenaeus was tutored by Polycarp, a first-century bishop and martyr, who knew St. John and heard him speak. Because of this connection, it is not surprising that Irenaeus would use the term *flesh* and other language similar to that found in the Gospel of John to support the belief that Jesus was truly human:

> For, according to [the Docetists], the Word did not originally become flesh. For they maintain that the Savior assumed an animal body, formed in accordance with a special dispensation by an unspeakable providence, so as to become visible and palpable. But flesh is that which was of old formed for Adam by God out of the dust, and it is this that John has declared the Word of God became. (*Against Heresies*, 3)

Jesus was sent into the world as a mediator between God and humanity. As the Second Vatican Council affirmed, "Since he is God, all divine fullness dwells bodily in him. . . . He is the new Adam, made head of a new humanity, and full of grace and truth" (*Ad Gentes*, 3).

Jesus's Divinity Is Confirmed

The Church addressed the question of Jesus's divinity while answering the false teaching of Arius (see Chapter 1, Section 1). Recall that the heresy named after him, Arianism, denied that Jesus is God. This heresy spread throughout both the eastern and western parts of the Roman Empire.

In 325, about three hundred bishops, mostly from the East, met in the small town of Nicaea, in modern-day Turkey, in the Church's first ecumenical council, the Council of Nicaea. The council condemned Arianism and spelled out in a creed (see the subsection "Beliefs" in the Appendix) that Jesus is *consubstantial* with God the Father. This means that Christ possesses the same nature as God the Father. By stressing Jesus's full divinity, the council also upheld the doctrine of the Blessed Trinity, that the Father and the Son and the Holy Spirit are God.

The number of bishops that attended the First Council of Nicaea widely varies in historical accounts. Generally, it is believed there were three hundred bishops in attendance.

When Arianism was slow to die out, St. Athanasius, a bishop of Alexandria, defended the Church's teaching on Christ's divinity. He firmly taught that Christ "was made man that we may be made divine." He correctly held that if Christ is not God, then he cannot be Savior of humankind. Only God can restore people to communion with himself.

Church Councils Respond to Other Heresies

During her early centuries, the Church had to clarify several other teachings about Jesus, especially concerning his identity as the Second Divine Person of the Blessed Trinity and his relationship to his mother, Mary. Another heresy emerged when Nestorius, the patriarch (a bishop of special honor) of Constantinople, taught that there were two persons *in* Jesus—one divine, one human. He said that some of Jesus's traits and experiences were purely human, while others were purely divine. According to Nestorius, God could not be totally dependent upon a human being and therefore it was only Jesus's human self that was born of Mary; his divine self was not. Nestorius thus rejected Mary's title as "Mother of God."

St. Cyril of Alexandria contradicted Nestorius and defended Mary's title *Theotokos*, meaning "God-bearer." He said that it was perfectly correct to talk about Mary as the true Mother of God. St. Cyril argued that since the Son of God was conceived as man within the womb of Mary, the man born of Mary, her human son, was the Son of God. She did not give birth to God as God, but she did give birth to the Son of God existing as man, and so she is the Mother of God. To deny that Mary is the Mother of God is to deny the reality of the Incarnation—that is, that the Son of God actually came to exist as man within her womb.

A fourteenth-century Russian icon of the Theotokos.

St. Cyril also taught that Jesus was one Divine Person and the Second Divine Person of the Blessed Trinity. "Christ's humanity has no other subject than the divine person of the Son of God, who assumed it and made it his own, from his conception" (*CCC*, 466). Catholics worship one Jesus Christ, not separate beings, divine and human. The Council of Ephesus (AD 431) upheld St. Cyril's view and condemned Nestorianism.

Another heresy concerning the nature of Jesus that arose in the early Church is known as **Monophysitism**, from the Greek words for "one" and "nature." This heresy was put forth by Eutyches, a leader of a monastery outside Constantinople. Eutyches claimed that the divine nature of Jesus absorbed his human nature. He said that Christ's human nature was swallowed up "like a drop of honey into the water of the sea." In effect, Eutyches was denying that Jesus was truly human.

St. Leo the Great refuted this heresy in his work entitled *Tome*. St. Leo's teachings were canonized by the Council of Chalcedon (AD 451), which taught the famous Chalcedon formula: *Jesus is one Divine Person with two natures—a divine nature and a human nature* (see the subsection "Beliefs" in the Appendix). The Second Council of Constantinople (AD 553) confirmed this teaching. The Third Council of Constantinople (AD 680–681) also confirmed this teaching and added that because Jesus has two natures, he also possessed two wills.

The human will of Jesus, though distinct from his divine will, was not

St. Leo the Great

Monophysitism From the Greek words *monos*, which means "one" or "alone," and *physis*, which means "nature"; a fifth-century heresy that promoted the error that Jesus had only one nature, a divine nature. In response, the Church taught that Christ has two natures, divine and human.

opposed to it. Each nature retained its characteristic properties. For example, it was Jesus's humanity, properly speaking, that suffered. However, because of the unity of the two natures, everything in Christ's human nature can be attributed to his Divine Person: "He who was crucified in the flesh, our Lord Jesus Christ, is true God, Lord of glory, and *one of the Holy Trinity*" (Council of Constantinople II: DS 432, quoted in *CCC*, 468).

A Summary of What the Church Believes about Jesus

Have you ever heard someone say, "I'm not Christian, I'm Catholic"? Or maybe, "Catholics are not Christians"? If these statements sound ridiculous, then you understand correctly that Catholics are indeed Christians. A Christian is someone who believes in the divinity of Jesus Christ. Catholics clearly believe this to be true.

The Church's early ecumenical councils at Nicaea (325), Constantinople I (381), Ephesus (431), Chalcedon (451), Constantinople II (553), and Constantinople III (680–681) formalized several official teachings and clarified what Catholics believe about Jesus. These teachings are summarized here.

Jesus is the only Son of God.

Although Jesus had a natural human mother, Mary, he had no natural human father. The father of Jesus is the First Person of the Blessed Trinity, God the Father. Humans are children of God through the privilege of divine adoption that they receive in Baptism; only Jesus is the Son of God, who is consubstantial with the Father. Jesus shares in the very nature of God.

Jesus is true God.

The Father begets his Son, and the Son is begotten of the Father. This means that Jesus has the same nature as the Father. There was never a time when the Son of God did not exist.

The Son is true God, God from God, Light from Light.

Like the Father, the Son has a divine nature. The Son, proceeding from the Father, is of one substance with the Father. Jesus is true God just as light is identical to the light from which it comes.

The Son is begotten, not made, one in Being with the Father.

This teaching addressed a false belief of the time that Jesus's divinity was bestowed on him at some point during his earthly life. Rather, the always-existing Son "proceeds" from the Father. The Father did not generate the Son in the same way that human fathers generate their sons. The Son is not "made" by the Father because the Son is not a created being. What is made is always of a different nature than the maker. Ants make anthills but beget other ants. Birds build nests but beget other birds. Humans construct houses but beget other human beings. God made the world but begot his Son, and so the Son is of the same nature as the Father. If the Son were made, he would not be of the same nature of the Father and so would not be God. The one being of God, what the one God is, is the Father begetting his Son, and so the Son is consubstantial—that is, one in being—with the Father.

All things were made through the Son.

Since the Son is one in being with the Father, he also shares in the creation of the world. "All things came to be through him" (Jn 1:3).

There is only one Person in Christ, the Divine Person.

Because Jesus is the Son of God existing as man, all that he says and does humanly is said and done by the Son. The Son of God works miracles as man. The Son of God suffers and dies as man.

Mary, by conceiving God's Son, is truly the Mother of God.

Since Jesus never ceased to be God, either in the womb or after he was born, his mother, Mary, is *Theotokos*, or "God-bearer."

There are two distinct natures and one Divine Person of Jesus Christ.

Jesus has a divine nature and a human nature. The Son of God came to exist as man, and so Jesus is perfect in divinity and perfect in humanity. Jesus Christ is true God and true man. The union of the human and divine natures in the one Divine Person of Jesus is so perfect that it is said that, in Jesus, God truly shared in the experiences of humanity. The suffering and Death of Christ is attributed to his Divine Person but not strictly to his divine nature. "The distinction between the natures was never abolished by their union, but rather the character proper to each of the two natures was preserved as they came together in one person (*prosopon*) and one hypostasis" (Council of Chalcedon: DS 302, quoted in *CCC*, 467).

As true God and true man, Jesus has a human intellect and a human will.

Because the Son of God is man, he possesses a human intellect and a human will. Thus, as man, the Son of God always conforms his human will to the divine will of his Father through the light of the

Holy Spirit. The human nature of the Son of God in conformity with his divine will knew and shared everything that pertains to the Father. With his union to divine wisdom, in his human intellect Christ has immediate knowledge of his Father and of the secret thoughts of humans.

Jesus is Savior of the world.

Those who unite themselves to Jesus's Death and Resurrection through faith will share in the eternal life he has promised.

The missions of Jesus and the Holy Spirit are distinct but inseparable.

Whenever the Father sends his Son, he always sends his Spirit.

None of these teachings about Jesus came from thin air. Neither were they formulated by the Apostles, martyrs, or Church Fathers. These were teachings revealed by Jesus himself through the intercession of the Holy Spirit. Jesus, who is God-in-the-flesh, taught much more about what God is like, about his special relationship with the Father, and about how one God can be in three coequal Divine Persons—Father, Son, and Holy Spirit.

Bishop D. Stephen Lee shakes a thurible during the Mass at St. Dominic's Church to celebrate the Feast Day of Our Lady of Fatima in Macau.

SECTION Assessment

Comprehension

1. What role did the Church Fathers play in responding to heresies?

2. How did Arianism begin to spread?

3. "Jesus is true God." Explain this Church teaching in your own words.

Vocabulary

4. How did Pope Leo the Great answer the false teaching of *Monophysitism*?

Reflection

5. How is your life different because the Son of God came to exist as man?

Section Reviews

Focus Question

How is Jesus both true God and true man?

Complete one of the following:

- Compare Jesus's healing of Jairus's daughter in Luke 8:40–56 with his healing of the woman with a hemorrhage. How does faith play a crucial factor in both healings? What does this tell us about the necessity of faith in understanding Christ's divinity?

- Dietrich Bonhoeffer (1906–1945) was a Lutheran pastor and theologian who opposed Adolf Hitler and Nazism during World War II. He was also involved in a failed plot to assassinate Hitler in 1943. Bonhoeffer was brutally tortured and hanged in 1945 right before the war ended. He once wrote, "If Jesus Christ is not true God, how could he help us? If he is not true man, how could he help us?" Explain the meaning of Bonhoeffer's observation.

- Consider the following statements. Identify those that are false statements of the faith. Rewrite the false statements to make them accurate.

  1. Jesus became God's Son at Baptism.
  2. God the Father created the Son.
  3. It was impossible for Christ to really suffer pain.
  4. In knowing God the Father, Jesus grows in knowledge that he is the Son of God.

Introduction

God Reveals Himself to Us

Review

God himself reveals the depths of the plans he has for us through his Revelation of salvation history culminating with the birth of the Messiah, Jesus Christ. Jesus is a Messiah that no one could have imagined. He is both God and Man. He is unique in his one Divine Person that he brings together in the union of his human and divine natures. Studying the relationship between Christ's humanity and divinity is the focus of Christology.

Assignment

Read paragraph 469 of the *Catechism of the Catholic Church*. Summarize what this paragraph teaches about Christ's true identity.

Section 1

How Is Jesus True God?

Review

The Gospels provide evidence for Jesus's divinity. Beginning with its prologue, John's Gospel emphasizes that Jesus was always present with the Father. In the synoptic Gospels, Jesus tells his disciples that he is "I AM," indicating the traditional Jewish name for God. Jesus fulfilled prophecies from the Old Testament concerning the Messiah and also predicted himself how his mission would unfold. Other evidence for Jesus's divinity are the miracles he performed, his demonstration along with his miracles that he could forgive sins, and the greatest evidence of all—his Resurrection from the dead.

Assignment

Read Hebrews 10:5–7. Explain how you understand this passage related to the question, "Why did God become human?"

Section 2

How Is Jesus True Man?

Review

The Son of God became man without ceasing to be God. Jesus is like us in all things but sin. He possessed a human body and a human soul. Throughout his lifetime, Jesus had the physical and emotional experiences that all humans encounter. Because of this, Jesus helps us to understand how to live and the meaning of life.

Assignment

Write a response to the following: How do you think the reality that Jesus was both human and divine influenced his obedience to Mary and Joseph?

Section 3

Historical Evidence and Beliefs about Jesus from Outside of Christianity

Review

Ancient Roman, Jewish, and Greek historians, philosophers, and writers wrote about the life and teachings of Jesus of Nazareth and the actions of the earliest Christians, refuting any claims that Jesus never existed. The non-Christian sources do not provide detailed biographical information about Jesus or affirm his divinity, but they do run parallel to the chronology of history provided in the New Testament.

Assignment

Does the historical evidence presented from non-Christian sources make it easier for you to accept that Jesus actually lived? Why or why not?

Section 4

The Truth of Christ Is Preserved in the Church

Review

In response to heresies that had to do with the divinity and humanity of Jesus, Church Fathers—such as Sts. Irenaeus, Athanasius, Cyril of Alexandria, and Pope Leo the Great—helped to proclaim clear Church teachings at ecumenical councils. Among the heresies confronted were Docetism, Arianism, Gnosticism, Monophysitism, and Nestorianism.

Assignment

Write a one-sentence definition of each heresy. Take turns quizzing a classmate on the definitions. Eventually, take away the written definitions and recite each definition by memory.

Chapter Projects

Choose and complete at least one of the following projects to assess your understanding of the material in this chapter.

✿ 1. Connect Duccio's Madonna and Child with Other Art History Topics

Duccio was an Italian artist of the late Middle Ages. He was from Siena, Italy. Several other Italian painters addressed the subject of the *Madonna and Child*. The size of this painting is also worth further study—what exactly were these smaller paintings used for at the time they were made? Research and write a report that connects Duccio's *Madonna and Child* with the following topics. Refer to the Metropolitan Museum of Art to begin your research.

- Italian painters of the late Middle Ages
- How paintings were used for private devotion
- How Duccio influenced and was influenced by the Sienese school of artists
- How *Madonna and Child* compares to other Italian paintings of the Infant Christ with his mother

✿ 2. Analyze and Reflect on the Miracles of Jesus

Read the following gospel passages about four miracles of Jesus. Write answers to the questions associated with each miracle. Add your own personal reflection (i.e., "what the miracle means to me") for each example.

The Man Born Blind (John 9:1–41)

- Why did the blind man's parents react as they did when authorities questioned them?
- What did the man say that angered the authorities?

The Healing of the Gerasene Demoniac (Mark 5:1–20)

- What did people want Jesus to do after they heard about his healing of the possessed man?

- Why did they react this way?
- What did the possessed man want to do?
- How did Jesus answer him?

The Raising of the Widow's Son (Luke 7:11–17)

- What motivated Jesus to bring this man back to life?
- How did the people react to this miracle?
- What did they say about Jesus?

The Feeding of the Four Thousand (Matthew 15:32–39)

- What motivated Jesus to perform this miracle?
- What was left over after everyone had eaten?

⚙ *3. Respond to Questions about Jesus*

Below are several questions about Jesus. In your own words, write a short response to each question. Support each of your responses with a reference from the *Catechism of the Catholic Church*. Possible references have been suggested. However, you may choose other references.

1. Is Jesus God?
   Hint: See *CCC*, 464, 469, 653, 663.

2. When you pray, do you pray to God or to Jesus?
   Hint: See *CCC*, 2598–2616, 2663–2672.

3. Is Jesus the Son of God in the same way that you are son or daughter to your own father?
   Hint: See *CCC*, 441–445.

4. Did Jesus create the world?
   Hint: See *CCC*, 290–292.

5. Is Jesus alive or dead right now? Was he dead at one time?
   Hint: See *CCC*, 624–627, 663.

6. Whom did Jesus talk to when he prayed? Himself?
   Hint: See *CCC*, 2746–2750, 2766.

7. Can you be a Christian if you don't believe that Jesus is God?
    Hint: See *CCC*, 425, 449, 463.

✿ *4. Research and Report on the Chalcedonean Creed*

The Chalcedonean Creed (see the subsection "Beliefs" in the Appendix) was adopted at the Council of Chalcedon in AD 451 in response to several heresies concerning the nature of Christ. The Western Church accepted this creed from the outset, as did most Eastern Orthodox churches since they were the main participants at this council. In fact, only some churches rejected this creed, including the Nestorians in present-day Iraq and the Coptic Church in Egypt. Research and read more about the development of this creed at the Council of Chalcedon. Write a report explaining the issues it addressed, telling how it was adopted, and summarizing what it taught.

✿ *5. Create a Collage of Words and Titles That Describe Jesus*

Words and titles used to describe Jesus in the New Testament give us many ways to answer questions like "Who is Jesus Christ?" "How can Jesus be both divine and human at the same time?" and "What does it mean to call Jesus the Son of God?" Look up some of these words and titles and the passages that accompany them. Then incorporate the words, titles, and passages in a colorful collage using an art medium of your choice. Include at least ten words, titles, and accompanying passages in your collage. Sample titles:

- Emmanuel—"God is with us" (Mt 1:23)
- The Word (*Logos*) of God (Jn 1:1–5)
- Lord (Jn 20:28)
- Messiah or Christ (Mk 8:27–33)

You may also choose Old Testament references that refer to the Messiah.

Faithful Disciple
Eusebius of Caesarea

It's hard for some of us to imagine doing research for a report without having the internet to look up sources. Just a generation ago, students had to peruse the shelves of a library, use card catalogs, and possibly use something called microfiche (sources recorded on film) to find references. Now, take the process back two centuries to a time when a Greek Christian named Eusebius set out to write the first history of the Church: "I feel inadequate to do church history justice as the first to venture on such an undertaking, a traveler on a lonely and untrodden path."

Nevertheless, Eusebius proceeded with the endeavor. Likely born in Palestine between AD 260 and 265, Eusebius was baptized in Caesarea and ordained a priest by his teacher and friend Pamphilus. Both men were followers of the early Christian scholar Origen. Before Origen died, he left his personal library to the Church in Caesarea. Pamphilus built a library in Caesarea that housed the greatest collection of Christian sources. During the Diocletian persecutions at the end of the Roman Empire, Pamphilus was martyred and Eusebius was imprisoned. While in prison, Eusebius began to compile the outline for a history of the Church. Around AD 315, when the persecutions had ended and Christianity had been legalized by Constantine, Eusebius was named bishop of Caesarea and his work on the Church history project continued.

Eusebius completed *Historia Ecclesiastica* (*Church History*) in about AD 323. It covers the history of the Church from the time of the Apostles to his day. Eusebius

Eusebius of Caesarea

chronicles the Church's history parallel to the Roman emperors, giving immense details. He also mentions bishops, martyrs, and other teachers of the Church at the time. Eusebius casts blame for the Crucifixion of Jesus on the Jews—a point that was corrected to "certain Jewish leaders" at the Second Vatican Council—but also states that forgiveness of those who put Jesus to death can be granted and the possibility of salvation exists for those who are absolved. *Historia Ecclesiastica* remains a valuable source of information on the early Church, especially since the references from the Caesarean library have all since been lost.

Eusebius wrote many other materials, including a biography of Emperor Constantine, whose Edict of Milan legalized Christianity. He was also instrumental in forging a compromise between the Arians and the Church's position regarding the nature of Christ at the Council of Nicaea. Prior to the council, the Church had temporarily excommunicated Eusebius because of his support for Arian Christology. But at the council itself, Eusebius moderated his stance and affirmed the Nicene Creed.

Later in life, Eusebius declined a promotion to become bishop of Antioch. Rather, he remained bishop of Caesarea until his death in approximately AD 339 or 340.

Comprehension

1.   What role does Pamphilus have in the creation of *Historia Ecclesiastica*?
2.   What was the scope of *Historia Ecclesiastica*?
3.   How was Eusebius's conjecture on the responsibility of Jews for Jesus's Crucifixion corrected at the Second Vatican Council?
4.   Why does *Historia Ecclesiastica* still remain a vital source for the history of the early Church?
5.   Why was Eusebius excommunicated? How did he correct his error?

Application

From your own knowledge, write down one key event from each of the first three centuries of the Church's history. Next, look up each event and write the correct date for when it occurred.

Prayer

Anima Christi (Latin for "Soul of Christ") is a well-known prayer that you might find in your parish missal and is often prayed in silence by Catholics on returning to the pew after receiving Holy Communion. The composition of the prayer dates from the first half of the fourteenth century, and it was possibly written by Pope John XII. For years the prayer was attributed to St. Ignatius of Loyola as it appears at the beginning of his *Spiritual Exercises*. However, the Anima Christi has been found in several sources that predate the *Spiritual Exercises*.

Anima Christi

Soul of Christ, sanctify me.
Body of Christ, save me.
Blood of Christ, inebriate me.
Water from the side of Christ, wash me.
Passion of Christ, strengthen me.
O good Jesus, hear me.
Within thy wounds hide me.
Suffer me not to be separated from thee.
From the malicious enemy defend me.
In the hour of my death call me
and bid me come unto thee,
that I may praise thee with thy saints
and with thy angels
for ever and ever.
Amen.

Jesus Reveals What God Is Like

Allegory of Divine Providence

➤Pietro da Cortona

The name of this painting with a myriad of colorful images is *Allegory of Divine Providence*. The Italian artist Pietro da Cortona (1596–1669) painted most of it over a three-year period beginning in 1633 and then reworked it until 1639. The relation of the subject of the painting to its title is more concrete than you might guess; the pope who commissioned the painting, Urban VIII, was said to have been bothered by the common narrative that his election to the papacy had been unfairly gained through his influential family, the Barberinis. Some felt that Pope Urban may have directed a painting with this title to remind the public that the choice of a pope is always due to **divine providence**.

It was common for popes of that era to build separate palaces away from the Vatican to use for secular functions. This painting, a fresco, fills the ceiling of the Barberini palace, more than four hundred meters wide. *Allegory of Divine Providence* is divided into five parts. In the center is the figure of Divine Providence, who sits on a cloud, holds a scepter, and directs the present and future. Around Divine Providence are justice, mercy, eternity, truth, purity, and beauty and others who are under her rule. Above Divine Providence are keys representing the papacy. Divine Providence is held up by Saturn and Fate, while other figures representing Truth and Eternity are also present. Fables like that of Hercules can also be seen. The inclusion of bees represents the Barberini family seal.

Allegory of Divine Providence is an apt representation of the baroque period, which began in the early seventeenth century and extended to the nineteenth century. Baroque paintings are dramatic, colorful, and designed to evoke emotion. *Allegory of Divine Providence* certainly fits that definition.

If you would like to examine other images in Allegory of Divine Providence, *see Chapter 2 Review, Chapter Project 1.*

---

divine providence God's loving and watchful guidance over his creatures on their way to their final goal and perfection.

What did Jesus reveal about God the Father?

Chapter Overview

Introduction
God Is Father

Section 1
God the Father Is Love and Truth

Section 2
God the Father Is Almighty

Section 3
God the Father Is Just

Section 4
God the Father Carries Out His Plan

GOD IS FATHER

Many people prefer to leave God completely a mystery. They are more comfortable with a God they do not really know. If they do not know God, they can imagine him in their own way and create for themselves a God in their own image. When God became incarnate in the Divine Person of Jesus Christ, it is not surprising that many were confused, disoriented, and ultimately angered by this intimate glimpse of God and direct encounter with him. Some of Jesus's neighbors and fellow Jews were extremely uncomfortable: "Is he not the carpenter's son?" (Mt 13:55). And they took offense at Jesus.

Even those who first believed that Jesus was God Incarnate might have wondered, "Who is minding the store?" In other words, they may have been confused about how God was on earth, knowing that the God of their ancestors was *everywhere* in all places and throughout all time. God had spoken to the Jewish people and revealed himself to them in dreams, in powerful actions, and directly to Moses at a burning bush when God said to Moses, "I am the God of your father . . . the God of Abraham, the God of Isaac, and the God of Jacob" (Ex 3:6). How was Jesus related to the God of heaven?

Christ revealed that the God of Israel was his Father. At the same time, God the Father revealed himself in Christ. In his book *Crossing the Threshold of Hope*, Pope John Paul II called the Father's self-Revelation in the Son the "zenith—the revelation of the invisible God in the visible image of Christ."[1] Besides telling his disciples that God was his Father, Christ also tells us that his Father is our Father. The words of the Lord's Prayer indicate this. God remains mysterious and will always be so. But through the Incarnation, Jesus has revealed more about the mystery of God than ever before.

How God Is Father

It is a beautiful and fundamental reality that Jesus called God "Father." Describing God as "Father" was not unique to Jesus. Many religions, including Judaism, have described God as Father. The Old Testament equates God as Creator with fatherhood: "Is he not your father who begot you?" (Dt 32:6). The Old Testament also compares God's parental role as Creator and caregiver to motherhood: "As a mother comforts her child, so I will comfort you" (Is 66:13).

Comparing God to human parents comes with a caution. Both human fathers and mothers make mistakes and do not live up to their responsibilities. Jesus understood this. After he healed a man on the Sabbath (and was vilified for it by some of the Jewish authorities), he explained why he did it: "Amen, amen, I say to you, a son cannot do anything on his own, but only what he sees his father doing; for what he does, his son will do also" (Jn 5:19). Isn't what Jesus said generally true? Children imitate their parents. Sons and daughters often take up the same profession as one of their parents. Negatively, the sins and poor behavior of parents are often perpetuated in their children.

In the Old Testament, God called out to Moses in a burning bush. When Moses asked God his name, God replied, "I am who am" (Ex 3:14).

When Jesus used "Father" to define God, he was doing so in a completely new and unique way: God is Father only in relation to Jesus, his Son. They share an eternal relation. **To understand and know God the Father is to understand and know the Son, Jesus. God transcends human fatherhood and motherhood.** This means that in order to truly know God as Father, we must believe in Jesus and so, by the power of the Holy Spirit, be transformed into children of God the Father. Only by living in Jesus, the Son, do we share in his filial knowledge of the Father and so know the Father's love. Only in Jesus and through the Holy Spirit can we address God as "Abba"—Father.

"Show Us the Father"

The *Catechism of the Catholic Church* reinforces that "Jesus revealed that God is Father in an unheard-of sense" (*CCC*, 240). The Father is not only Creator; he is eternally Father in relation to his only Son, Jesus. Because of this, in knowing the Son of God, examining his actions, and listening to his words, we can come to know the Father. Jesus said, "All things have been handed over to me by my Father. No one knows the Son except the Father, and no one knows

Pope John Paul II called the Father's self-Revelation in the Son "the zenith of the invisible God in the visible image of Christ."

the Father except the Son and anyone to whom the Son wishes to reveal him" (Mt 11:27).

Even by the time of the Last Supper, Jesus's closest disciples were still having trouble understanding the relationship between the Son of God and his Father. Jesus told them, "I am the way and the truth and the life" (Jn 14:6), and added, "No one comes to the Father except through me. If you know me, then you will also know my Father. From now on you do know him and have seen him" (Jn 14:6–7).

The Apostle Philip requested an epiphany: "Master, show us the Father, and that will be enough for us" (Jn 14:8). Many years later, Pope John Paul II asked this question as well, wondering if God couldn't have gone even further in revealing himself to humankind. However, Pope John Paul II realized, "In truth, it seems that he has gone as far as possible. He could not go further. In a certain sense God has gone too far! Didn't Christ perhaps become 'a stumbling block to Jews and foolishness to Gentiles' (1 Cor 1:23)? Precisely because he called God his Father, because he revealed him so openly in himself he could not but elicit the impression that it was too much."[2]

Whenever you wonder how to know and see God the Father, reread Jesus's response to Philip's demand that Jesus show him and the others the Father: "Whoever has seen me has seen the Father. . . . The words that I speak to you I do not speak on my own. The Father who dwells in me is doing his works" (Jn 14:9–10). A careful reading of the Gospels in whole, focusing on the words and actions of Jesus, is a way to know the Father and what he is like. The next sections focus on some of the important ways Jesus reveals God the Father.

SECTION Assessment

Comprehension

1. What is new and unique about the way Jesus described God as "Father"?

Reflection

2. Assess your willingness to know God intimately. What keeps you from doing so?

3. Why do you think Pope John Paul II believed that Jesus could not go further in revealing God the Father?

4. What are positive images of fathers (and mothers) you associate with God the Father?

GOD THE FATHER IS LOVE AND TRUTH

Throughout the course of salvation history, the one thing God's people could be sure of was that God loved them. What other reason could he have for always coming to their rescue and forgiving them of their unfaithfulness and sins? God's love for them was stronger even than a mother's love for her child. His love is everlasting. It has no end. God told his people through the prophet Jeremiah, "With age-old love I have loved you; so I have kept my mercy toward you" (Jer 31:3).

By becoming incarnate in the Divine Person Jesus in order to offer humans a chance to recover from the Original Sin that plagued the world, the Father revealed even more about love: The Father's very being is love. Jesus said, "No one has ever seen God. Yet, if we love one another, God remains in us, and his love is brought to perfection in us" (1 Jn 4:12). There is an eternal exchange of love among the Divine Persons of the Blessed Trinity: Father, Son, and Holy Spirit. The Incarnation of Christ allows humans to witness this love in the flesh.

God is also truth. As the First Letter of John states, Jesus came to confirm this: "We also know that the Son of God has come and has given us discernment to know the one who is true" (5:20). Every word from the mouth of God is true. Everything God created conforms with the mind of God. His truth is his wisdom, "which commands the whole created order and governs the world" (*CCC*, 216). Because the Son of God is one with the Father, he too is the truth.

God So Loved the World

John 3:16 is one of the most cited Bible verses. This Scripture verse may be the best summary of God's love:

> For God so loved the world that he gave his only Son, so that everyone who believes in him might not perish but might have eternal life.

This message is truly remarkable. God showed his love for people who were sinners and did not earn his love in any way (see Romans 5:8). By sending his Son to redeem a world that was both ignoring and disobeying him, the Father confirms that his love is benevolent. It is "not that we have loved God, but that he loved us and sent his Son as expiation for our sins" (1 Jn 4:10). This doesn't mean that because God has loved us in such depth, we don't have any responsibility. **God's love is a grace that he will never take back. We don't have to earn God's love. But we must not resist God's love or oppose it in our actions.** John 3:36 is a passage that should be read in accompaniment to John 3:16: "Whoever believes in the Son has eternal life, but whoever disobeys the Son will not see life, but the wrath of God remains upon him."

God's wrath should only be considered under the heading of God's love, which is boundless. Jesus told about the vastness of his Father's love and about his compassion and mercy. Jesus's message in the parable of the lost sheep (see Matthew 18:10–14) is that God's love is personal and caring. The Father does not abandon those he loves, and his love does not exclude anyone. At the end of the parable, Jesus explained, "It is not the will of your heavenly Father that one of these little ones be lost" (Mt 18:14).

When we understand that the Father loves us so much that he is willing to send his Son to die for us whether or not we merit this saving gift, it also becomes easier to understand Jesus's new commandment: "As I have loved you, so you also should love one another"

(Jn 13:34). Recall also Jesus's instruction that we should not only love those who love us back; we must also love our enemies and pray for those who persecute us (see Matthew 5:44). This resembles what the Father did in offering his love by sending his Son to redeem the world, even though the world is hostile to him.

It may seem impossible to love as the Father loves. It is true that such love is impossible on our own; it is only by God's grace that we can love others with the kind of love he asks of us. Fortunately, God understands this challenge and accepts the way we love or the degree to which we love. A conversation between the Risen Jesus and Peter in John 21:15–19 reveals this:

After fishing on the Sea of Tiberias and eating breakfast on the shore, Jesus asked Peter, "Simon, son of John, do you love me more than these?" (Jn 21:15). (By "these," he was probably referring to the other disciples or perhaps to fishing.) John's Gospel records Jesus using the most intimate form of the word *love* in his question, the Greek *agapes me*.

Peter answered Jesus, "Yes, Lord, you know that I love you," using another Greek term for love, *philo se*. Whereas *agapes me* describes a deep, intimate love, *philo se* equates more with the love one would have for a friend.

Jesus repeated the question a second time. *"Agapes me*, Simon?" He wanted to know if Peter loved him deeply and without reserve.

Again Peter responded, *"Philo se."*

When Jesus asked Peter a third time whether he loved him, Jesus restated the question using *philo se*. Jesus understood the difficulty of loving another completely and fully in the way that the Father does. By using Peter's term for love, Jesus accepted the current degree of love Peter was able to offer.

And yet, the story does not end there. Eventually, at the end of his life, Peter cooperated with God's grace to show the ultimate form of *agape* love. He was martyred for his love of Christ in Rome by being crucified upside down. He chose to be hung upside down on the cross out of humility; he did not feel worthy to be crucified in the exact way that Christ was.

The eternal love between God the Father and God the Son is meant to be shared with us and by us: "Remain in my love," said Jesus. "If you keep my commandments, you will remain in my love, just as I have kept my Father's commandments and remain in his love" (Jn 15:9–10). Much of our journey in this life involves entering more deeply into a love of God in all Three Divine Persons: Father, Son, and Holy Spirit.

What Is Truth?

Jesus was brought before Pontius Pilate by Jewish leaders who charged him with a crime that his accusers did not explain (see John 18:28–40). Pilate himself wasn't sure of the crime, so he questioned Jesus, "Are you the King of the Jews?" As the conversation persisted, Jesus explained to Pilate that he had come into the world to testify to the truth. "Everyone who belongs to the truth listens to my voice," Jesus said. Pilate was dumbfounded. He responded, "What is truth?"

This incident brings up a common issue for those who struggle to know God. Is there an answer to Pilate's question about the definition of truth? When two people in the same conversation have completely different understandings of what is being said and what is taking place, it's very difficult to

Christ before Pilate.

ascertain an answer. Jesus, the Son of God, was standing right in front of Pontius Pilate, yet Pilate could not understand his message or recognize to whom he was really speaking.

There are different ways to understand the meaning of truth. One way is to have a correct understanding of reality, which comes over time from experience and knowledge. For example, humans have come to understand that a mouse is not a snake and that a door is not a window. Truth, in these examples, has to do with the perception of an object that matches up with what the object actually is. From there, understanding what is truthful can extend to the realms of grammar, math, science, and art. Truth in these areas has grown as human history has progressed and the human capacity to understand truth has grown. Truth is also more than just objective facts. Humans are expected to be truthful with one another. This definition equates with being sincere and honest. Truthfulness becomes part of our identity, instead of being untrue or a liar.

The definition of truth that describes God is mostly the second type of truth. At the Last Supper, the Son of God said to his disciples: "I am the way and the truth and the life. No one comes to the Father except through me" (Jn 14:6). But the first definition also applies. Think of what you know to be the meaning of truth. The word *truth* signifies something that is real, something that is honest, something that really exists. The Divine Persons of the Blessed Trinity can be described in all of those ways.

Understanding God as truth can help you to look at the entire picture of your life, from beginning to end. You can see your life through the eyes of God, meaning that you can take a "big picture" view of what is happening to you now. **The virtue of truth helps you to make an honest assessment of your life, to see how all the events of your life—good and bad, joyful and painful—from childhood to the present and into the future have value.** This is the way God sees your life. In uncovering the truth, you are able to view life more as God does. Doing so helps you to know the Triune God, Father, Son, and Holy Spirit.

It is up to you to do the opposite of what Pilate did. Accept the offer of truth. Accept that it is Jesus, the Son of God, standing before you making the offer.

SECTION Assessment

Comprehension

1. How does the parable of the lost sheep show that God's love is personal and caring?

2. Name the New Commandment.

3. How is God the Father's very being love?

4. How does *truth* describe God?

Reflection

5. Why do you think Jesus used the term *philo se* the third time he questioned Peter?

6. Recall that Pilate had an inscription, "King of the Jews," placed on the Cross of Christ. How might Pilate's conversation with Jesus about truth have affected this action?

7. How can growing in the virtue of truth help you to make an honest assessment of how you are living your life?

GOD THE FATHER IS ALMIGHTY

Of all the attributes of God the Father (e.g., holy, wise, loving), only one is named in the Catholic creeds. We say, "I believe in God the Father, the *Almighty*, Creator of heaven and earth." We believe God's power is universal; the "God who created everything also rules everything and can do everything" (*CCC*, 268). God can do whatever he pleases. Nothing is impossible for God. We believe God is not only a God of love and truth; he is also omnipotent, or all-powerful. This power of God means several things:

He created the entire universe.

He rules over creation.

He is the Lord of history.

He governs the events of history according to his will.

Different than the world typically thinks of power, God the Father's power is loving. His fatherhood and power work together. God the Father shows us his "fatherly omnipotence" (*CCC*, 270) by taking care of our needs, both physical and spiritual; adopting us as his children and not as his slaves; and especially by the great mercy he shows us by forgiving our sins. God's power is not random. He uses his power according to his just providence and his wise intellect.

A person's faith in Almighty God may be put to the test by the presence of evil and suffering in the world. For example, we might wonder: "How can I accept an omnipotent God who seems to be temporarily impotent as so many atrocities—war, murder, genocide, cancer, sexual abuse—occur?" Ultimately, how can we accept an omnipotent God who himself suffers the brutality of Crucifixion and Death on the Cross? Given that the words and actions of Jesus reveal what God is like, what do they reveal about why there is evil and suffering in the world? The next subsections examine some of these issues and answers.

What Did Jesus Teach about Suffering?

If you were given devastating news about your health—for example, that cancer had invaded your body—you would have questions for the doctor about how to treat the illness and rid your body of the disease. But in the same conversation and later, during often-painful treatment and recovery, you might also ask *why* you had contracted the

A crucifix on the wall of a home or a hospital room reminds us to unite our suffering with the suffering of Christ.

cancer. Was it your diet? Was it heredity? Or was the illness and suffering something from God that he intended for you to endure for your own good?

No one can escape suffering in this world, and everyone has questions about why people must suffer. Jesus did not explain as much with words about the reasons people suffer. Rather, his whole life, and particularly the Paschal Mystery itself, revealed the meaning of suffering. **To understand the origins of evil and suffering, we must fix the eyes of our faith on him "who alone is its conqueror"** (*CCC*, 385). Primarily, Jesus *acted* on the suffering. He did this from the very beginning of his ministry. Entering the home of Simon (Peter) and his brother John, he found Simon's mother-in-law ill with a fever. "He approached, grasped her hand, and helped her up. Then the fever left her and she waited on them" (Mk 1:31). Jesus didn't spend time explaining to her the exact reasons why she was ill or the larger question of why humans suffer.

Mostly because of a lack of understanding of communicable sickness and disease, sick people in Jesus's time were treated as outcasts. They were kept separate from the family, often confined to one room or to their homes. Those with leprosy were among the most isolated. This condition was not the form of leprosy we now call Hansen's disease. The Hebrew word *sara'at* was the ritualistic term used in the Bible to describe this condition, which may have manifested itself as boils, scabies, eczema, or a fungus infection.

Lepers—and also the blind, deaf, and crippled—in Jesus's time were forced to live outside the city walls, often settling around a public garbage dump where they could scavenge for food. Lepers had to identify themselves when they saw another person coming by either ringing a bell or shouting "unclean" to warn of their condition. Under Mosaic Law, Jews would become "unclean" themselves if they touched a sick person or a corpse.

Jesus did not obey these religious laws or local customs. He used human signs and touch to heal. He laid hands on the sick and, in one case of a man born blind, "made clay with the saliva, and smeared the clay on his eyes" (Jn 9:6).∞ Through these actions, the sick and outcast concretely felt God reaching out to them to be with them in their suffering. Jesus performed these healing miracles to cure physical, mental, and spiritual ailments. The Son of God acted on his Father's behalf, fulfilling the words of Exodus 15:26: "I, the LORD, am your healer."

∞ Note

Scripture scholar Dr. Brant Pitre points out that "if you try to make something from dust, you can't do it. You can't mold a statue of dust. You have to have some liquid in order to hold the dirt together. So the Jews had this tradition that when God made Adam, he made him from spit and clay. He made him from his own spit, and the Dead Sea Scrolls actually have a line that said that Adam, or man, was made from 'spat saliva, molded clay.' So think about that for a second. If in Jewish tradition God makes Adam from spit and dust from the clay, what is Jesus doing here? Jesus is acting like God acted in the Old Testament. In other words, he is performing an act of a new creation. Just as Adam was given his body from the clay, so Jesus now gives the man born blind sight. He gives him, in a sense, new eyes from the clay and his own spittle. So this is like a divine action for Jesus to spit on the ground and make clay and give this man sight" (*Mass Readings Explained*, Fourth Sunday of Lent, Cycle A).

The closest Jesus ever came to explaining with words why people suffer was when he healed a man who was born blind (see John 9:1–41). Recall that many people in Jesus's time thought that suffering was a punishment for sin. Jesus's disciples asked him, "Rabbi, who sinned, this man or his parents, that he was born blind?" Jesus answered them clearly: "Neither he nor his parents sinned; it is so that the works of God might be made visible through him" (Jn 9:2–3).

What do Jesus's words and actions about suffering teach us about how an Almighty God the Father allows for suffering? For one, though God doesn't punish us with illness for our sins, it is important to understand that our sins themselves do cause us to suffer. For example, pride, selfishness, arrogance, lust, and an unwillingness to forgive cause us to suffer and become unhappy. Two consequences of sin are the loss of divine grace and the incurring of a debt of punishment. *Mortal sin* deprives a person of sanctifying grace and brings about the debt of eternal punishment. *Venial sin* deprives a person of some of God's grace and requires temporal punishment. These two kinds of punishment are not the action of a vengeful God but the consequence of a person's own sin. Also, some suffering is the direct result of the work of Satan. Natural disasters can, in part, be understood as a result of Original Sin: "Harmony with creation is broken: visible creation has become alien and hostile to man" (*CCC*, 400).

There are other intricacies of human suffering to consider. For example, self-discipline and self-control cause suffering in one sense (e.g., the "suffering" of an athlete who endures a difficult workout) but in the end bring joy, peace, and happiness (see Hebrews 12:1–13). And some suffering is, in fact, good. Standing up for what is right and just or being ridiculed and persecuted for doing good is positive suffering. This is what Jesus and the saints did. This is the kind of suffering we should expect as Christians and rejoice in.

An important lesson we can draw from Jesus's explanation after the healing of the blind man and from his other healing miracles is the Father's willingness to be with humans in their suffering. (This is also the message of the famous story from the Book of Job from the Old Testament.) Human suffering and death itself are consequences of Original Sin. Through his Passion and Death, Christ "took upon himself the whole weight of evil and took away the 'sin of the world,' of which illness is only a consequence" (*CCC*, 1505). These saving actions of Jesus give new meaning to suffering. They help to form us to

ST. JOSEPH: THE EARTHLY SHADOW OF GOD THE FATHER

Focus Question:
What did Jesus reveal about God the Father?

To celebrate the 150th anniversary of Pope Pius IX's proclamation of St. Joseph as the patron of the Church, Pope Francis wrote the apostolic letter *Patris coerde* (*With a Father's Heart*) in 2020, which also marked the start of the Year of St. Joseph. Whereas in Jesus, as the Lord said to the Apostle Philip, we have "seen the Father," it is in St. Joseph that God the Father sent a human representative to be the model of himself for his Son. In the letter, Pope Francis writes that "in his relationship to Jesus, Joseph was the earthly shadow of the heavenly Father."∞ St. Joseph continues to be a human representative helping us to know more about what God is like as Father. Through St. Joseph, according to Pope Francis, we learn some of these things about God the Father:

1. He was a sacrificial father.

St. John Chrysostom pointed out that Joseph placed himself "at the service of the entire plan of salvation." Pope John Paul II said that Joseph expressed his fatherhood "by making his life a sacrificial service" to the

∞ Note

The image of Joseph as the "earthly shadow" of God the Father originated in a book by Polish writer Jan Dobraczyński, *The Shadow of the Father*, which tells the story of St. Joseph's life in the form of a novel.

life of Jesus and Jesus's mission to redeem the world. St. Joseph devoted his life to service of Jesus and Mary.

2. He was a tender and loving father.

In Joseph, Jesus was able to experience in the flesh a father who had compassion, who prayed, and who never lost hope. Pope Francis speculates that Jesus may have modeled the merciful father in the parable of the prodigal son on Joseph. God is the Father who welcomes our return to him, willing to show us mercy and be reconciled with us. God the Father will embrace us, kiss us, and rejoice with us when we are with him.

3. He was an obedient father.

Joseph obeyed the will of God the Father, which he heard in dreams. In the first dream, God told Joseph to take Mary into his home and make her his wife. He did that. In the second dream, an angel of God told Joseph to escape with Mary and Jesus to Egypt to avoid the murderous rage of King Herod. He followed the angel's command. From Joseph, Jesus learned obedience. After he was found in the Temple, Jesus returned home with his parents and was "obedient to them" (Lk 2:51).

4. He was an accepting father.

Joseph did not do a lot of explaining. In the Gospels we do not hear him speak. Rather, he trusted the angel's words to him. According to Pope Francis, "Even though he does not understand the bigger picture, he makes a decision to protect Mary's good name, her dignity, and her life." He accepts God's will courageously, not passively, and is firmly proactive. God the Father is an active God, fully engaged in his plan of salvation.

5. He was a creatively courageous father.

When he arrived in Bethlehem to find no lodging for his expectant wife, Joseph located a stable where the Son of God could be born. "He was the true 'miracle' by which God saves the child and his mother. God acted by trusting in Joseph's creative courage," wrote Pope Francis. God is a Father who cooperates with us and our own freely chosen ingenuity to protect and defend his Son in the world.

6. He was a working father.

St. Joseph the Worker is an aspect of Joseph that has been emphasized throughout the history of the Church. Joseph was a carpenter. Jesus learned the value, dignity, and joy of work from Joseph. God the Father values our work and wishes that everyone be given the opportunity to use their particular talents to work and provide for themselves and their families.

7. He was a father in the shadows.

Pope Francis uses the image of a "father in the shadows" for Joseph, explaining that "being a father entails introducing children to life and reality" and "not holding them back, being overprotective or possessive, but rather making them capable of deciding for themselves, enjoying freedom, and exploring new possibilities." Our Father in heaven is like that; one of his great gifts to us is our freedom, even though it is a gift that risks us turning away from him. Joseph never tried to possess Jesus but continued instead to point him to the Father he came from.

"No one is father as God is Father" teaches the *Catechism of the Catholic Church* (239). It is true that human parents are not perfect and can diminish the face of fatherhood (and motherhood). But in his modeling of human fatherhood, St. Joseph provides a glimpse into what God is like as Father.

Comprehension

1. On what occasion did Pope Francis write *Patris coerde*?
2. In what ways was St. Joseph an obedient father?
3. What is meant by Joseph being a "father in the shadows"?
4. How is God the Father a "father in the shadows"?

Reflection

Though God is a spirit, and neither male nor female, he has characteristics resembling both human fatherhood and motherhood in the best sense. How do you imagine these characteristics in a human parent?

him and unite us to his Passion. John Paul II offered the reminder that God "is Emmanuel, God-with-us, a God who shares man's lot and participates in his destiny."[3]

God Reveals His Almighty Power through Suffering

Pope John Paul II said that in a certain sense the Almighty God *did* choose to become impotent when he became fully human. Think back again to Jesus coming before Pontius Pilate (see the subsection "What Is Truth?" in Chapter 2, Section 1). Jesus told Pilate, "My kingdom does not belong to this world. If my kingdom did belong to this world, my attendants [would] be fighting to keep me from being handed over to the Jews. But as it is, my kingdom is not here" (Jn 18:36).

Jesus attempted to explain to Pilate that he had come into the world to testify to what is really true. Pilate didn't understand this and had Jesus condemned. Here is the irony: the Almighty God who had good reason to offer judgment for the sinfulness of humanity was instead being judged himself by a human judge who had no idea of how to answer his own question, "What is truth?" (Jn 18:38).

Jesus was taken away, scourged, crowned with thorns, forced to carry his Cross, and then nailed to it. People continued to mock him: "Save yourself by coming down from the cross" (Mk 15:30). The chief priests and the scribes added, "He saved others; he cannot save himself" (Mk 15:31). These incidents are some of the reasons people have questioned God's power.

But don't forget: as Jesus told Pilate, all of Pilate's power came directly from God. Jesus's kingdom was not an earthly one. In the

Jesus told the women he met while carrying his Cross, "Daughters of Jerusalem, do not weep for me; weep instead for yourselves and for your children" (Lk 23:28).

end, God could have crushed all of his human enemies. But he didn't. Jesus stayed on the Cross until the very end. He cried out with words echoed by countless people who have experienced the loss of a close friend or relative to death, been told of a terminal illness, been cast jobless and homeless into the street, been trafficked and abused, and in so many other unimaginable situations of suffering in this world: "My God, my God, why have you forsaken me?" (Mk 15:34).

These words of the Son of God and his complete acceptance of the human condition—even suffering and death—invert the meaning of omnipotence. Pope John Paul II explained, "Yes! God is love and precisely for this he gave his Son, to reveal himself completely as love. Christ is the one who '*loved . . . to the end*' (Jn 13:21). 'To the end' means to the last breath. 'To the end' means accepting all the consequences of man's sin, taking it upon himself."[4]

Even the Roman soldiers jeered and belittled Jesus.

It may still seem impossible or foolish that the suffering and Death Christ experienced were really signs of God's power and strength. St. Paul wrote to the Corinthians that the "message of the cross is foolishness to those who are perishing," but added that "to us who are being saved it is the power of God" (1 Cor 1:18). The *Catechism of the Catholic Church* teaches that "only faith can embrace the mysterious ways of God's almighty power" (273). When we unite our own suffering to Jesus's suffering, it too becomes redemptive for ourselves and for others (see *CCC*, 1851).

Jesus's violent Death "was not the result of chance in an unfortunate coincidence of circumstances" (*CCC*, 599), but the way God chose to redeem humankind. Jesus died in this way so that sins could be forgiven and so that suffering due to sin could be overcome. God the Father knew that Jesus's

Death was not the end of the story. God knew that Jesus would descend to the dead to save the just who had already died. God knew that he would raise Jesus from the dead on the third day so that the world could receive the Holy Spirit and so that humans could be free to live good lives. This confident hope in Christ's saving act allows us to seek and live a life of happiness in spite of human suffering. After his Resurrection, Jesus explained the meaning of all that had happened to him to his disciples on the way to Emmaus and then to his Apostles (see Luke 24:13–35).

In overcoming sin and the evil and suffering it causes, the Almighty God, acting in the Divine Person of Christ, the Son of God, overcame death—the ultimate evil and suffering. The fullness of this joy is only found in the new heaven and the new earth, where God "will wipe every tear from their eyes, and there shall be no more death or mourning, wailing or pain, [for] the old order has passed away" (Rv 21:4).

SECTION Assessment

Comprehension

1. What did Jesus do after he healed Peter's mother-in-law?

2. What was unusual about how Jesus treated lepers and the blind and lame?

3. What was the closest Jesus came to explaining the existence of human suffering?

4. What did Jesus say was the reason for human suffering?

Reflection

5. Why do you think Jesus did not offer much explanation in words for why God allows human suffering?

6. How do you think that God the Father chose to be, in a certain sense, "impotent" when he became fully human?

7. How do the events around the Paschal Mystery invert the understanding of omnipotence a full 180 degrees?

GOD THE FATHER IS JUST

God the Father created the world in justice. Adam and Eve were created in a state of grace known as **original holiness and original justice**. Original holiness was a grace for people to share in the life of God. Original justice was a grace so that people would not have to suffer and die. Original justice also guaranteed an inner harmony of the human person, the harmony between man and woman, and the harmony between humans and all of creation.

The graces of original holiness and original justice were lost with the sin of Adam and Eve, the Original Sin. Original holiness is restored through the Sacrament of Baptism. But the gift of original justice is not restored. Only with the help of God's grace can we do what is right and grow in holiness, truth, and life. It is a spiritual battle to live a life of justice on earth. Love and compassion provide a basic path.

Through his parables and other teachings, the Son of God revealed much about the Father's true nature. He shared lessons in word and action for how the Father intends for us to live. Love and compassion for the "least ones" are the hallmarks of the Father's justice. Jesus cared for those who were both poor materially and poor in spirit and addressed how we are to treat them. In reading the Gospels, there is little doubt that Jesus had a special concern for

---

original holiness and original justice The state of man and woman in paradise before sin. The grace of original holiness was to share in the divine life (see *CCC*, 375). "The inner harmony of the human person, the harmony between man and woman, and finally the harmony between the first couple and all creation, comprised the state called 'original justice'" (*CCC*, 376). "From [Adam and Eve's] friendship with God flowed the happiness of their existence in paradise" (*CCC*, 384).

the poor. Part of this was likely due to the fact that his own life was steeped in poverty in several ways. From the time of his birth in a stable, Jesus was poor:

> He had no place to call home (see Matthew 8:20).

> He relied on others for generosity and support (see Luke 8:3).

> He died with no possessions (see John 19:23–24).

Jesus also chose to befriend the poor and the outcast. For example, he defended a destitute woman who was condemned for adultery (see John 8:1–30) and reached out to Zacchaeus, the despised tax collector—even going to his home and sharing a meal with him (see Luke 19:1–10). These examples of love and compassion are also criteria on which God will judge us at the time of our death.

The Father's Justice Differs from the World's Justice

When Jesus was handed the scroll in his hometown synagogue and declared from the reading of the prophet Isaiah that the "Spirit of the Lord" was upon him, he continued by quoting his mission, saying that the Spirit "has anointed me to bring glad tidings to the poor" (Lk 4:18–19).

Jesus certainly revealed a God who cares for the poor and loves them for who they are and not what they can produce. In the familiar parable of the workers in the vineyard (see Matthew 20:1–16), the laborers who are hired early in the morning and work a full day are paid the same amount as those who work only one hour. The landowner in the parable tells the workers who complain, "What if I wish to give this last one the same as you? [Or] am I not free to do as I wish with my own money? Are you envious because I am generous?" (Mt 20:14–15).

This form of justice seems illogical to many. An understanding of justice today revolves around what people can produce *and* consume. The poor and vulnerable of society—including the unborn, immigrants, the homeless, the unemployed, the disabled, and the sick and elderly—are often viewed and

"Children are the first among those to pay the heavy toll of emigration, almost always caused by violence, poverty, environmental conditions, as well as the negative aspects of globalization" (Pope Francis).

treated as a weight on society because they do not "do their fair share" to contribute to the economic pie.

God's idea of justice is completely different. The Father values all people and is generous with the gifts he gives. He provides to people not according to their skills or talents or what they produce but according to what they need. **Additionally and surprisingly, God equates poverty with happiness. Jesus said so in his preaching of the eight Beatitudes in the Sermon on the Mount (see Matthew 5:3–12).** The word *beatitude* means "supreme happiness." The type of happiness described here is not temporal or fleeting. This type of happiness draws us to God, the only one who can fulfill this desire for supreme happiness. The Beatitudes and how to live them will be covered in more detail in chapter 8.

The Hebrew name for the poor in Jesus's time was *anawim*. This term described people without many material possessions who nevertheless kept a positive attitude, realized their helplessness, and sought God for all their needs, material and spiritual. Most important, the "poor in spirit" trusted that God would take care of all their needs. This is the type of poverty of spirit that God calls us to. With this trust comes more than personal easiness and satisfaction. The real reward is supreme happiness.

The Father Assigns Judgment to the Son

Both the Apostles' Creed and the Nicene Creed remind the Church that Jesus, the Son of God, has been assigned the role of judge by his Father: "He will come again to judge the living and the dead." In describing the work of the Son, Jesus said, "For just as the Father raises the dead and gives life, so also does the Son give life to whomever he wishes. Nor does the Father judge anyone, but he has given all judgment to his Son, so that all may honor the Son just as they honor the Father" (Jn 5:21–23).

Christ's primary mission in coming to the world was to save souls, and the full right to judgment of all people belongs to him as Redeemer of the world. The criteria for judgment are not secrets. Jesus referred to a person's **particular judgment** in the parable of the rich man and Lazarus (see Luke 16:19–31). In the parable, because of ignoring the starving Lazarus, the rich man went to hell while Lazarus went to a peaceful resting place.

The Rich Man and Lazarus.

particular judgment The individual judgment of every person right after death, when Christ will rule on one's eternal destiny in heaven (after purification in Purgatory, if needed) or in hell.

The particular judgment will occur immediately at the time of your death, when your soul separates from your human body. At this one-to-one meeting between you and Christ, Christ will decide whether or not your soul will proceed directly to the blessedness of heaven, or to heaven after first being purified in Purgatory, or immediately to hell and eternal damnation.∞

At the Last Judgment, our bodies will come back to life, united with our souls.

∞ Note

Heaven is eternal happiness in union with the Blessed Trinity, Mary, the saints (including your friends and relatives who are saints in heaven), and the angels. "What eye has not seen, and ear has not heard . . . what God has prepared for those who love him" (1 Cor 2:9). Time and space will be different in heaven; they won't be measured by days or years or confined areas. The Father's house has many rooms. *Purgatory* is the name for the state of being of those who died in God's grace and friendship without mortal sin on their souls, which would deprive them of eternal life, but are still in need of purification. There is work and pain in Purgatory as these souls rid themselves of sin. Yet there is consolation as well, knowing that when the purgation is complete, the souls will be made capable of enjoying the bliss of heaven. *Hell* is a separation from God forever due to one's own free choice to commit, and not repent of, mortal sin. It is replete with everlasting physical, emotional, and spiritual suffering and filled with absolute hate, interminable anger, and boundless rage. The existence of hell is consistent with a merciful and loving Father who truly has made humans free. God respects our freedom even if, out of pride, we choose to reject his love, grace, and mercy.

A modern fresco of the Last Judgment.

The **Last (or General) Judgment** will occur on the last day of human history when Jesus returns in glory to earth. On that day, good will ultimately triumph over evil. The resurrection of all the dead will occur, both "the righteous and the unrighteous" (Acts 24:15). All bodies of those who have died will rise and be reunited with their souls, both those souls in heaven and those souls in hell.∞ In Jesus's presence, the saved and the condemned will be separated from one another like the sheep and the goats in his concluding discourse, the judgment of the nations, in Matthew 25:31–46. This separation will be based on how each person responded to the needs of the poor and suffering in their midst.

∞ Note

At the Last Judgment our bodies will be transformed into spiritual bodies, similar to the way Jesus's body appeared after his Resurrection. He was recognizable to his disciples yet his spiritual body was different; for example, he could pass into rooms through locked doors.

Last (or General) Judgment Jesus Christ's judgment of the living and the dead on the last day, when he will come again to fully establish God's Kingdom.

SECTION Assessment

Comprehension

1. What is meant by "poor in spirit"?

2. Provide an example from Scripture of how Jesus treated someone who was poor.

3. What are the criteria Jesus uses for judging a person's life?

Vocabulary

4. Explain the difference between the *particular judgment* and the *Last (or General) Judgment*.

Reflection

5. In your own words, write one-sentence descriptions of heaven, Purgatory, and hell.

GOD THE FATHER CARRIES OUT HIS PLAN

All of creation is "in a state of journeying toward an ultimate perfection yet to be attained, to which God has destined it" (*CCC*, 302). The name for this action is divine providence. God's plan for you and the world will not be denied. He cares for all things from the least to the greatest, down to the most minute of details. Jesus spoke of divine providence. To help his disciples ignore the anxieties that came with being persecuted, he pointed out that even the sparrows in the sky are cared for by the Father. "Even all the hairs of your head are counted," Jesus said. "So do not be afraid; you are worth more than many sparrows" (Mt 10:30–31).

Understanding how divine providence works remains difficult. Think about how you ask God for important things with your prayers and then experience some of your prayers going unanswered. For example, have you ever known anyone like

- the sophomore who prayed to make the baseball team but got cut,

- the mother who prayed for a healthy child but gave birth to an infant with Down syndrome, or

- the soldier who prayed to come home from the war safely (and did), only to be diagnosed with a rare cancer shortly after?

There is no doubt that it is very difficult to accept the Father's will when it is different from our own, but in reality God's ways, in general, are not our ways (see Isaiah 55:8).

In the situations mentioned, the former baseball player turned his talents to sports writing, which earned him a full college journalism scholarship. The child with Down syndrome was the family's seventh and youngest child. The mother is now fond of saying, "She is the one who taught us all about the joy of life." The ex-soldier with cancer eventually died of the disease but not before he met regularly with a Catholic hospital chaplain, and not before he was baptized into the Church a few days before he died.

"She is the one who taught us all about the joy of life."

Recall from the subsection "God Reveals His Almighty Power through Suffering" in Chapter 2, Section 2, how God allows suffering and evil and can make good come from them. This section delves further into what the Son of God taught about how the Father reveals his will and how he always acts out of the best intentions for us in combination with our gift of freedom. Our own journeying in life is to lead us to be like Jesus himself, who completely followed his Father's will from the time of the Incarnation until his Death on the Cross.

The Father's Will

Amid all the commotion of speaking with a Samaritan woman and asking her for water (see John 4:4–41), Jesus explained that his mission in life (and our mission too) is to do the Father's will. Jesus's disciples were in for another surprise when they tried to make sure he had eaten. Jesus told them, "I have food to eat of which you do not know" (Jn 4:32). The disciples wondered if someone could have brought him something to eat when they were not present. Jesus responded to their question succinctly: "My food is to do the will of the one who sent me and to finish his work" (Jn 4:34).

Jesus always did his Father's will, to the point of accepting his own Death on the Cross. It wasn't always easy for him. In the Garden of Gethsemane, he prayed, "Father, if you are willing, take this cup away from me," but added, "still, not my will but yours be done" (Lk 22:42). On the Cross, Jesus cried out in a loud voice, "Father, into your hands I commend my spirit" (Lk 23:46), quoting Psalm 31:6, which is an expression of his confidence in the Father's offer of redemption.

Jesus's conversation with the Samaritan woman at the well was surprising to his disciples because the Samaritans were viewed by Jews as foreigners, even though they had Jewish ancestry from their intermarriage in history with the old northern Israelite tribes at the time of the Assyrian conquest of the Northern Kingdom. Jews and Samaritans recognized Abraham as their common father. Samaritan women were regarded by Jews as ritually impure, making it even more remarkable Jesus would drink from any vessel she handled. God's providence was moving in new ways. Jesus is the Living Water who brings new and everlasting life.

Many people today have difficulty believing in a divine providence that allows all things to work for the Father's plan. God *is* able to make good from bad. There is nothing that he does not control. As St. Augustine wrote, "Nothing happens that the Almighty does not will should happen, either by permitting it or by himself doing it." God does not will the evil of war or sickness like cancer, but he is so good, wrote St. Augustine, "that in his hand, even evil brings about good. He would have never permitted evil to occur if he had not, thanks to his perfect goodness, been able to use it."

From Jesus's example of obedience to his Father's will, we can learn that we, too, are meant to seek and obey divine providence. We should also understand that, apart from sin, everything that happens in our life—big and small, bad and good—is part of God's plan for us and our salvation. (God does use even our sin and the suffering it causes to turn us away from sin and toward goodness.) The difficulty in accepting and following divine providence is that doing so is often in direct opposition to our own will or the will of others nearby (people, Satan) who are able to influence us.

Jesus Offers Ways to Follow God's Providence

The gifts of freedom and human intellect help us to analyze our choices and what happens in the course of our day in accordance with the will of God.∞ These gifts also help us to battle Satan and the various temptations he places before us.

Jesus gives us guidance about how to recognize and follow God's providence in our life:

1 Become like a child.

Talking with his disciples, Jesus called a child forward and then told them "unless you turn and become like children, you will not enter the kingdom of heaven" (Mt 18:3). This message does not mean we are to be naïve but rather we are to be dependent on and trust in God just as young children are dependent on and trust in their parents.

2 Don't worry.

Jesus wondered, "Can any of you by worrying add a single moment to your life-span?" (Mt 6:27). He gave several examples to make his point that worry is fruitless. Birds don't worry, yet God feeds and shelters them. Fields adorned with wildflowers are more beautiful than anything a person could purchase to wear. The point here is not to deny the reality of human needs but to not be anxious about them. St. Teresa of Avila said, "Let nothing disturb you. Let nothing frighten you." St. Pio of Pietrelcina likewise said, "Pray, hope, and don't worry." Jesus himself reminds you that God will care for you. He knows all that you need. "Seek first the kingdom [of God] and his righteousness, and all these things will be given you besides" (Mt 6:33).

∞ Note

God's gift of freedom always allows for the possibility of opposing God and choosing evil and thus sinning. However, the more we choose what is good and orient ourselves toward the ultimate good that is God, the freer we become. It is a wonderful feeling to be free in this way and gives us a hint of our life in eternity. See *CCC*, 1730–1742.

③ Let God handle the details.

In speaking of not being afraid in the face of persecution, Jesus pointed out that the Father's providence extends to the most minute of details: "Even the hairs of your head have all been counted. Do not be afraid" (Lk 12:7).

The best way to live in accord with God's will and to accept his providence is to encounter him in daily prayer. Pray as Jesus taught that his Father's will "be done, on earth as in heaven" (Mt 6:10). God answers the prayers of those who keep asking, keep seeking, and keep knocking: "For everyone who asks, receives; and the one who seeks, finds; and to the one who knocks, the door will be opened" (Lk 11:10).

SECTION Assessment

Comprehension

1. In his conversation with the Samaritan woman, what did Jesus say was his life's mission?

2. What did St. Augustine say about God being able to make good from bad?

3. How do the gifts of freedom and human intellect help a person to follow God's providence?

Reflection

4. How can a childlike approach to life help you to follow God's will?

5. Name one small event from your daily life in the past few days when you recognized God's presence.

Section Reviews

Focus Question

What did Jesus reveal about God the Father?

Complete one of the following:

- Psalm 23 is beloved for its imagery of a caring, loving God who shepherds his people. Carefully read this psalm. Then rewrite it using different imagery that still represents the Father's loving-kindness and care for his people.

- Review the meaning of the following attributes of God: holy, omnipotent, infinite, eternal, immense. Look up the following passages from the Old Testament. Decide which attribute of God each describes: Jeremiah 10:10–12; Psalm 139:1–6; Isaiah 55; Jeremiah 32:17, 27; Psalm 139:7–12.

- Read each of the following gospel passages: Matthew 18:1–5; Matthew 6:25–34; Luke 12:2–9; Luke 11:9–13. Summarize what each passage says about following God's will in your own life.

Introduction
God Is Father

Review

Christ revealed that God is Father in a unique way: God is Father only in relation to his Son. When we come to know the Son, Jesus, through the power of the Holy Spirit, it is also possible to intimately know God the Father. Jesus said, "Whoever has seen me has seen the Father" (Jn 14:9)

Assignment

What are three qualities you associate with a good father? (Note that there can also be spiritual expressions of fatherhood.) How can these qualities also be connected to God the Father?

Section 1

God the Father Is Love and Truth

Review

The very essence of God is love. We are meant to share in the eternal love between God the Father and God the Son, a love that manifests itself in the Holy Spirit. God's truth is his wisdom with which he created and governs the world.

Assignment

Read the *Catechism of the Catholic Church*, paragraphs 214–221. Use this information to complete these two sentences: (1) God is truth because . . . and (2) God's love for his people is like . . .

Section 2

God the Father Is Almighty

Review

God is omnipotent or all-powerful, yet as he reveals, his true power was to embrace human weakness and human suffering in order to redeem the world. Jesus's entire life and particularly the Paschal Mystery shed light on the mystery of suffering. Jesus ministered to the sick and suffering. He explained in his healing of a blind man that the man's condition was not punishment for the sinfulness of his parents. Some suffering is traced directly to the evil of Satan. Human suffering and death are the direct result of Original Sin.

Assignment

When was a time in your own life when something good happened after a period of trial, setback, or suffering?

Section 3
God the Father Is Just

Review

Jesus, commanded by the Father to be the judge of humankind, explained that the criterion for our judgment is how we treat the poor. Jesus shared the Father's special love and care for the poor. He himself was poor. Jesus quoted the Old Testament, explaining that his mission was "to bring glad tidings to the poor" (Lk 4:18). In the Beatitudes—especially the first Beatitude, "Blessed are the poor in spirit"—Jesus equated lasting happiness with being poor enough to rely on God always for all of our needs.

Assignment

Research the following terms and tell how they relate to the particular judgment and the Last (or General) Judgment: *Second Coming, resurrection of the body,* and *beatific vision.*

Section 4
God the Father Carries Out His Plan

Review

Jesus explained the importance of remaining close to God the Father and following his will. God always acts with our best intentions in mind in combination with our gift of freedom. Through childlike dependence on the Father, giving over to him all anxiety and worry, remembering that he is in control of all the details of our life, and especially through daily prayer, we can be open to and follow God's will.

Assignment

Look up the definition of *divine providence* contained in the *Catechism of the Catholic Church,* paragraph 302. Summarize it in your own words.

Chapter Projects

Choose and complete at least one of the following projects to assess your understanding of the material in this chapter.

⚙ 1. Identify Items in Allegory of Divine Providence

Allegory of Divine Providence has an overwhelming number of intricate details and requires time to study. Develop a key that labels each of the following items in the painting. You might make a printed copy of the painting and glue it to a poster board with lines or arrows pointing to the items, and then number the items and provide a corresponding key. Or you could overlay tracing paper on the painting and record the names of the items on the tracing paper. Ten items are listed below. Add two other items not on the list. Write an explanation of the meaning of six items of your choice.

1.   Golden maidens holding papal keys
2.   Golden bees
3.   Man with a scythe
4.   Twelve stars
5.   Mermen, nymphs, garlands, and bucrania (ox skulls)
6.   Small wreath
7.   Hercules
8.   Venus (the goddess)
9.   Scipio Africanus the Younger
10. Woman on a cloud (Divine Providence)

⚙ 2. Film a Video Interview on the Meaning of Life

At one point in William Shakespeare's famous play *Macbeth*, the forlorn king says he is disenchanted with life and has a pessimistic view of it. In contrast to his negative judgment is the Christian view, which says that human life is good and that all people are created precious sons and daughters of a loving God.

Make a video recording of an interview with a person who is actively engaged in public ministry in the Church. The person might be a priest, a religious sister or brother, a parish youth minister, or a theology teacher at your school. Ask the person about what makes life beautiful and how even fallen human beings can find redemption. You could also investigate why human beings often do bad things or why evil exists in the world. Share the video on a social media site approved by your teacher so that you can play all or part of it to your classmates. Write a one-page essay that includes biographical information on the interviewee, a summary of the interview, and a brief commentary on what you learned.

⚙ *3. Highlight St. Teresa of Avila's Reflections on St. Joseph*

Sixteenth-century mystic St. Teresa of Avila is one of many saints with a devotion to St. Joseph. Create a video, slide, or printed journal compilation of at least five quotations of St. Teresa about St. Joseph. Highlight each quotation separately. After each quotation, write your own reflection on St. Joseph. Provide images for each quotation and reflection. Add an introductory page with brief biographical information on St. Teresa of Avila with an explanation of her devotion to St. Joseph.

⚙ *4. Create a Mind Map of God's Providence*

Jean-Pierre de Caussade was an eighteenth-century French Jesuit priest best known for his book *Abandonment to Divine Providence*. There he writes, "All things exist and live in the hand of God. Our senses perceive only creaturely action, but through faith we see the action of God in everything. Through faith we believe that Jesus Christ is alive in everything and works throughout the course of the centuries."

Create a mind map that connects the simple everyday actions, joys, sufferings, people, and experiences of your day to a revelation of how God is working in your life. For example, maybe through an illness or disappointment you came to a better understanding of the meaning of Jesus's suffering for you. Or maybe through a random traffic stoplight or a missed turn you encountered a homeless person who brought God's face alive to you. Connect experiences like these using words, pictures, and an art medium of your choosing. Be prepared to explain the connections of the items and their significance to you in learning more about God.

⚙ *5. Summarize and Illustrate the Petitions of the Our Father*

Arguably the most famous Christian prayer is the Our Father. Given to his disciples directly from Christ, this prayer offers great insight into how we should relate to God the Father.

Read the important treatise on the Our Father in the *Catechism of the Catholic Church*, paragraphs 2759–2865. Write a one-page summary of these paragraphs. Also, create a visual, artistic depiction of the Our Father. You can create original artwork or make a collage of pictures. Use poster board or a PowerPoint presentation for display.

Faithful Disciple
St. Alphonsus Liguori

St. Alphonsus Liguori (1696–1787) suggested that when anything disagreeable happens, one should say, "This comes from God," and then be at peace. He said that a person should direct all thoughts and prayers, all receptions of Holy Communion, and all visits before the Blessed Sacrament to this request: "My God, behold me in your presence; do with me and all that I have as you please."

Alphonsus Marie de Liguori was born in Naples, Italy. He originally became a lawyer but was unhappy in the profession. One day he heard an interior voice say to him, "Leave the world, and give yourself to me." He then desired to enter the seminary and study to be a priest. His father was disappointed and only agreed if Alphonsus would complete his studies while living at home. Alphonsus was ordained in 1726. One of his first ministry efforts was to work with the unemployed and idle in Naples. He was committed to offering them the Sacrament of Penance and religious instruction. In 1732 he founded the Redemptorist order, which was dedicated to preaching in the poorest areas of cities.

St. Alphonsus Liguori was also a poet and a musician, who used these gifts to calm his scruples. He was obsessed by his least faults and often overcome with guilt. However, St. Alphonsus viewed his scrupulous temperament as a blessing, explaining that scruples "cleanse the soul, and at the same time make it careful." St. Alphonsus evolved and eventually became a moral theologian noted for opposing legalism and strict rigor, which he now saw as contrary to the

St. Alphonsus Liguori

love of Christ and the Gospel. His multivolume masterpiece, *The Moral Theology*, provides concrete answers to practical questions posed by Catholics. The insights gathered here were born from the saint's work as a parish priest, and especially with the poor and incorrigible.

In all things, St. Alphonsus was moved to obey God's will. In approximately 1755, he wrote an essay entitled "Uniformity with God's Will," in which he reminds Catholics that everything comes from God—things we deem good and things we consider bad—all working for our own good:

> The essence of perfection is to embrace the will of God in all things, prosperous or adverse. In prosperity, even sinners find it easy to unite themselves to the divine will; but it takes saints to unite themselves to God's will when things go wrong and are painful to self-love. Our conduct in such instances is the measure of our love of God. St. John of Avila used to say, "One 'Blessed be God' in times of adversity, is worth more than a thousand acts of gratitude in times of prosperity." Furthermore, we must unite ourselves to God's will not only in things that come to us directly from his hands, such as sickness, desolation, poverty, death of relatives, but likewise in those we suffer from man—for example, contempt, injustice, loss of reputation, loss of temporal goods and all kinds of persecution. On these occasions we must remember that whilst God does not will the sin, he does will our humiliation, our poverty, or our mortification, as the case may be. It is certain and of faith, that whatever happens, happens by the will of God.

Later in life St. Alphonsus was consecrated as bishop of Sant'Agata de' Goti. He tried to refuse the appointment due to his advanced age, but once he became bishop, he devoted himself to correcting abuses in the diocese. He reformed the seminary and suspended any priest who did not celebrate Mass reverently or who rushed through Mass under fifteen minutes.

St. Alphonsus suffered through the last eighteen months of his life. He died just before his ninety-first birthday. Pope Pius VII beatified Alphonsus Liguori in 1816. He was canonized on May 26, 1839, by Pope Gregory XVI. In 1950 he was named patron saint of confessors and moral theologians by Pope Pius XII. Always, the saint recommended recourse to prayer in order to understand God's will: "Our Savior says, if you have not received the graces that you desire, do not complain to me, but blame yourself, because you have neglected to seek them from me."

Comprehension

1. What condition did Alphonsus's father place on his entering the seminary?
2. What is the name of the religious order founded by St. Alphonsus?
3. How does sin play a factor in the will of God according to St. Alphonsus?
4. Name a reform St. Alphonsus accomplished as bishop.

Application

Look up and read St. Alphonsus's essay "Uniformity with God's Will." Write down two of your favorite quotations from the article. Explain why you chose them.

Prayer

St. Jane Frances de Chantal (1572–1641) was born in Dijon, France. Her husband, the Baron de Chantal, died when she was twenty-eight years old, leaving her with four young children. Her father-in-law threatened to evict her from the castle she had shared with her husband. At age thirty-two, Jane met St. Francis de Sales. He encouraged her to found a religious community for women who had been previously denied religious life owing to age, illness, or other issues. St. Jane founded the Visitation community to fulfill that purpose. St. Jane's life was plagued by suffering. One of her sons was killed, and she lived through the plague that traversed France. Through it all she trusted in God's providence, as reflected in the following prayer.

An Act of Abandonment to Divine Providence

O sovereign goodness of the sovereign Providence of my God! I abandon myself forever to thy arms. Whether gentle or severe, lead me henceforth whither thou wilt; I will not regard the way through which thou wilt have me pass, but keep my eyes fixed upon thee, my God, who guidest me. My soul finds no rest without the arms and the bosom of this heavenly Providence, my true Mother, my strength and my rampart. Therefore I resolve with thy divine assistance, O my Savior, to follow thy desires and thy ordinances, without regarding or examining why thou dost this rather than that; but I will blindly follow thee according to thy divine will, without seeking my own inclinations. Hence I am determined to leave all to thee, taking no part therein save by keeping myself in peace in thy arms, desiring nothing except as thou incitest me to desire, to will, to wish. I offer thee this desire, O my God, beseeching thee to bless it; I undertake all it includes, relying on thy goodness, liberality, and mercy, with entire confidence in thee, distrust of myself, and knowledge of my infinite misery and infirmity. Amen.

Jesus Reveals More about God in Three Persons

Return of the Prodigal Son

Rembrandt

We learn quite a bit about the compassionate nature of God the Father in the parable of the prodigal son, told by Jesus and recorded only in the Gospel of Luke (15:11–31). The parable has a Trinitarian dimension as there is a family living under the roof of the father of the parable, including the older son and the wayward younger son, but also likely a mother and possibly other siblings and hired workers. When the younger son decides to return home, he is returning more to his loving family than to a place. The connection with the Holy Trinity is that the Three Divine Persons are a communion who operate like a loving family. As the father in the parable is compassionate and prays for his son's return, God in all Three Divine Persons wants us to remain in his everlasting love.

Dutch artist Rembrandt (1606–1669) was significantly moved by the parable of the prodigal son and created many sketches and paintings around its theme. *Return of the Prodigal Son* was completed within two years of Rembrandt's death in 1669, making it one of his last paintings. There are several figures in the painting. The highlighted father and son stand out against the dark background. Notice the son's ragged clothing and balding head; he has wasted his life in foreign lands, which has left his appearance disheveled. The father appears grateful and somewhat shocked to have his son home, and his embrace is one of love. Standing at the right is the older brother of the parable, who crosses his hands in judgment. The seated figure is thought to be an assistant of the father. In the shadows is thought to be the mother of the two young men.

Our God, who is a God of reconciliation and love, always calls us home to the loving communion of himself in Three Divine Persons: Father, Son, and Holy Spirit. Twentieth-century Dutch spiritual writer Henri Nouwen wrote a book on this painting, describing Rembrandt as a man who had at one time been both the judging older son and the lost younger son. "Both needed to come home. Both needed the embrace of a forgiving father," Nouwen wrote.

Return of the Prodigal Son is now housed in the State Hermitage Museum in St. Petersburg, Russia.

If you would like to compare two other Rembrandt works on the prodigal son with this one, see Chapter 3 Review, Chapter Project 1.

How can we understand the mystery of the Holy Trinity?

Chapter Overview

Introduction
One God, Three Persons

Section 1
The Church Teaches about the Blessed Trinity

Section 2
Understanding More about the Relationship between God the Father and God the Son

Section 3
Tracing an Understanding of the Holy Spirit

Section 4
Entering the Life of the Blessed Trinity

ONE GOD, THREE PERSONS

God had revealed himself to the Jewish people as the only God. By the time Jesus entered into the world, *monotheism*, the belief in one supreme God, was still treated as an odd belief among the Roman occupiers and the Greek-based culture in which the Jews lived. More typical among these Gentiles was some form of *polytheism*, the belief in many gods.

The Icon of the Trinity *painted by Russian artist Andrei Rublev in the early fifteenth century is of three angels who visisted Abraham at the Oak of Mamre (see Genesis 18:1–8). The angels represent the community of Persons of the Holy Trinity who embody spiritual unity, peace, harmony, mutual love, and humility.*

This course has already introduced the unique relationship that Jesus had with the one, true God, the same God of his Jewish faith. Jesus referred to God as Abba, or "Father." In addition, Jesus spoke of the Holy Spirit, "the Spirit of truth, which the world cannot accept, because it neither sees nor knows it" (Jn 14:17). How was this reference to be understood? In fact, when you make the Sign of the Cross—"In the name of the Father, and of the Son, and of the Holy Spirit"—are you aware that through these simple words you are expressing the most essential Christian doctrine? You are also recognizing one of the most difficult mysteries about God that you could possibly attempt to comprehend: the mystery of the Blessed Trinity. Though it is a mystery that human minds cannot solve, the Blessed Trinity is the source of our life and love and therefore a mystery we should glory in.

The mystery of the Blessed Trinity is essentially this: **There is only one God, but there are Three Divine Persons in this one God.** There are not three Gods "but one God in three persons, the 'consubstantial Trinity'" (*CCC*, 253). The Church has always striven to understand the concept of Three Persons in one God. The Council of Florence (1338–1445), for example, addressed the mystery in some detail. The council taught four essential points:

There is **1** nature in God.

There are **2** processions. The Son proceeds from the Father. The Holy Spirit proceeds from the Father and the Son.

There are **3** Persons: Father, Son, and Holy Spirit.

There are **4** relationships between the Three Divine Persons: (1) God the Father *generates* the Son; (2) God the Son *is generated* by the Father; (2) The Father and Son *bring about* the Holy Spirit through their love; and (4) The Holy Spirit *is brought about* from the love of the Father and Son.

The important overall point is that God is a community of love. Just as the Three Divine Persons have one and the same nature, the Trinity also acts as one. We can partially understand this through our participation in human relationships that grow in love in families. The love of a man and woman produces a child. In love, moms and dads and brothers and sisters share in sorrows, challenges, and joys. Love in a family is relational; the family members care for one another. Likewise, the Three Divine Persons are relative to one another. However, just as moms, dads, sisters, and brothers are unique individuals in a family, each Divine Person—God the Father, God the Son, and God the Holy Spirit—"performs the common work according to his unique personal property" (*CCC*, 258) that leads to the creation, redemption, and sanctification of the world. Nevertheless, all of God's action is always accomplished by all Three Persons of the Blessed Trinity.

Gospel Examples of the Blessed Trinity

On four separate occasions, the Gospels describe the Three Divine Persons of the Blessed Trinity coming together and being clearly revealed by Jesus. The Gospels present evidence of the Trinitarian nature of God from the very beginning of Jesus's life. The Gospels also share several examples of how the Divine Persons reveal their own distinct properties in work that is done by the whole Blessed Trinity.

At the Annunciation, when Jesus was conceived, God the Father sent the angel Gabriel to Mary. The angel told her she would conceive a son and that her Son would be called Son of the Most High. When Mary asked how this could be since she was not married, Gabriel responded that "the holy Spirit will come upon you, and the power of the Most High will overshadow you" (Lk 1:35). In the conception of Jesus, all the Persons of the Blessed Trinity are acting and all are revealed. God the Father sends the angel Gabriel to announce that his Son is coming into the world as a man. By the power of the Holy Spirit, God the Son becomes a man in the womb of Mary. So, in the one act by which the Son of God becomes man, all Three Persons of the

Fresco of Annunciation scene by Karl von Blaa.

Blessed Trinity are contributing—the Father sending his Son, the Holy Spirit acting by his power to conceive the Father's Son as man, and the Son of God being conceived as man.

At the beginning of his public ministry, when Jesus appeared at the Jordan River to be baptized, John the Baptist recognized him as God's Chosen One: "I need to be baptized by you, and yet you are coming to me?" (Mt 3:14). After Jesus was baptized, the Holy Spirit became visible in the form of a dove (Mt 3:16). Finally, the voice of God the Father was heard from heaven: "This is my beloved Son, with whom I am well pleased" (Mt 3:17). Thus, at his Baptism, the Father sent the Holy Spirit upon Jesus, empowering him to be the Messiah, the anointed one of God, so that by the power of the Holy Spirit, Jesus would be able to perform saving acts throughout his ministry, especially in his Passion and Death. Throughout his life, Jesus, as the Father's Son, always did his Father's will by the power of the Holy Spirit.

All three Divine Persons of the Blessed Trinity were present at the Baptism of Jesus.

Later, during the heart of his public ministry, Jesus gave another glimpse of the Blessed Trinity when he showed his divine glory to the Apostles Peter, James, and John on a mountain and appeared in the company of the Old Testament prophets Moses and Elijah. During this event, called the *Transfiguration*, Jesus revealed his divine Sonship, and the Father vocally confirmed that Jesus was indeed his beloved Son. All Three Divine Persons were evident in this event (see Matthew 17:5): the Father in the voice, the Son in Jesus, and the Holy Spirit in the shining cloud.

Finally, after Jesus's Resurrection and just before his Ascension to heaven, he instructed the eleven Apostles to carry on his work:

> All power in heaven and on earth has been given to me. Go, there-fore, and make disciples of all nations, baptizing them in the name of the Father, and of the Son, and of the holy Spirit, teaching them to observe all that I have commanded you. And behold, I am with you always, until the end of the age. (Mt 28:18–20)

Note three key points:

1. **Jesus commissioned his Apostles to share the Gospel to the ends of the earth.**

2. **He instructed them to baptize in the name of the Father, and of the Son, and of the Holy Spirit.**

3. **He said he would be with the Church until the end of time.**

In this commissioning of the Apostles, Jesus revealed that there is one God in Three Divine Persons. This passage points to a clear connection between the Sign of the Cross, Baptism, and faith in the Blessed Trinity. The Rite of Baptism "signifies and actually brings about death to sin and entry into the life of the Most Holy Trinity through configuration to the Paschal mystery of Christ" (*CCC*, 1239). From the mystery of the Blessed Trinity come all other mysteries of faith.

A fresco of the Transfiguration by Lattanzio Gambara.

In other examples in the Gospels, Jesus explained more truths of each Divine Person: Father, Son, and Holy Spirit. Inspired by the Holy Spirit, the Church has delved more deeply into this mystery from her beginning. Reflecting the faith articulated at the Council of Nicaea in 325, St. Athanasius clearly stated that "we worship one God in Trinity, and Trinity in Unity. . . . The Father is God, the Son is God, and the Holy Spirit is God, and yet there are not three gods but one God."

This chapter explores more about the Blessed Trinity, the mystery central to Christian faith.

SECTION Assessment

Comprehension

1. Summarize the four points on the Blessed Trinity from the Council of Florence in your own words.

2. How were the Three Divine Persons of the Trinity represented in the account of Jesus's Baptism?

3. What were the main tasks Jesus assigned to his Apostles when he commissioned them after his Resurrection?

Vocabulary

4. Define *Transfiguration* as it pertains to the example in the synoptic Gospels.

Reflection

5. Explain the statement made by St. Athanasius, "We worship one God in Trinity, and Trinity in Unity," using a concrete example from your own life.

THE CHURCH TEACHES ABOUT THE BLESSED TRINITY

The Church addressed the mystery of the Blessed Trinity from its earliest days. For example, St. Paul shared a Trinitarian formula for greeting fellow Christians: "The grace of the Lord Jesus Christ and the love of God and the fellowship of the holy Spirit be with all of you" (2 Cor 13:13).

Also, early Church councils and the Church Fathers developed a vocabulary that remains associated with the Blessed Trinity:

- *Substance* is used to describe the unity of God. *Substance* is often substituted for "nature" or "essence." God is one divine being. All Three Persons of the Trinity—Father, Son, and Holy Spirit—have the same divine substance. All Three Persons share the same attributes—for example, all-loving and eternal. St. Gregory of Nazianzus wrote, "Each person considered in himself is entirely God . . . the three considered together. . . . I have not even begun to think of unity when the Trinity bathes me in its splendor" (*Oratio* 40, 41: PG 36, 417, quoted in *CCC*, 256).

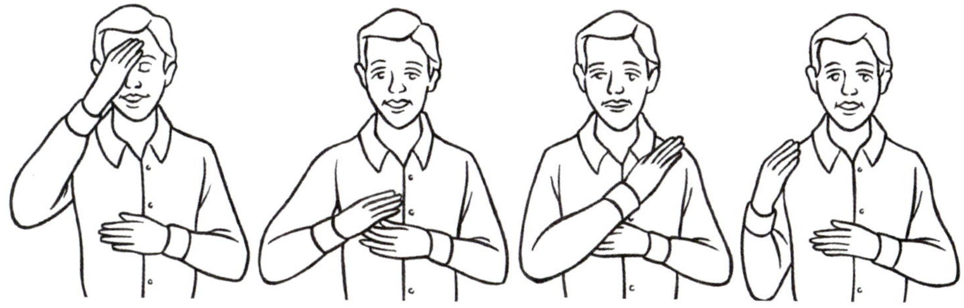

"In the name of the Father, and of the Son, and of the Holy Spirit. Amen."

- *Person* (or "hypostasis")[∞] is used to make distinctions among Father, Son, and Holy Spirit.

- *Relation* designates that the distinction of the Three Divine Persons is due to the relationship of each Person to the others.

As the centuries went on, theologians used this vocabulary to teach even deeper truths about the Blessed Trinity.

Ways to Understand the Mystery of the Blessed Trinity

God created human beings with minds that want to know the truth and that are attracted to God, the source of all truth. That is why theologians—including St. Augustine of Hippo[≈] and St. Thomas Aquinas—guided by the Holy

∞ Note

Hypostasis is a Greek word that means an individual, complete substance existing entirely in itself. Each Person of the Holy Trinity is an individual substance, but there is one essence and one nature in all three: each Divine Person is God. However, each Divine Person is a separately existing being and a substance (hypostasis), a free spiritual being with its own existence and character. God the Father is the principal being; he is the only Divine Person able to beget, that is, capable of causing other persons to proceed from him. The Father is the "first cause" from which the Son and Holy Spirit find their being.

≈ Note

A story is told about St. Augustine walking along the seashore, deep in thought, trying to figure out the mystery of the Trinity. "How could there be one God and yet three distinct Persons?" he pondered. He was so engrossed in thought that he almost stumbled over a little boy who was pouring a pail of water into a hole he had dug in the sand. Augustine stopped to chat with the boy. "What are you doing?" he asked. "I'm going to empty the ocean into this hole," the boy replied. Augustine laughed. "You'll never get the whole ocean into that little hole," he said. The boy stood up and looked directly at Augustine and said, "And you, sir, will never put the whole mystery of the Blessed Trinity into your little mind."

Spirit, have struggled to explain, even if in a partial way, the mystery of the Blessed Trinity. The Church has described God's *immanence*, or inner life, as determining the active and inseparable work of the Triune God in salvation history. The way the Divine Persons act in salvation history is called the salvific or economic expression of the Trinity.

God's immanence refers to how "God exists in God." The inner life of God is a starting point for understanding the mystery of the Blessed Trinity. Several points follow here:

1 **God is eternal; he exists without beginning or end.** The Father is eternally the Father, and so from all eternity the Father begets his Son.

2 **The Father gives fullness of divine life to his Son so that the Son is the perfect image of the Father, which is why he is the Son.**

3 **Because the Son is the perfect image of the Father, the Son contains all the truth of the Father, and so the Son is also the perfect Divine Word of the Father.** Recall from the very first verse of the prologue of John's Gospel how the Father and Son were together from eternity:

> In the beginning was the Word,
> and the Word was with God,
> and the Word was God. (Jn 1:1)

4 Also, as the Father begets his Son in the love of the Holy Spirit, so the Son, in turn, loves the Father in the same Holy Spirit. **Thus, the Holy Spirit *proceeds* or ensues from the Father as the paternal love of the Father for the Son, and *proceeds* or ensues from the Son as the filial love of the Son for the Father.** You may recognize the verb *proceeds* from the Nicene Creed.

What is discovered in God as a Trinity of Divine Persons is the awesome mystery of life and love. God is not an impersonal divine power—he is not just some kind of supernatural force—but rather he is the fullness of life and love. The Father begets his Son in the love of the Holy Spirit, and the Son, in turn, loves the Father in the same Holy Spirit. It is precisely because the Blessed Trinity is the fullness of life and love that the Divine Persons can, in

Three generations of Cuban farmers: father, son, and grandson.

love, create humans in their image and likeness so that we can also share in their divine life and love.

In other words, God shares the mystery of the Blessed Trinity to help us to understand how he gives his life and his love. In the Old Testament, God prefigured the fullness of life and love present in the Blessed Trinity. But it was only fully revealed in Jesus Christ, the Son of God. The prologue of John's Gospel concludes,

> And the Word became flesh
> and made his dwelling among us,
> and we saw his glory,
> the glory as of the Father's only Son,
> full of grace and truth. (Jn 1:14)

Jesus makes it possible for us to receive the Holy Spirit so that we can be children of the Father and know the Father's love for us and love the Father in return. While we can never fully grasp the mystery of the Blessed Trinity, we can glory and rejoice in the mystery, knowing that it is the *source* of all life and love as well as the *goal* of life and love.

SYMBOLS FOR THE TRINITY

Focus Question: How can we understand the mystery of the Holy Trinity?

Catholic theologians, teachers, and artists have often used symbols to express the mystery of the Triune God. Here is some information on three of the symbols.

Shield of the Trinity

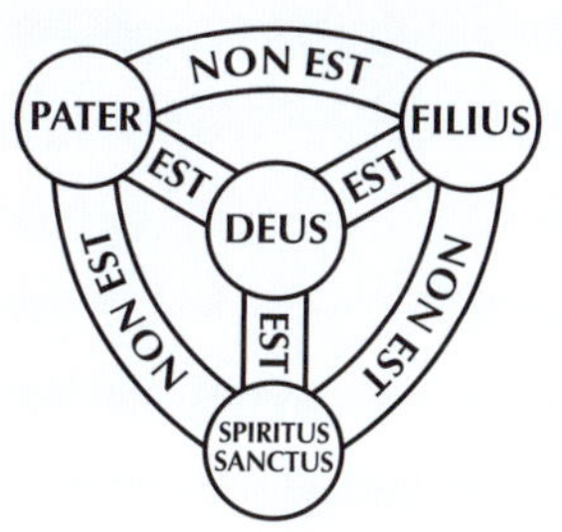

The exact origins of this symbol are unknown, though it likely originated in the twelfth century, when artists experimented with symbolizing the Trinity in abstract form. There are several different variations of this symbol. The translation of the Latin words in this example read: the Father (*Pater*) is (*est*) God (*Deus*); the Son (*Filius*) is God; and the Holy Spirit (*Spiritus Sanctus*) is God. Thus God's unity is expressed.

Equality among the Divine Persons is symbolized by the equilateral triangle. The distinction between each Person of the Trinity is again conveyed by the Latin: the Father is not (*non est*) the Son or the Holy Spirit; and the Son is not the Father or the Holy Spirit; and the Holy Spirit is not the Father or the Son.

Shamrock

It is easy to see the connection between the shamrock and the Trinity. The legendary story related to this symbol traces to the preaching of St. Patrick, the first bishop of Ireland, in the fifth century. Challenged by the Druid people to prove how God could be one yet Three Persons, St. Patrick picked a shamrock and asked whether he held up one leaf or three leaves. "If three, then why one stem? If one stem, then why three leaves?" he asked. Those who questioned him could not answer. St. Patrick continued, "If you cannot explain such a simple mystery as a shamrock, how can you hope to understand such a profound one as the Blessed Trinity?"

While the symbol is ancient and traditional in the Church, it is important to note some ways the symbol is inaccurate. For example, the shamrock does indeed have three leaves and one stem, but the Persons of the Trinity are not three parts that form one God. Rather, the whole of God is the Three Persons, and each Divine Person is the whole of God. Each Divine Person is not one-third of God.

Tree and Sun

St. John Damascene taught with two famous images for the Trinity. The first is a tree where the Father is the root, the Son is the branches, and the Holy Spirit is the fruit. The substance of each (root, branch, and fruit) is the same—that of a tree. And yet there is also a distinction. So it is with the Blessed Trinity. Each Divine Person has the fullness of divine nature, yet there is a distinction: one God, Three Persons.

The second metaphor or symbol St. John used was that of the sun. The Father is the sun, the Son is the rays, and the Holy Spirit is the heat. There is a distinction between the parts but the same substance.

A More Profound Image

Human families are called to image the Trinity in concrete ways. A husband loves a wife and receives her love; a wife loves a husband and receives his love; and their love is so great that it actually pours forth another person—that is, their child. The *Catechism* explains,

The Christian family is a communion of persons, a sign and image of the communion of the Father and the Son in the Holy Spirit. In the procreation and education of children it reflects the Father's work of creation. It is called to partake of the prayer and sacrifice of Christ. Daily prayer and the reading of the Word of God strengthen it in charity. (2205)

Comprehension

1. Why is an equilateral triangle used in the Shield of the Trinity?
2. What is one way the shamrock symbol is an inaccurate description of the Trinity?
3. How do the tree and sun images of the Trinity communicate sameness and distinction of the Three Divine Persons?

Reflection

- What are three ways in which families in today's world can deny their calling to image the Trinity? Give specific examples and explain.
- What are three ways in which families in today's world can uphold their calling to image the Trinity? Give specific examples and explain.

Understanding the Economic Expression of the Blessed Trinity

It is because God is a Trinity of Persons that he acts in time and history. **The action of the Divine Persons in salvation history—that is, Divine Revelation—is called the salvific or economic expression of the Blessed Trinity.** "The whole divine economy is the common work of the three divine persons" (*CCC*, 258).

Understanding what the Divine Persons of the Trinity "do" begins with knowledge of and faith in Jesus, the Second Divine Person of the Trinity. He was sent by the Father to reveal the Father to the world. He and the Father are one. After his earthly life ended and he returned to the Father, he fulfilled his promise in union with the Father by sending the Holy Spirit. Distinct from one another in relation to their origins, it is

The **Father** who made all things and who continues to give life and being to all

The **Son** who taught about this Father's love, and whose Passion, Death, and Resurrection brought the gift of salvation

The **Holy Spirit** whose loving presence would be with the Church always as Sanctifier

"Father," "Son," and "Holy Spirit" are not names to describe a sense of God. "God is one but not solitary" (*Fides Damasi*: DS 71, quoted in *CCC*, 254). Thus it is the economic expression or the work of salvation that reveals the Trinitarian nature of God. We can know God by the way he has acted as Father, Son, and Holy Spirit. The ultimate work of the Blessed Trinity is to bring all creation into unity with the one God in Three Divine Persons. As Jesus told his disciples, "Whoever loves me will keep my word, and my Father will love him, and we will come to him and make our dwelling with him" (Jn 14:23).

An early image of the Trinity carved in stone.

Comprehension

1. What does the Church mean by the word *Person* in reference to the Blessed Trinity? How is this meaning different from the word's usual meaning?

2. What are four points that help to describe the immanence or inner life of the Blessed Trinity?

3. What work does each Person of the Blessed Trinity do according to the understanding of the salvific (or economic) expression of the Trinity?

Reflection

4. Write one succinct definition of the Blessed Trinity. Do not merely repeat one of the definitions you created in your notes. Start with one sentence on each Person of the Trinity. Edit and incorporate parts of each of your three sentences into one new sentence.

5. To which Person of the Blessed Trinity do you usually address your prayer? Why do you think this is so?

UNDERSTANDING MORE ABOUT THE RELATIONSHIP BETWEEN GOD THE FATHER AND GOD THE SON

Several aspects of the identity, work, and relationship of God the Father and God the Son have previously been explored. You may recall from previous courses that the Old Testament tells a great deal about what God is like. For example, the Old Testament reveals that YHWH, a name that translates to "I AM," is the only God. He is the Creator of the universe who brought everything into existence.

In the Old Testament, God cared for the Chosen People, the Jews. He freed them from slavery in Egypt and formed them into a special nation. He gave them a land of their own. God established the kingdom of David, from which God promised the future Messiah was to come.

In time, Jesus the Christ was born. During his earthly ministry, Jesus taught that the God he called Abba, or "Father," was the same God who had made covenants with the Chosen People in the Old Testament. To highlight his unique relationship as God's only Son, Jesus referred to God as "my heavenly Father" (Mt 15:13). But he also talked about "your heavenly Father" (Mt 5:45).

The parable of the tenants illustrates even more clearly the uniqueness of God the Son's identity and his relationship with the Father. The parable is set during the time of Jesus's third journey into Jerusalem, detailed in the Gospel of Mark. At the Temple, Jesus's authority to teach is questioned by the religious leaders. Jesus not only refuses to tell them "by what authority" he has taught and performed miracles; he also tells them the pointed parable of the tenants (see Mark 12:1–12).

In the parable, evil tenants cheat a vineyard owner. They beat and kill the owner's servants who come to collect some of the produce of the vineyard. Finally, as Jesus tells the story, "He had one other to send, a beloved son. He

"The stone that the builders rejected has become the cornerstone; by the Lord this has been done, and it is wonderful in our eyes" (Mk 12:10–11).

sent him to them last of all, thinking, 'They will respect my son'" (Mk 12:6). The parable is really an allegory because it tells how God sent prophets in Old Testament times (servants in the story) to the Jewish people (the tenants). The prophets were abused; some were killed. Then, as the story continues, the vineyard owner decides to send someone with even more authority. This representative would be special and unique. God decided to send his Son into the world.

The meaning of this allegory was not lost on the Temple leaders. They knew Jesus was associating himself with the beloved son of the vineyard owner—and by connection claiming to be the beloved Son of God. By telling this parable, Jesus was predicting his future arrest and Death. The chief priests, scribes, and elders understood that Jesus was criticizing them. The postscript to the parable is that the religious leaders "were seeking to arrest him, but they feared the crowd, for they realized that he had addressed the parable to them. So they left him and went away" (Mk 12:12).

Through the parable of the tenants and his other teachings, Jesus taught that God is eternally the Father because of his relationship with the Son and vice versa. In fact, we only learn about the identity and work of God the Father in relationship to God the Son.

The Father's Love and Compassion

Foremost, Jesus's teachings reveal the Father's unconditional and total love for humanity. God is like the Good Shepherd who went out of his way to find a lost sheep (see Matthew 18:10–14). (Jesus is the Good Shepherd.) God is like the father in the parable of the lost son (see Luke 15:11–32, also known as the

"Coming to his senses he thought, 'How many of my fathers' hired workers have more than enough food to eat, but here am I, dying from hunger. I shall get up and go to my father and I shall say to him, "Father, I have sinned against heaven and against you. I no longer deserve to be called your son; treat me as you would treat one of your hired workers"'" (Lk 15: 17–19).

parable of the prodigal son) who welcomed back his wayward child with open arms—no questions asked.

Notice that the younger son of the parable is indeed "prodigal" (profligate, wasteful). When he is completely destitute, he wants to return home. He is broke and hungry. When the father sees his son and hurries across the field to embrace him, it is the father's turn to be prodigal: foolishly spendthrift with his love, giving his son the symbols of a free man (shoes) and the privileges of being a member of the family (robe and ring). Jesus has already told his audience that the return of sinners brings great joy in heaven (Lk 15:7). God the Father has only love for sinners.

The connection between the Trinitarian formula—"in the name of the Father, and of the Son, and of the Holy Spirit"—and Baptism is also related to the theme of the parable of the lost son.[∞] It is at this sacrament that God welcomes sinners, adopts them as his own, and clothes them in the purest and finest garments of holiness. God is Father to all the baptized through and in his Son. In fact, his mercy and love as Father also extend to those who are

∞ Note

The Sign of the Cross has a long history in the Church. In the fifth century, the gesture was made from the right shoulder to the left shoulder; at the instruction of Pope Innocent III in the early thirteenth century, the order shifted from left to right because Christ descended from above to below (forehead to chest) and from the Jews (right) to the Gentiles (left).

unbaptized and who are able to experience mercy and love fully if they come to the faith and are baptized (see *CCC*, 1257, 1260–61).

Likewise, the healing miracles of Jesus detailed in the Gospels reveal a compassionate Father. And the sacrifice of Jesus on the Cross shows a Father who gave his own Son for the redemption of humankind. The Father is a saving God who redeems the world through his Son, Jesus Christ, in the Holy Spirit. The Father brought his beloved Son back to life, and through him he promised resurrection to all who believe. St. Paul writes assuredly, "Thanks be to God who gives us the victory through our Lord Jesus Christ" (1 Cor 15:57).

Revelation about God the Son

The Old Testament uses variations of the title "son of God" in a different of ways. For example, the title refers to Israel (Ex 4:22), to a king (2 Sm 7:14), and to angels (Jb 1:6). In the New Testament, "Son of God" is used directly in reference to Jesus. Immediately after St. Peter identified Jesus as "the Messiah, the Son of the living God," Jesus replied, "Blessed are you, Simon son of Jonah. For flesh and blood has not revealed this to you, but my heavenly Father" (Mt 16:16–17). Peter's statement of faith shows Jesus to be different from Israel and the kings and angels for whom the title was used in the Old Testament. Jesus is Son in a unique way to God the Father. Jesus, as the Son, is the human face of the Father.

Jesus also makes special connections between himself and God the Father in several places in John's Gospel, apart from those in his Last Supper discourse. John's Gospel is also noted for the inclusion of several "I AM" statements spoken by Jesus. In using this name, Jesus clearly connected himself to the name YHWH, or God himself. For example, examine Jesus's words in relation to the following Old Testament passages:

"I am the bread of life" (Jn 6:35).

In the Old Testament, YHWH gave manna to the Chosen People (see Exodus 16).

"I am the light of the world" (Jn 8:12).

In the Genesis creation accounts, God is the author of light (see Genesis 1:3).

> ### *"I am the gate for the sheep" (Jn 10:7), and "I am the good shepherd" (Jn 10:11).*
>
> Both of these images recall God's promise to be the shepherd of his people (see Psalm 23).

> ### *"I am the resurrection and the life" (Jn 11:25).*
>
> The Old Testament reveals God as the one who authors life and restores life (see Genesis 2:7 and Isaiah 26:19).

> ### *"I am the way and the truth and the life" (Jn 14:6).*
>
> The psalms tell of God providing a "path to life" (Ps 16:11).

> ### *"I am the true vine" (Jn 15:1).*
>
> The prophets Isaiah and Ezekiel both use the image of the vineyard owner to describe God as the one who planted the vine and Israel as an image of the vine itself (see Isaiah 5:1–7 and Ezekiel 17:1–8).

The "I AM" statements of Jesus reveal a deep connection between Jesus and God the Father. Nevertheless, both his disciples and his enemies had a difficult time recognizing Jesus as the unique Son of God. In a pivotal exchange between Jesus and the Jewish leaders recorded in John's Gospel, Jesus explains when the world will finally know that he and the Father are one:

> When you lift up the Son of Man, then you will realize that I AM, and that I do nothing on my own, but I say only what the Father taught me. The one who sent me is with me. He has not left me alone, because I always do what is pleasing to him. (Jn 8:28–29)

The connections between the "I AM" statements became clearer to Jesus's Apostles and other disciples after his Resurrection and after the coming of the Holy Spirit at Pentecost. They realized that Jesus did things that only God could do, miraculous actions that revealed his identity as God's only Son, the Second Divine Person of the Blessed Trinity.

SECTION Assessment

Comprehension

1. How did Jesus highlight his unique relationship with God the Father?

2. In the parable of the lost son, how is the father also "prodigal"?

3. In what way does the parable of the lost son connect with the Sacrament of Baptism?

4. Why did Jesus use "I AM" statements to refer to God?

5. How was the title "son of God" used in the Old Testament?

Reflection

6. How do the qualities and characteristics of Jesus represent what God the Father is like?

7. What do these qualities and characteristics reveal about any differences between God the Father and God the Son?

TRACING AN UNDERSTANDING OF THE HOLY SPIRIT

The Holy Spirit, the Third Divine Person of the Blessed Trinity, is often the least understood. Yet it is the Holy Spirit who is active and at work in the Church and the world today. St. Gregory of Nazianzus wrote of the Revelation of the Blessed Trinity and particularly the Holy Spirit in this way: "The Old Testament proclaimed the Father clearly, but the Son more obscurely. The New Testament revealed the Son and gave us a glimpse of the divinity of the Spirit. Now the Spirit dwells among us and grants us a clearer vision of himself" (quoted in *CCC*, 684). One of the reasons the Holy Spirit seems hidden, especially in the Old Testament, is that the Spirit does not speak of himself. His sole activity is to manifest the love of the Father for the Son and the love of the Son for the Father, as well as their love for all humanity. In actuality, this love was always present.

The Hebrew word *ruah*, meaning "wind" or "breath," is often used in the Old Testament to speak of God's mysterious, powerful, and life-giving presence. For example, this word was used to describe the Spirit's presence in the work of creation. Genesis 1:2 names a "mighty wind" that swept over the earth when it was a dark wasteland. In discussing the creation of the first man, the second creation story tells of how God "blew into his nostrils the breath of life, and the man became a living being" (Gn 2:7).∞ God's Spirit was present in the anointing of Israel's prophets, including Elijah (see 2 Kings 2:9) and Elisha (see 2 Kings 2:15). The Holy Spirit was also witnessed in *theophanies*—that is,

∞ Note

Recall that creation is the common work of the Blessed Trinity. The Father is the source of the creative activity, whereas the Son brings the creation into existence through the Holy Spirit.

visible manifestations of God—for example, in the cloud and fire that led the Chosen People to the Promised Land (see Exodus 13:21) and at the giving of the Law to Moses at Mount Sinai (see Exodus 19:16–25).

As St. Gregory of Nazianzus taught, the Old Testament more clearly reveals God the Father and points to the coming of God the Son. In the New Testament, Jesus alluded to the Spirit on several occasions before the Last Supper, when he finally named the Holy Spirit and promised his disciples he would send the Spirit to them. It was not until the disciples witnessed and experienced Jesus's Paschal Mystery—his Passion, Death, Resurrection, and Ascension—that they were prepared for the coming of the Holy Spirit at Pentecost and for a new understanding of the Holy Spirit as a distinct Person of the Blessed Trinity.

Jesus Prepares the World for the Holy Spirit

A careful reading of the Gospels clearly points to the presence of the Holy Spirit throughout Jesus's life, especially in his public ministry. For example:

Jesus was conceived by the power of the Holy Spirit (see Luke 1:35 and the Apostles' Creed in the subsection "Beliefs" in the Appendix). "Through Mary, the Holy Spirit begins to bring [humanity], the objects of God's merciful love, *into communion* with Christ" (*CCC*, 725).

At the Presentation in the Temple, the Holy Spirit moved the prophet Simeon to recognize Jesus as the Promised One (see Luke 2:22–38).

The Holy Spirit was present at Jesus's Baptism (see Luke 3:21–22). The Holy Spirit took the form of a dove and descended on Jesus, accompanied by the Father's declaration that Jesus is his "beloved Son."

The Holy Spirit was with Jesus through his temptations in the desert (see Luke 4:1–13). "Filled with the holy Spirit," Jesus was prepared to overcome the devil.

Jesus began his public ministry "in the power of the Spirit" (see Luke 4:14). The ensuing healings, driving out of demons, raisings from the dead, and displays of power over nature were all performed through the power of the Holy Spirit.

Jesus gradually taught about the Holy Spirit. He told Nicodemus he would have to be born again in water and the Spirit (see John 3:5–8). To the Samaritan woman at the well, he spoke of worshipping "the Father in Spirit and truth" (see John 4:1–42). In his instructions to the crowd about the Eucharist, he taught about the Spirit giving life (see John 6:27, 51, 62–63).

It was at the events surrounding the Paschal Mystery that Jesus most clearly referred to the coming of the Holy Spirit. At the Last Supper, Jesus promised to send the Holy Spirit to comfort and teach the disciples: "I will ask the Father, and he will give you another Advocate to be with you always, the Spirit of truth, which the world cannot accept, because it neither sees nor knows it. But you know it, because it remains with you, and will be in you" (Jn 14:16–17).

Jesus also connected his impending suffering and Death with the Spirit coming to bring comfort. Jesus used the term *Advocate* to describe the Holy Spirit as Comforter. He said, "But I tell you the truth, it is better for you that

I go. For if I do not go, the Advocate will not come to you. But if I go, I will send him to you. . . . When he comes, the Spirit of truth, he will guide you to all truth" (Jn 16:7, 13). Finally, after his Resurrection and before his Ascension, Jesus told the Apostles, "You will receive power when the holy Spirit comes upon you, and you will be my witnesses in Jerusalem, throughout Judea and Samaria, and to the ends of the earth" (Acts 1:8).

Jesus's promise was intended not only for his Apostles but for all who believe. **The Holy Spirit comes to each of us to teach the meaning of Divine Revelation in our lives and help us to recognize it.** The Holy Spirit also gives us the grace to understand and accept Jesus's gospel message. Finally, the Holy Spirit gives us the strength to proclaim the Gospel to others.

The Coming of the Holy Spirit at Pentecost

The promises Jesus made to send the Holy Spirit were fulfilled on Pentecost Sunday. *Pentecost* is a Greek word that means "fiftieth day." Pentecost was a Jewish harvest feast that happened fifty days after the Passover.∞ Jews from all over the Roman Empire, many of whom spoke different languages, gathered in Jerusalem to celebrate this first harvest of summer. Meanwhile, the eleven Apostles were in hiding after the events around Jesus's Death and Resurrection. They were in the place where they had shared the Last Supper. Jesus's mother, Mary, was with them. **The Holy Spirit was poured out upon them and appeared to them as tongues of fire.** The sound from the sky was like a strong, driving wind. The tongues of fire rested on each one of them. The Acts of the Apostles (2:2–4) describes the event.

This event changed the Apostles. They were no longer afraid. They began to preach in different languages to the gathered crowds. Peter recounted all

∞ Note

From Jesus's time through today, Jews celebrate Pentecost as *Shavout* (Hebrew for "weeks"), a day commemorating when God gave the Torah to all of Israel (though there is no mention of this occasion in Scripture). There is a likely reference in the New Testament of Jesus marking this festival. In the story of Jesus's healing of a man on the Sabbath, the Gospel of John reports that it occurred on "a feast of the Jews, and Jesus went up to Jerusalem" (Jn 5:1). The fiftieth day after Passover would fall on the Sabbath.

A Cameroon expression of the Feast of Pentecost. Note that Mary, the Mother of Jesus, is present.

of salvation history to convince them that Jesus was the Messiah promised in Scripture. Three thousand people were baptized that very day. St. Peter explained that what happened on Pentecost was promised by the prophet Joel:

> "It will come to pass in the last days," God says,
> "that I will pour out a portion of my spirit upon all flesh.
> Your sons and your daughters shall prophesy,
> your young men shall see visions,
> your old men shall dream dreams. . . .
> and it shall be that everyone shall be saved who calls on the name of the Lord."
> (Acts 2:17, 21, quoting Joel 3:1–5)

Most significant, on the day of Pentecost the "Holy Trinity is fully revealed" (*CCC*, 732). The coming of the Holy Spirit at Pentecost caused the world to enter into the "last days." The "last days" refers to the entire historical time of the Church. The Kingdom of God was initiated at Pentecost, though not fully completed. Because of the events of Pentecost, it is sometimes called the "birthday of the Church."∞

What Is the Holy Spirit Like?

Recall that the Holy Spirit is of the same substance (nature) as the Father and the Son. The image of the Holy Spirit from Scripture as *ruah*, or "breath," is a helpful way to understand more of what the Holy Spirit is like. The Holy Spirit is the breath of the Father with whom Jesus is totally filled. Although images like breath, wind, and fire are helpful in understanding the role of the Holy Spirit, it is important to remember that the Holy Spirit is not part of the created world. He is fully God, coequal with the Father and the Son.

The Sacrament of Confirmation imparts the fullness of the gifts of the Holy Spirit.

A related question is, "What does the Holy Spirit do?" The Holy Spirit advocates for us, defends us, and consoles us. He makes us holy so that we are his temples. He transforms us into children of the Father in the likeness of Jesus the Son. He makes us a new creation in Christ. These actions of the Holy Spirit and many more define the meaning of the term *Paraclete*, or Advocate.

Our lives are linked with the Holy Spirit at Baptism. Because of the Holy Spirit, we become "new creatures," adopted children of God. Other effects of the Holy Spirit's presence in our lives are these:

- We are members of Christ and his Body, the Church.

- We are coheirs with Christ, the children of God.

- We are temples of the Holy Spirit (see *CCC*, 1265).

- We are justified before God.

∞ Note

Pentecost is the day the sacraments of the Church were inaugurated. "Through the Church's sacraments, Christ communicates his Holy and sanctifying Spirit to the members of his Body" (*CCC*, 739).

Being justified means that our sins are forgiven and we are able to enter into a right relationship with God through faith in Jesus. This justification begins a lifelong process of conversion to God that leads us to eternal life with him and enables us to share in his own nature.∞

The Holy Spirit showers many gifts on the Church to make her holy and to help us understand more about what he is like. Seven particular *gifts of the Holy Spirit* were promised by Jesus. A special outpouring of these gifts comes to those who receive the Sacrament of Confirmation:

- *Wisdom* enables us to look at reality from God's point of view.

- *Understanding* helps us to reflect on the deeper meaning of our faith.

∞ Note

Justification is the movement from the state of sinfulness to the state of grace. But this is not a one-time event (as some Protestants believe). We must assist God, working through the Holy Spirit, to remain sinless and to achieve our justification. St. Augustine wrote, "God created us without us: but he did not will to save us without us" (quoted in *CCC*, 1847). St. Paul also reminds us, "So then, my beloved, obedient as you have always been, not only when I am present but all the more now when I am absent, work out your salvation with fear and trembling" (Phil 2:12).

- *Knowledge* shows us how God is working in our life and in the world. It allows us to see that God knows us as we really are.

- *Counsel* (*right judgment*) helps us form our conscience in light of Church teaching.

- *Fortitude* (*courage*) provides us with strength to follow our Christian convictions.

- *Piety* (*reverence*) moves us to show respect to God through praise and worship. It also enables us to respect the dignity and worth of others and ourselves.

- *Fear of the Lord* (*wonder and awe*) keeps our life balanced. It helps us to be attentive to the ongoing reality of sin in our lives.

Of course, the gifts of the Holy Spirit are limitless. St. Paul wrote, "There are different kinds of spiritual gifts but the same Spirit" (1 Cor 12:4). St. Paul also named *fruits of the Spirit*—that is, spiritual perfections that result from the Holy Spirit living in a person. According to Galatians 5:22–23, these are the first fruits of eternal glory. The *Catechism of the Catholic Church* (1832) identifies these fruits as charity, joy, peace, patience, kindness, goodness, generosity, gentleness, faithfulness, modesty, self-control, and chastity. There are also *charisms*—that is, "graces of the Holy Spirit which directly or indirectly benefit the Church" (*CCC*, 799). Charisms are meant to be given away to others by those who receive them. St. Paul refers to charisms in 1 Corinthians 12:4–11, including wisdom, knowledge, faith, healing, mighty deeds, discernment, and speaking in **tongues** (see 1 Corinthians 14). Obviously, some charisms are more common than others. Working mighty deeds and speaking in tongues are "extraordinary" charisms (*CCC*, 2003) and occur rarely.

All the gifts, fruits, and charisms of the Holy Spirit are related to one another. When we use them, we show that we are united to Jesus, the True Vine (see John 15:1). The Holy Spirit is the great Gift-Giver. Without the Holy Spirit, it would be impossible to live as disciples of Christ.

---

tongues Private speech directed toward God in inarticulate terms. Needs interpretation to be understood by others.

SECTION Assessment

Comprehension

1. How is *ruah* used in the Old Testament?

2. Share two examples of the Holy Spirit's presence or involvement in the Old Testament.

3. Give two examples of the Holy Spirit's presence or involvement in Jesus's earthly ministry.

4. When did Jesus say the Holy Spirit would come to the Apostles?

5. Name three things the Holy Spirit does for a baptized Catholic.

Vocabulary

6. How did St. Paul allude to the gift of tongues in 1 Corinthians 14?

Reflection

7. Why is justification a lifelong process?

8. Share concrete examples of how three of the gifts of the Spirit have been manifested in your life.

ENTERING THE LIFE OF THE BLESSED TRINITY

While it is both interesting and beneficial to study the individual Persons of the Blessed Trinity, it's also important to keep in mind that although they are distinct, the Father, the Son, and the Holy Spirit are in eternal relationship with one another. It's always accurate to call this eternal relationship of the Divine Persons a mystery, but we humans have been gifted by God with talented and inquisitive minds that have sought answers and actually solved many of life's mysteries in other areas. There is nothing to prevent us from attempting to understand more about the mystery of the Blessed Trinity as well.

Twentieth-century saint Maximilian Kolbe, a Franciscan priest martyred by the Nazis at Auschwitz, was devoted to Mary, especially under the title she used with St. Bernadette when she appeared at Lourdes, France in 1858. **Mary said in the apparition, "I am the Immaculate Conception."** Kolbe meditated on this interesting choice of words. Mary did not say, "I was conceived immaculately." Instead she named herself the Immaculate Conception. Kolbe eventually connected this title of Mary to the Holy Spirit. The Third Person of the Trinity was also immaculately conceived from the love that flows between the Father and the Son. The Holy Spirit was not created;

The Militia of the Immaculata (MI) was founded by St. Maximilian Kolbe in 1917 as a means to promote total consecration to Mary as a most effective way to live one's Baptism and Confirmation.

rather, as Kolbe said, he is the "Uncreated, Eternal Immaculate Conception." And Mary is the *created* Immaculate Conception. Just as the love between Father and Son immaculately conceived the Holy Spirit, the love of the Holy Spirit that came to Mary at her Annunciation conceived the Incarnate Second Divine Person of the Trinity. Further, Kolbe explained that the Holy Spirit is

> the flowering of the love of the Father and the Son. If the fruit of created love is a created conception, then the fruit of divine Love, that prototype of all created love, is necessarily a divine "conception." The Holy Spirit is, therefore, the "uncreated, eternal conception," the prototype of all the conceptions that multiply life throughout the whole universe.[1]

Our own parents participated in our conception in a similar way, sharing in the love between God the Father and God the Son that resulted in the conception of the Third Person of the Trinity, the Holy Spirit. This means that we entered into the life of the Blessed Trinity from our very beginnings. It also means that the Blessed Trinity was, is, and will always be part of our DNA.

There are many other ways we encounter the Blessed Trinity throughout our life. To consider some of these ways, it is helpful to review how the Three Divine Persons function as one (see also Chapter 3, Introduction):

The Father

The First Person of the Trinity is absolutely without origin. From all eternity he begets the Son, the Second Divine Person of the Trinity. The Son proceeds from the Father. There was never a time when the Son did not proceed from the Father. Therefore, the Father is in relationship to the Son from all eternity.

The Son

We can think of the Father's begetting of the Son as God knowing himself perfectly. The Father expresses himself perfectly to himself, and this is the Son, the Word of God. Thus, the Son is the Father's perfect, divine expression of himself. They are one yet distinct. The Son of God is in relationship to the Father from all eternity. As the Son of God, he is true God and consubstantial with—that is, "having the exact divine nature as"—the Father.

The Holy Spirit

The relationship of the Father and Son is a perfect relationship. The Father and Son love each other with an eternal, perfect, and divine love. The love that proceeds from the Father and the Son is the Third Person of the Blessed Trinity. The Holy Spirit proceeds from both the Father and the Son as the perfect expression of their divine love for each other. Since the Holy Spirit proceeds from the Father and the Son eternally, the Holy Spirit is consubstantial with the Father and the Son.

The early Church summarized the relationship of the Divine Persons in the classic Athanasian Creed, named for St. Athanasius,∞ who lived in the fourth century:

> The Father is not made by anyone, nor created nor begotten. The Son is from the Father alone, not made, not created, but begotten. The Holy Spirit is from the Father and the Son, not made, not created, not begotten, but proceeding. The entire Three Persons are co-eternal with one another and co-equal, so that . . . both Trinity in Unity and Unity in Trinity are to be adored.

The next subsection discusses how the Divine Persons of the Blessed Trinity work throughout salvation history in order to help us understand more about how God acts in the world today and in our own lives.

∞ Note

The Athanasian Creed is no longer officially attributed to St. Athanasius, although it is still a valid creed in the Church. It is sometimes recited as part of Lauds (Morning Prayer) in the Divine Office.

Ways We Can Encounter the Work of the Blessed Trinity

A deeper study uncovers that the Father, the Son, and the Holy Spirit reveal themselves through their deeds within salvation history. Whatever action God undertakes is always done by all Three Persons of the Blessed Trinity. In the same way that the Three Persons have only one divine nature, so too they have only one divine operation.∞ Yet, "each divine person performs the common work according to his unique personal property" (*CCC*, 258).

How do these two truths work together? Specifically, while *creation* is attributed to the Father, the Father creates through his Son and in the loving breath of the Holy Spirit. While *salvation* (redemption) is attributed to the Son, the Son performs all of his saving acts in accordance with his Father's will and in the power of the Holy Spirit. While *sanctification* (holiness) is attributed to the Holy Spirit, it is the Father and the Son who pour out the Holy Spirit upon humankind so as to transform men and women into the likeness of Jesus the Son so as to make them children of the Father.

We encounter the Blessed Trinity most clearly in Jesus, who is the Son of God Incarnate. By being united to him, we encounter the divine life of the Holy Spirit and the love of God the Father. Jesus, the Second Divine Person of the Blessed Trinity, is God in the flesh who redeemed the world from sin. As Savior, he is always with us as a faithful companion. But there are many other distinct ways we can encounter the work of the Blessed Trinity. For example, God the Father can be experienced through the beauty of creation. The Father is

Love is the answer to deepening our relationship with the Blessed Trinity.

∞ Note

Operation means "works." When God performs an action, it is done at once by all Three Persons of the Trinity. The individual Persons do not work separately.

Creator of everything in the universe, large and small, from the tiniest insect to the widest ocean to the most encompassing galaxy. And, gifted with the Holy Spirit at Baptism, we can experience the many graces of the Third Divine Person through the way he directs us to live in imitation of Jesus.

God's Revelation as a Trinity of Divine Persons took place gradually through salvation history. Catholic philosopher Peter Kreeft notes that this same pattern applies to how the Trinity reveals himself to each person:

> First as the transcendent Creator "outside" us; then as the "incarnate" Savior "beside" us; then as the indwelling Spirit "inside" us. The reason for this progression is God's very being, which is love (1 Jn 4:18), and in the purpose and motive for God's self-revelation to [you], which is love. For love's aim is always greater intimacy, deeper union with the beloved; so the stages of God's self-revelation are stages of increasing intimacy with [you] (from "outside" to "beside" to "inside").[2]

Love really is the answer to deepening our relationship with the Blessed Trinity. An encounter with the Blessed Trinity leads us to love in imitation of God. And yet, we are called to more than just imitation; indeed, we are called to actually participate in the exchange of love of the Trinity. This is our life's purpose. The *Catechism of the Catholic Church* boldly reminds us:

> But St. John goes even further when he affirms that "God is love": God's very being is love. By sending his only Son and the Spirit of Love in the fullness of time, God has revealed his innermost secret: God himself is an eternal exchange of love, Father, Son and Holy Spirit, and he has destined us to share in that exchange. (221)

Yes, you are personally destined to share in the life and the love of the Trinity. When you partake in this life and love, you come to understand that the Divine Persons form a family among themselves that unites you with them and in love to all the people of the world. Pope John Paul II said, "God in his deepest mystery is not a solitude, but a family, since he has in himself fatherhood, sonship, and the essence of family, which is love."

SECTION Assessment

Comprehension

1. Explain how the Holy Spirit is the "Uncreated, Eternal Immaculate Conception" and Mary is the "created Immaculate Conception."

2. How is the Father, the First Person of the Blessed Trinity, related to the Son?

3. How is the Son, the Second Divine Person of the Blessed Trinity, related to the Father?

4. How is the Holy Spirit, the Third Person of the Blessed Trinity, related to the Father and the Son?

5. How does the Athanasian Creed summarize the relationship of the Divine Persons?

Reflection

6. How does St. Maximilian Kolbe's comparison between the Holy Spirit and Mary help you to understand the mystery of the Blessed Trinity? What questions do you have about this comparison?

7. How do you experience God's action differently through each Person of the Blessed Trinity?

8. Describe a time when you experienced an encounter with God through creation.

Section Reviews

Focus Question

How can we understand the mystery of the Holy Trinity?

Complete one of the following:

- Read the following Scripture passages. Each tells something about what Jesus revealed about God the Father. Answer each of the questions.
    - Matthew 18:19–20. What does Jesus say to do? What is the reward?
    - Matthew 18:21–35. What is the meaning of this parable?
    - Luke 11:1–13. What will the Father do for you if you follow Jesus's teaching?
- Create a collage illustrating Jesus's "I AM" statements from the Gospel of John (see subsection "Revelation about God the Son" in Chapter 3, Section 2).
- Write a short essay on the seven gifts of the Holy Spirit. Address the following questions: What do these gifts mean to me? How are they part of my life? How can I share them with others?

Introduction

One God, Three Persons

Review

Through his words and actions, Jesus revealed the central mystery of the Christian faith: that in the one God there are Three Divine Persons: Father, Son, and Holy Spirit. Whenever God acts, the common work of the Divine Persons of the Blessed Trinity is always present. In several places in the Gospels, the distinct properties of the Three Persons are manifest; for example, Three Persons are evident at both Jesus's Baptism and his Transfiguration. Jesus's commissioning of his Apostles recorded in Matthew 28:18–20 reveals in a single verse the names of the Divine Persons.

Assignment

Compose a prayer to the Blessed Trinity that addresses each Divine Person.

CHAPTER 3 REVIEW

Section 1

The Church Teaches about the Blessed Trinity

Review

The Church in every age has contemplated the mystery of the Blessed Trinity. Early Church Fathers developed a vocabulary of terms (*substance*, *Person*, *relation*) that continues to be used to describe the Trinity. It is God's inner life that determines that active and inseparable work of the Blessed Trinity. The way the Divine Persons act in salvation history is the salvific or economic expression of the Trinity. God's Revelation of himself in the Divine Persons of the Blessed Trinity helps us to understand the mystery of how he shares his life and love and the gift of creation with others.

Assignment

Re-create a drawing of one of the symbols of the Holy Trinity introduced in this text. Write a caption that explains its meaning.

Section 2

Understanding More about the Relationship between God the Father and God the Son

Review

The identity and work of God the Father can only be understood in relationship with God the Son. In the Old Testament, God established a series of covenants with the Chosen People and promised to send a Messiah. Jesus the Christ is that Messiah. Through several teachings in which he described himself as YHWH, or "I AM," Jesus established his identity as the unique Son of God. Jesus's words and actions provide the best way to know what God the Father is like. Jesus revealed the Father to be loving and compassionate.

Assignment

Read Psalm 68. Tell how this image of God as Father compares to how Jesus portrayed God the Father.

Section 3
Tracing an Understanding of the Holy Spirit

Review

Through the inspiration of the Third Person of the Blessed Trinity to the Church, the Holy Spirit's presence in the Old Testament can be recognized. The Holy Spirit played a key role in Jesus's public ministry. Jesus referred to the Holy Spirit in his teaching and promised that the Spirit would come after his Ascension. This promise was fulfilled on Pentecost.

Assignment

Imagine you were present at Pentecost, and share your own account of the dramatic descent of the Holy Spirit.

Section 4
Entering the Life of the Blessed Trinity

Review

God's Revelation as a Trinity of Divine Persons took place gradually throughout salvation history. Basic teachings about the inner life of God reveal that the Father has no origin and begets the Son from all eternity, that the Son is the perfect expression of the Father and is in eternal relationship with the Father, and that the love that proceeds from the Father and Son is the Third Person of the Blessed Trinity, the Holy Spirit. The Father, Son, and Holy Spirit are one, and whatever work is done by the Holy Trinity is done by all Three Divine Persons. However, each Divine Person performs the common work (creation, salvation, and sanctification) according to his unique personal property. The fundamental truth about the Blessed Trinity is that the Trinity—in other words, God—is love.

Assignment

Read and succinctly summarize the teaching on the mystery of the Holy Trinity found in paragraph 234 of the *Catechism of the Catholic Church*.

Chapter Projects

Choose and complete at least one of the following projects to assess your understanding of the material in this chapter.

⚙ 1. Compare and Contrast Three Works by Rembrandt on the Prodigal Son

Create a chart like the following. Complete each of the columns listed for three works by Rembrandt on the parable of the prodigal son. Add two columns of your own with additional points of comparison and complete those as well. Make sure to include a copy of the image of each work in the first column.

TITLE OF WORK	*The Prodigal Son in the Brothel*	*Return of the Prodigal Son* (drawing)	*Return of the Prodigal Son*
DATE			
MEDIUM			
CURRENT LOCATION			
SUBJECT DESCRIPTION			

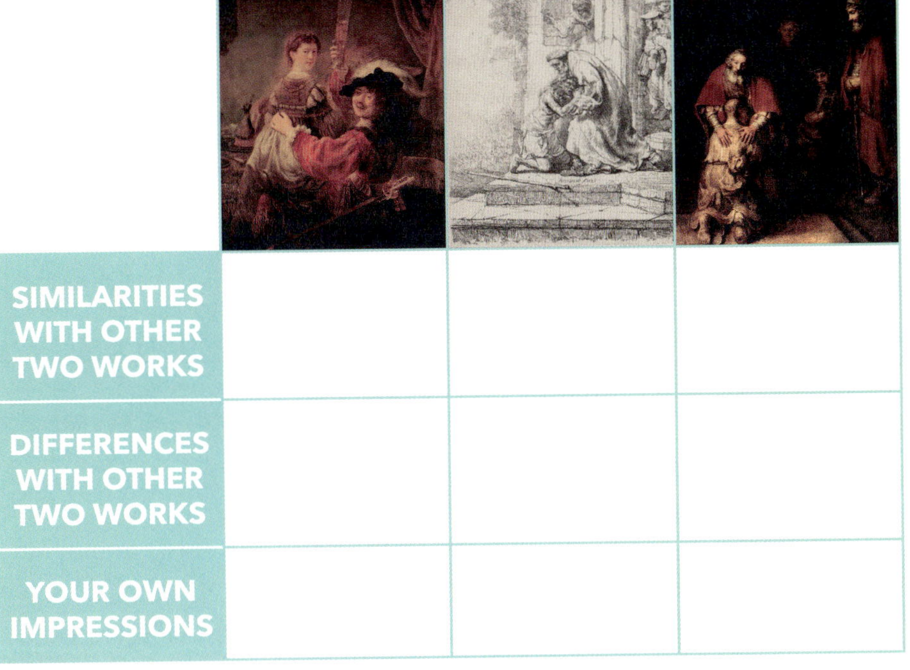

SIMILARITIES WITH OTHER TWO WORKS			
DIFFERENCES WITH OTHER TWO WORKS			
YOUR OWN IMPRESSIONS			

⚙ 2. Look for Evidence of Spiritual Fruit and Moral Vices in Today's World

If we live by the Holy Spirit, good fruit will show itself in our lives. If we ignore the Holy Spirit and live according to our vices, then moral deformities or bad habits will fill our lives instead. See how these statements are true by completing each of the following steps.

- Read and copy five of the Bible verses listed in the category "Spiritual Fruit" below. Do the same for the category "Moral Vices."

SPIRITUAL FRUIT	MORAL VICES
Love (Jn 13:35)	Sexual Promiscuity (1 Cor 5:1)
Joy (Rom 15:13)	Idolatry (1 Pt 4:3)
Patience (Rom 2:4)	Sorcery/Witchcraft (Rv 9:21)

SPIRITUAL FRUIT	MORAL VICES
Kindness (2 Cor 6:6)	Hatred (Rom 8:7)
Goodness (Rom 15:14)	Jealousy (Rom 13:13)
Faithfulness (Mt 23:23)	Self-Seeking (2 Cor 12:20)
Gentleness (1 Cor 4:21)	Heresy/Factions (1 Cor 11:19)
Self-Control (Acts 24:25)	Drunkenness (Lk 21:34)

- For three days, check the news from various sources to find evidence of both the spiritual fruits and the moral vices you chose. Provide links to the examples.

- Summarize your findings in a one-page report or a three-minute oral presentation. Include in your summary observations of which examples were easiest and most difficult to find and why you think this is so.

⚙ *3. Teach the Trinity to Children*

The Trinity can be difficult to explain. However, even children can grasp the basic relationship of the Father, Son, and Holy Spirit. For this assignment, create a lesson plan on how to teach the Trinity to second graders (ages seven and eight). Make sure to include some creative examples and illustrations. (For example, you might hand out candy corn and explain that there are three colors in each piece of candy, but the candy is still one piece.) The lesson plan should include notes on what you would say to the children and what you would show on the board, along with any creative techniques to help them grasp this core Christian belief.

⚙ *4. Participate in the Work of God*

Do all three of the following parts to this assignment.

First, review the tasks associated with God the Father, God the Son, and God the Holy Spirit (creation, salvation, and sanctification) described in the subsection "Ways We Can Encounter the Work of the Blessed Trinity" in Chapter 3, Section 4.

Second, respond to the following questions:

1. How can a person physically, emotionally, or spiritually cooperate with the Father's grace for a fresh start in his or her life?

2. How can one person cooperate with Christ's salvific plan by sharing his offer of redemption with another person (e.g., through forgiveness)?

3. How can one person cooperate with the Holy Spirit to inspire another person to love better, to be more courageous, or to be more generous?

Third, write a three-paragraph essay about each task, using the following format:

- *Paragraph 1*: Define the term.

- *Paragraph 2*: Tell how you personally have done the action or how someone has done the action to you.

- *Paragraph 3*: Summarize the results of the action. Tell what happened next.

⚙ *5. Develop a Holy Trinity Quiz Game*

Develop a Holy Trinity quiz game in the style of the popular game show *Jeopardy*, featuring twenty-five answers and their corresponding questions. You will need three different colors of three-by-five-inch index cards. Begin by creating the "answers" about the Holy Trinity and record them. Next, go back and write the questions for each of the answers. Define the questions in three levels of difficulty, from easy to average to difficult. Then print each question on one side of an index card and its corresponding answer on the other side. Use the different colors of index cards to note the appropriate level of difficulty. For example:

Easy

A: The central mystery of the Christian faith.

Q: What is the Blessed Trinity?

Average

A: The Baptism of Jesus and the Transfiguration of Jesus.

Q: What are two examples from the Gospels when all Three Divine Persons of the Holy Trinity were manifest?

Difficult

A: A Greek term to designate the real distinction between Father, Son, and Holy Spirit.

Q: What is hypostasis?

As time permits, host a demonstration of this game with three classmates while the rest of the class takes the role of the audience.

Faithful Disciple
St. Elizabeth of the Trinity

St. Elizabeth of the Trinity (1880–1906) was a French Discalced Carmelite nun who lived a short but eventful life. As her name indicates, she had a special devotion to the Blessed Trinity. But this wasn't always so. Born Elizabeth Catez at a French military camp at Avord, about two hundred miles south of Paris, she experienced two tragic losses at age seven: the death of her grandfather, followed by the unexpected death of her father. Her mother moved the family to an apartment in Dijon in Burgundy. In response to the traumas and upheaval in her life, Elizabeth often acted out in anger and with terrible tantrums.

Elizabeth experienced a conversion on her First Communion day. On her way out of church, she told a friend, "I'm no longer hungry. Jesus has fed me." Also on that day, she met the prioress of a nearby convent, the Carmel of Dijon. The prioress told Elizabeth that her name meant "house of God" and that it "hides a mystery, accomplished on this great day."

Elizabeth took steps to conquer her bad temper. "From the day of First Communion and afterward, Elizabeth had no more fits of anger," her mother remembered. Elizabeth also felt the first stirrings of a call by God to join the Discalced Carmelites.

Elizabeth began to teach the catechism to younger children. She sang in two choirs in her parish. She organized a daycare for the

St. Elizabeth of the Trinity

children of local factory workers. She also read and studied the first edition of St. Thérèse of Lisieux's autobiography, *Story of a Soul*, which had just been published. It was around this time that Elizabeth began to be aware that not just Christ "but all Three of the Trinity—Father, Son, and Spirit" were present in her life. With the grace of the Blessed Trinity, Elizabeth entered the Carmelite order in 1901, at age nineteen.

On becoming a Discalced Carmelite, Elizabeth was given the name "Elizabeth of the Trinity" as her awareness and experience of the Triune God continued to grow. Through contemplative prayer, Sr. Elizabeth of the Trinity came to understand that all people are created to be united with Jesus in order to share in his relationship with the Father and the Holy Spirit. On November 21, 1904, the Feast of the Presentation of Mary, Elizabeth composed a prayer to the Trinity that remains treasured today. It is quoted in the *Catechism of the Catholic Church* (260):

> O my God, Trinity whom I adore, help me forget myself entirely so to establish myself in you, unmovable and peaceful as if my soul were already in eternity. May nothing be able to trouble my peace or make me leave you, O my unchanging God, but may each minute bring me more deeply into your mystery! Grant my soul peace. Make it your heaven, your beloved dwelling and the place of your rest. May I never abandon you there, but may I be there, whole and entire, completely vigilant in my faith, entirely adoring, and wholly given over to your creative action.

Sr. Elizabeth of the Trinity died from Addison's disease, a disorder of the adrenal glands, two years after writing this prayer, after suffering for many months. On November 25, 1984, Pope John Paul II beatified Elizabeth of the Trinity. He described her as a person "who led a life hidden with Christ in God." Pope Francis canonized Elizabeth of the Trinity on October 15, 2016. Her feast day is November 8. Because of her vow to silence as a Discalced Carmelite, the Church has validated the importance of silent prayer. Elizabeth reminds us that "everything is a sacrament that gives us God." She thought of the Trinity as the furnace of excessive love and calls on us to ingrain the Trinity into our lives: the Father beholding the Son in the fire of the Holy Spirit.

Comprehension

1. How did Elizabeth begin to experience a conversion when she celebrated her First Communion?
2. What does Elizabeth's name mean?
3. What did St. Elizabeth of the Trinity want to remind all people of?

Application

For her first Christmas in the convent, Elizabeth wrote this poem about the Blessed Trinity:

> He comes to reveal the mystery
> To give all the Father's secrets
> To lead from glory to glory
> Even unto the bosom of the Trinity.

Write your own short poem to express your love for, and faith in, the Blessed Trinity.

Prayer

St. Catherine of Siena, a theologian and mystic of the Church from the fourteenth century, understood the Trinity to be unified with the Holy Eucharist. She taught that when we receive Holy Communion, we not only receive the Body and Blood of Christ but are infused with the graces of each Divine Person of the Trinity—God the Father, God the Son, and God the Holy Spirit. The following prayer or tribute to the Blessed Trinity written by St. Catherine of Siena is part of a longer prayer read each year on April 29, her feast day.

Prayer to the Holy Trinity

> Eternal God, eternal Trinity,
> You have made the Blood of Christ so precious
> through his sharing in your Divine nature.
> You are a mystery as deep as the sea;
> the more I search, the more I find,
> and the more I find, the more I search for you.
> But I can never be satisfied;
> what I receive will ever leave me desiring more.
> When you fill my soul, I have an ever greater hunger,
> and I grow more famished for your light.
> I desire above all to see you,
> the true Light, as you really are.
> Amen.

4

Jesus's Own Life Reveals More about the Nature of God

Tree of Jesse

➤*Unknown*

The Tree of Jesse has appeared in religious art for centuries, representing the ancestors of Jesus as named in his genealogy in the Gospel of Matthew (1:1–17). This stained glass window mosaic of the Tree of Jesse is in the Cathedral of Our Lady of Chartres, about fifty miles southwest of France. This famous cathedral was constructed mostly between 1194 and 1220. The mosaic is very similar in style to one that appears in the Saint-Denis Basilica and was created by a French priest, Abbot Suger, in 1142. The Chartres mosaic has no known artist.

Chartres, a Gothic cathedral, has over 170 stained glass windows that were created to not only tell the story of faith but also to let more light into the darkened nave. The process for creating these windows was an innovative one: metal oxides were added to the glass when it was still being fused, allowing for a range of colors. The pieces were cut with a hot iron in order to create the desired design. On certain pieces, images were painted onto the glass with a brush in gray scale, a process that involved measuring the quality of light from dark to gray to light. This process allowed for the ability to create details on the glass such as faces and drapes.

Several expert glassmakers of the time had mastered the techniques of grayscale, and there were likely dozens of artists who composed the stained glass windows at Chartres. Their style and work was masterful; their use of a combination of colors resulted in a mosaic that changes in appearance based on the amount of light and time of day.

In this mosaic, Jesse is sleeping. Note the vine that emanates from his body, representing his descendants. Within the branches are four kings, each one forming the centerpiece of one of the square central panels. David appears first, followed by Solomon and Rehoboam and Abijah. The latter two kings are meant to represent the entire royal line that extends to Mary and to Christ. Jesus is depicted at the top of the tree.

If you would like to investigate the history of the Jesse tree, see Chapter 4 Review, Chapter Project 1.

What can we learn about God from the human nature of Jesus?

Chapter Overview

Introduction

God Enters History in the Person of Jesus Christ

Section 1

The Cultural and Historical Context of Jesus's Life

Section 2

Jesus Was Formed in the Jewish Faith and Tradition

Section 3

Events in the Life of Jesus

Section 4

We Know Jesus through the Gospels

GOD ENTERS HISTORY IN THE PERSON OF JESUS CHRIST

By now you know well that Jesus Christ is both true God and true man. This means that he was, indeed, a true historical figure. St. Paul said that God sent his Son to this world in "the fullness of time" (Gal 4:4). What this means is that the Incarnation happened at the perfect time, appointed by God. God could have become man earlier in history or later in history, but he did not. The moment he entered was purposefully chosen by the wisdom of God.

Thus, it is important to examine the facts and details surrounding Christ's historical presence. However, when studying his historicity, we must be careful not to forget about his divinity. The heresies previously described (see Chapter 1, Section 4) became heresies because people misunderstood this great mystery of the hypostatic union. This said, while keeping in mind his divinity, you must understand there was a Divine Person who entered history named Jesus who lived in a small village called Nazareth near the eastern shores of the Mediterranean Sea. This isn't a made-up place. It still exists today. Check out the map and photos of Nazareth, all taken within the past few years.

Likewise, don't read the details of Jesus's historicity from Christian sources (most prominently the Bible) as less than true because they were composed by faithful believers. The Bible itself remains one of the most reliable—and

161

Cityscape of Nazareth (left). Jezreel Valley from the Mount Precipice (right).

scrutinized—historical sources of the first century. Put the accuracy of the Bible alongside that of non-Christian historical sources (see Chapter 1, Section 3) confirming that a person called Jesus Christ indeed lived, and we have a perfect starting point to examine the life of Jesus Christ, the Incarnate God who came to earth.

When Did Jesus Live?

Jesus not only lived in an actual place; he also lived in a real time. See if you can approximate the time period when Jesus lived based on the total age of the planet Earth. Scientists estimate that Earth is approximately 4.6 billion years old. Science has also estimated that the first humans appeared on the planet about two hundred thousand years ago. If the timeline were drawn to scale (4.6 billion total years), where would the first humans appear on it? From what you already know about the life of Jesus, where would his life fall on the timeline?

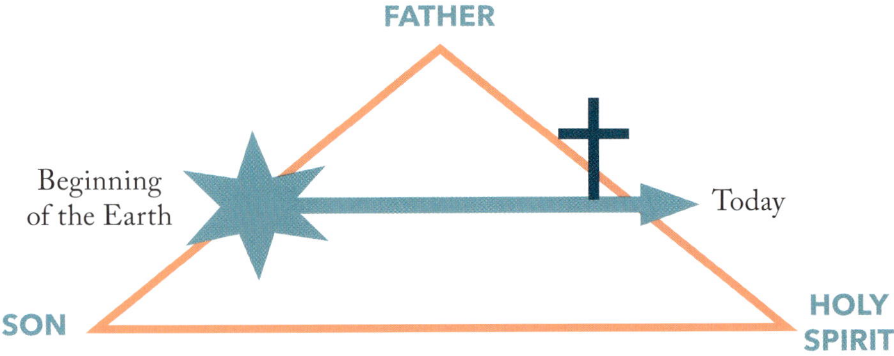

It would not be an exaggeration to label the Incarnation as the greatest event in history. What about some other significant world events? Where would they fall on the timeline? The European discovery of America occurred around AD 1500. Roman civilization had its origins around 500 BC. The invention of the wheel and primitive writing both took place around 7000 BC. The life of Abraham from the Old Testament is often dated around the twentieth century BC. As you can tell, in relationship to the entire life of this planet, human history is condensed. The appearance of Jesus Christ on Earth actually occurred late in the life of both the planet and the human race.

The next sections of this chapter present more evidence for the historical life of Jesus. However, before moving on, return to the timeline. What if you were asked to situate God on the timeline? As the image below represents, God is present before all time, after all time, above all time, and beyond all time. God is the origin of time and the final end of time. The historical life of Jesus can only be examined in light of Jesus's identity as the Second Divine Person of the Blessed Trinity made man.

SECTION Assessment

Comprehension

1.   At what point did the Blessed Trinity appear in creation?

2.   Where did Jesus live?

Reflection

3.   Explain God's presence in any era on your timeline.

4.   Why is it important to study Jesus of Nazareth's time and place in history?

THE CULTURAL AND HISTORICAL CONTEXT OF JESUS'S LIFE

Jesus was born into a human family. Though he was conceived without a human father, through the power of the Holy Spirit, Jesus was born of a woman like every other human being. Likewise, he came into this world as a hungry, helpless infant, the same way that everyone else did. He was dependent on his parents for food, clothing, shelter, and education.

This section examines more closely some of the gospel passages that stress the true humanity of Jesus Christ.

Jesus's Ancestry

Jewish people living under Roman occupation in first-century Palestine had various ideas and expectations for the coming of a messiah who would save them. Most Jews strongly believed that God would send his Chosen One, the Messiah, very soon. The Hebrew word *masiah* translates to the Greek word *Christos* (Christ), which means "anointed one." At first, the title *messiah* applied to the king of Israel (i.e., King David and his successors). However, David's successors were mostly weak and corrupt.

Even when the monarchy era ended for the Jews, the belief in God's promise to provide a messiah did not die. After the Babylonian Exile, the Jews increasingly believed that a messiah would usher in God's Kingdom or reign. Various Jewish sects in Jesus's day (e.g., Sadducees, Pharisees, Zealots, and Essenes) had different expectations about who or what kind of person the Messiah would be. However, most Jews expected a political or military leader like King David, who would lead them to reestablish the prominence of Israel as an independent nation and help establish God's Kingdom on earth.

Also, by the first century, some Jews (possibly including John the Baptist) fully expected the coming of the Messiah to be accomplished by an apocalyptic event. This **apocalypse** would be dramatic, pointing to the Messiah's identity and the glorious establishment of God's Kingdom. All Jews of the first century expected the Messiah to hold the ancestry of King David, as prophesized in Jewish Scripture. Two of the synoptic Gospels, Matthew and Luke, provide genealogies of Jesus, each connecting him in a particular way to his ancestry among the Chosen People. Luke takes the additional step of tracing Jesus's lineage back to the first man, Adam.

Genealogy in Matthew's Gospel (1:1–17)

The Gospel of Matthew begins with a genealogy listing Jesus's ancestors. Matthew, writing for a Jewish Christian audience, wanted to show explicitly that Jesus was part of the Jewish people, God's Chosen People who traced their lineage back to the great figures of Jewish history. Matthew called Jesus the "son of David" and the "son of Abraham" (Mt 1:1). In both cases, the word *son* means "descendant."

Imagine Jesus's first disciples. Most had been raised as faithful Jews. Many would have to explain to their families why they had decided to believe that Jesus was the Chosen One called for by their traditional Jewish faith. It was important to Matthew to establish that Jesus was a legal heir to the throne of King David. The Old Testament records the prophet Samuel, who anointed David king, saying,

> When your days have been completed and you rest with your ancestors, I will raise up your offspring after you, sprung from your loins, and I will establish his kingdom. He it is who shall build a house for my name, and I will establish his royal throne forever. (2 Sm 7:12–13)

Matthew takes great effort to show that Jesus is part of the Davidic line. He traces the ancestors of Jesus from Abraham, the father of the Jewish faith, to Joseph, Jesus's foster father but not his blood relative. Jewish people regarded adopted children as full heirs, and this citation would not have raised any

---

apocalypse A word meaning "revelation" or "unveiling" and often associated with the end times or the Second Coming of Christ. Also, *apocalyptic writing* is the name of the literary genre in the Bible that uses inspired, highly symbolic language to bolster faith by reassuring believers that the current age, subject to forces of evil, will end when God intervenes and establishes a divine rule of goodness and peace.

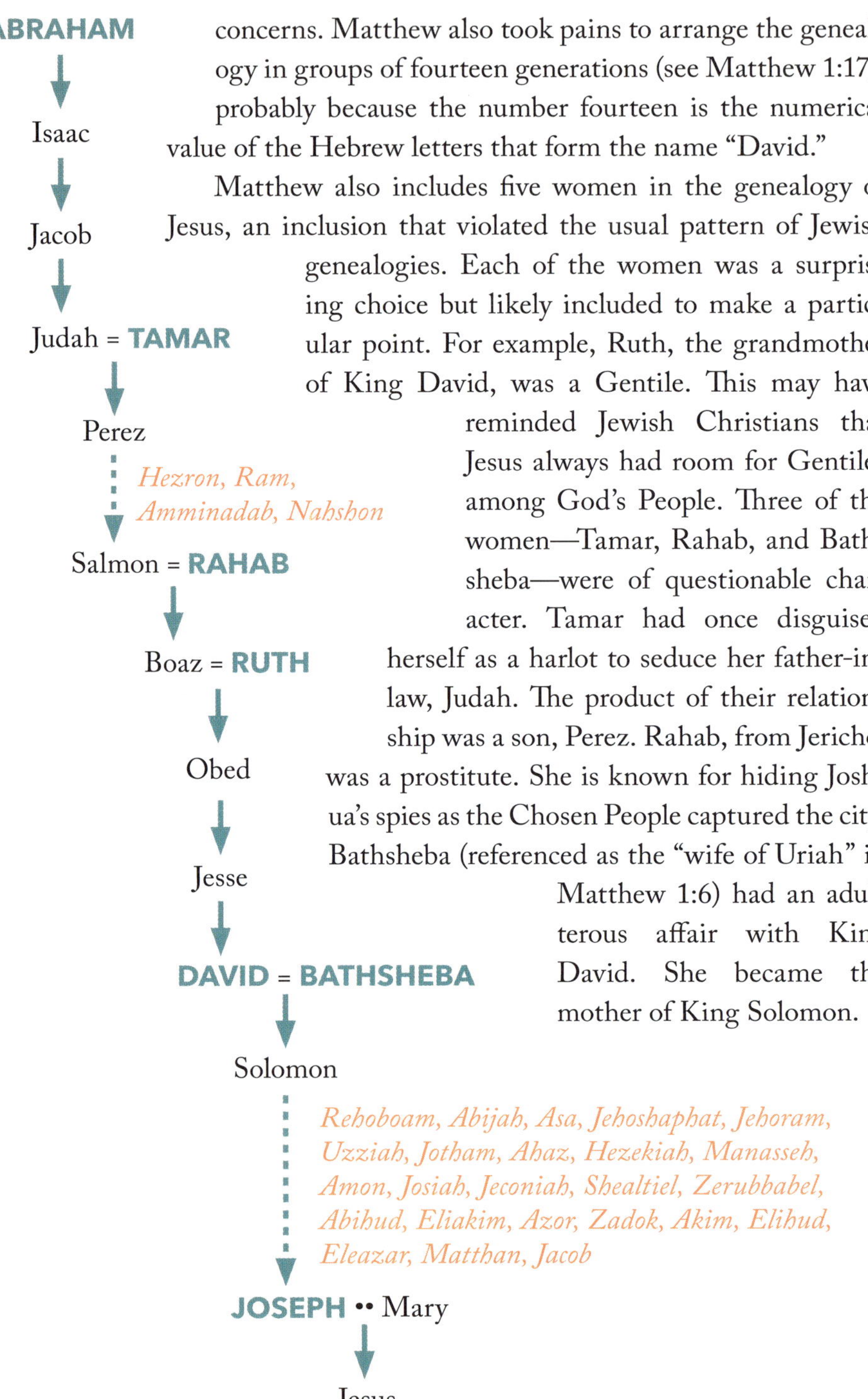

concerns. Matthew also took pains to arrange the genealogy in groups of fourteen generations (see Matthew 1:17), probably because the number fourteen is the numerical value of the Hebrew letters that form the name "David."

Matthew also includes five women in the genealogy of Jesus, an inclusion that violated the usual pattern of Jewish genealogies. Each of the women was a surprising choice but likely included to make a particular point. For example, Ruth, the grandmother of King David, was a Gentile. This may have reminded Jewish Christians that Jesus always had room for Gentiles among God's People. Three of the women—Tamar, Rahab, and Bathsheba—were of questionable character. Tamar had once disguised herself as a harlot to seduce her father-in-law, Judah. The product of their relationship was a son, Perez. Rahab, from Jericho, was a prostitute. She is known for hiding Joshua's spies as the Chosen People captured the city. Bathsheba (referenced as the "wife of Uriah" in Matthew 1:6) had an adulterous affair with King David. She became the mother of King Solomon.

Why did Matthew include these women in his genealogy? Perhaps he wanted to show that God is in control. **God's actions do not always coincide with the preconceptions people have about how he should act.** In his own ministry, Jesus included some rather ordinary people among his disciples. There were sinners in Jesus's family tree. The fact is that God chooses whomever he wants to do his work, sinners included. This theme is supported throughout the Gospels. Jesus associated with the poor, with people whom society rejected, with prostitutes, and with sinners of all kinds. Jesus came to save everyone: Jews, Gentiles, men, and women alike.

Genealogy in Luke's Gospel (3:23–38)

Luke wrote for Gentiles who had become Christian. For this reason, Luke's genealogy of Jesus traces his ancestry through David and Abraham all the way back to Adam, the first human, and then to God. Luke is making two important theological points here. First, he is stressing that Jesus is a descendant of the first humans. The Son of God assumed a human nature with a human body and a human soul. Jesus was like all humans except that he was not touched by Original Sin, nor did he commit any personal sins. Second, Luke highlights the truth that Jesus came to redeem not only the Chosen People but all people. This theme is extended in Luke's Gospel.

Luke wanted to state clearly that Jesus is, in fact, the Son of God. Significantly, Luke inserted the genealogical background of Jesus right after his Baptism. At Jesus's Baptism, God says, "You are my beloved Son; with you I am well pleased" (Lk 3:22). **Luke's Gospel makes the clear point that Jesus, the Son of God, became a human being and a human being with a family tree.** The Son of God became a son of Adam so that he could be the New Adam, inviting all people to be children of his Father.

Like Matthew's Gospel, Luke's traces the line of ancestry to Joseph. Jesus had the legal right to claim himself as a descendant of King David. Luke makes this clear by stating, "He was the son, as was thought, of Joseph" (Lk 3:23).

Jesus's Formative Years

The family tree of Jesus would not be noteworthy except that it leads to the Incarnation, the birth of God's Son, the coming of the Savior into the world. This event was the election and fulfillment of Israel in the Person of Jesus:

Nazareth today. Note the mosque in the forefront, right.

"All this took place to fulfill what the Lord had said through the prophet: 'Behold, the virgin shall be with child and bear a son, and they shall name him Emmanuel,' which means 'God is with us'" (Mt 1:22–23).

Born in Bethlehem, Jesus grew up and lived most of his life in Nazareth, a small village of about 1,200 people about two miles off the main road through southern Galilee. This had to be an established and well-noted fact in the first century, because if it wasn't, his first followers and the gospel authors may have wanted to disassociate Jesus from Nazareth. **In Jesus's day, Nazareth was off the beaten path. It was a small and insignificant rural village.** The disparaging remark about Nazareth—"Can anything good come from Nazareth?" (Jn 1:46)—made by Nathanael, when Philip declared that Jesus of Nazareth was the Promised One, may have reflected a common sentiment of the time.

Matthew validates what was a firmly established tradition—that Nazareth was the hometown of Jesus—with this passage: "He shall be called a Nazorean" (Mt 2:23). Though the town of Nazareth is never mentioned in the Old Testament, Matthew may have connected Nazareth with certain Old Testament texts having words similar to the name of that town (e.g., Isaiah 11:1). In any case, it was in this simple village that Jesus grew up among good, hardworking, but largely poor people. This is where Jesus learned to work, to read, and to interact with friends and family. Nazareth is where Jesus was taught the Jewish faith. Luke's Gospel reports that it was in Nazareth that Jesus "grew and became strong, filled with wisdom; and the favor of God was upon him" (Lk 2:40).

Jesus Was the Son of a Carpenter

Jesus was known as the "carpenter's son" (Mt 13:55) and the "son of Joseph, from Nazareth" (Jn 1:45; 6:42; Lk 4:22). It is likely that Joseph died before Jesus began his public ministry. Evidence for this is that when Jesus returned to Nazareth with a new reputation for preaching and healing and went to his hometown synagogue, he was identified as "the carpenter, the son of Mary" (Mk 6:3). It would have been unusual to refer to Jesus by his mother's name unless Joseph had already died.

Jesus used many metaphors and analogies from the carpentry trade in his teaching. He spoke about entering by the narrow gate (see Matthew 7:13–14) and of building one's house on rock, not sand (see Matthew 7:24–27). In one parable, he told of a vineyard owner who built a tower for produce (see Matthew 21:33).

During his public ministry, Jesus extended one of his warmest invitations to those who were burdened by the law when it was dealt out harshly by the Pharisees and scribes. Jesus compared this to a yoke that was fastened to two animals and attached to a heavy plow: "Come to me, all you who labor and are burdened, and I will give you rest. Take my yoke upon you and learn from me, for I am meek and humble of heart; and you will find rest for yourselves. For my yoke is easy, and my burden light" (Mt 11:28–30).

Jesus must have understood work. Rather than speaking and acting as a harsh taskmaster, he promised to provide rest for those worn down by burdens. Jesus himself likely had many days of grueling, hard, and dusty work.

The Language and Dialect of Jesus

Jesus spoke Aramaic, a Semitic language closely related to Hebrew and originally spoken by tribes from parts of ancient Syria and Mesopotamia. More precisely, the Gospels hint that Jesus spoke a Galilean version of Western Aramaic, considered mainly as a regional dialect by Aramaic speakers in Judea. Recall, for example, how Peter's dialect betrayed him when he denied

Before the Roman Empire, most ancient roads were dirt paths that were often muddy and pockmarked. Roman engineers changed that and constructed an interconnected road system paved with stones. The most famous of the roads was the Appian Way, which began construction in 312 BC. Eventually there were twenty-nine highways connected by 372 road links, a total of about 250,000 miles of road system. This system would have been present in Jesus's time; certainly both St. Peter and St. Paul traveled along these roads ending in Rome. Along the way a variety of languages and dialects would have been spoken by travelers of all cultures.

knowing Jesus: "Surely you too are one of them; even your speech gives you away" (Mt 26:73).

Aramaic was the common language of the Jews in Palestine since the sixth century BC, after they returned from captivity in Babylon. Although the Scriptures were read in Hebrew in Jesus's day, many people did not understand Hebrew. So the Scriptures were translated into Aramaic paraphrases known as **Targums** when the sacred Hebrew texts were read aloud in the synagogues.

The Gospels themselves, though written in Greek, retain several Aramaic sayings of Jesus, including *Ephphatha* ("Be opened") and *Talitha koum* ("Little girl, get up"). The Gospels also contain Aramaic place names such as *Gethsemane* ("Oil Press") and *Golgotha* ("Place of the Skull"). They also use the Aramaic word *bar* for "son of," as in Bar-Jonah, Bartholomew, and Barabbas. The most important use of an Aramaic word is when Jesus addresses God as *Abba* ("Father").

Jesus also likely learned to read and write in Hebrew, as the passage from Luke 4:16–17 suggests. The language might have still been spoken commonly in his lifetime, especially in the southern part of the province of Judea. Jesus may have learned Hebrew in the synagogue and spoken it on visits to Jerusalem. He may have used it in debates with the learned scribes and Pharisees.

Targums The name for Aramaic paraphrases or translations of the Jewish Bible that came into prominence in the first century when Hebrew was declining as the spoken language in and around Palestine.

The common language of the Roman Empire during Jesus's time was a colloquial Greek known as *Koine* ("common") Greek.[1] It was the favored spoken language in the Near East because of Alexander the Great's conquests in the fourth century BC. Jesus may have had limited knowledge of this language, finding it useful if his trade was indeed carpentry, especially if he did any work in a large nearby city such as Sepphoris. He may have spoken Greek when he was brought before Pontius Pilate.

Finally, some Latin was probably spoken in Palestine, because of the presence of the Roman occupation forces. But Latin was more likely spoken only by, and for, Roman officials. Almost certainly Jesus did not speak Latin.

SECTION Assessment

Comprehension

1. Name two differences between Matthew's and Luke's genealogies of Jesus.

2. What was the common first-century Jewish belief concerning the messiah?

3. What do both genealogies have in common?

4. Who were the women included in Matthew's genealogy of Jesus? Why was their inclusion surprising?

5. What is one metaphor or analogy from carpentry that Jesus used in his teaching?

Reflection

6. Jewish people accepted adopted children equally with their natural children. How is this a lesson for how God views and treats you?

JESUS WAS FORMED IN THE JEWISH FAITH AND TRADITION

Luke's Gospel makes it clear that Jesus was raised in the Jewish faith and tradition. According to Jewish law, Jesus was circumcised on the eighth day after his birth (see Luke 2:21). He was then given what was perhaps the most common name for Jewish boys of his time—Jesus or "Yeshua." (The name Joseph or "Yoseff" was the second most popular name for males, while Mary or "Miryam" was the most common female name.) **While the name Jesus was a common name, from the moment it was bestowed on the Son of God Incarnate, it took on a forevermore unique meaning. The literal meaning of "Jesus" is "YHWH saves."** Jesus is truly the Son of God who brought salvation to the world. Jesus's practice of his Jewish faith revolved around the Temple, synagogue, and religious feasts.

Jesus and the Temple

For Jews, the one and only Temple was in Jerusalem. The Temple was where the Jews offered sacrifices to God. It was the holiest place where Jews believed God dwelt in a special way. Only the priestly caste had a role in Temple worship. It was the priests who were able to sacrifice the unblemished lamb to YHWH on a daily basis. Only the high priest could enter the most sacred space inside the Temple—the Holy of Holies—once a year, on Yom Kippur, the Day of Atonement.

The Temple standing during Jesus's life was the third one constructed in Jerusalem. The First Temple, Solomon's Temple, was destroyed by the Babylonians in 587 BC. The Second Temple, that of Zerubbabel, was replaced by Herod the Great's magnificent Temple. Construction to replace the Second Temple began in 20–19 BC (see John 2:20). It took ten thousand workers, supervised by one thousand priests, to finish building the Temple in ten years.

However, the work of decorating the Temple was still going on in Jesus's day. The Temple was completely finished in AD 64, only six short years before the Romans leveled it (except for the Wailing or Western Wall, which remains today) during the First Jewish Revolt (66–70).

The Temple was a marvelous structure, 2,350 feet in its perimeter, with eight main gates. Around the altar was a courtyard reserved for priests. Next were the courtyard of Israel (for males) and then the courtyard for women. Beyond that was the courtyard of the Gentiles. No Gentile could cross beyond this outer courtyard, under penalty of death. The Mosaic Law required Jews to pay a Temple tax and obligated Jewish men to make a pilgrimage to Jerusalem on the three major feasts of Passover, Pentecost, and Tabernacles. However, not all Jews could make it to the holy city for all the feasts.

The Gospels mention Jesus's presence at the Temple on a few key occasions. As was customary, he was presented in the Temple as an infant (see Luke 2:22) in order to fulfill the requirements of the Mosaic Law, in which an offering was made on the infant's behalf. Typically the offering was a lamb, but exceptions were made for those who could not afford this offering. Mary and Joseph offered two doves or young pigeons in accord with this exception (see Luke 2:24). This was another indication that Jesus was not from a wealthy family.

When Jesus was twelve years old, his parents took him to the Temple for the Feast of Passover. There, it is reported that he astounded the teachers of his day with insights and knowledge (see Luke 2:46). After his parents found him in the Temple, Jesus returned with them to Nazareth, where "he was obedient to them" (Lk 2:51).

Jesus and the Synagogue

Jesus learned his Jewish religion from his parents and from praying and studying in the synagogue in Nazareth. *Synagogue* comes from the Greek word for "assembly." Many larger towns had more than one synagogue, and Jerusalem may have had hundreds. The synagogue served three main purposes:

1. It was a house of prayer where Scriptures were read and YHWH was worshipped.

2. It was a place of discussion for settling legal disputes.

3. It was the local school.

Synagogues were often built near rivers or springs so that worshippers could purify themselves in running water before entering. Inside the synagogues were stepped stone benches on three sides, with higher seats set aside for those in more prestigious positions. The scrolls containing the Law (Torah) and the writings of the prophets were kept in a cabinet called an ark.

Synagogues were opened three times a day for those who wished to pray. There were special services on market days—Mondays and Thursdays. The most important day for regular worship was the Sabbath (Saturday). Once ten men over the age of thirteen assembled, the simple service could begin. Sacrifices were not offered, nor did priests or Levites play any special role. Ordinary townspeople conducted the service, although a "leader of the synagogue" (e.g., Jairus in Luke 8:41) was appointed to organize the meetings as well as to maintain the building. His assistant was in charge of the sacred scrolls, which he handed to the readers for the day.

Typically, the congregation stood facing Jerusalem and recited various prayers beginning with the confession of faith known as the **Sh'ma** (see Deuteronomy 6:4). The key part of the service was the careful reading of the Torah in Hebrew, followed by selected readings from the prophets, again in Hebrew. These readings were translated simultaneously during the respective readings. All of this was done while worshippers remained standing. Then, the leader of the synagogue invited one of the guests—preferably someone well educated or well traveled—to explain the readings in a homily.

Jesus preached in synagogues in the region early in his ministry (see Luke 4:15). Apparently, his earliest ministry took place in Capernaum, a village in Galilee near Nazareth that runs along the Sea of Galilee (see Luke 4:23). Its ruins are still visible today. When Jesus first came to his hometown synagogue in Nazareth, the people had already heard of his Capernaum ministry.

It is in the Nazareth synagogue that Jesus is portrayed as a prophet whose ministry is compared with those of the Old Testament prophets Elijah and Elisha. He is chosen to read from the scroll a passage from the prophet Isaiah. After reading the passage that includes the words "The Spirit of the Lord is upon me, because he has anointed me" (Lk 4:18), Jesus declares that those words apply directly to him. Because the people understood that Jesus was naming himself as God's prophet, they rejected him, led him out of town, and attempted to throw him over a hill. After all, they wondered, "Isn't this the son of Joseph?" (Lk 4:22).

Luke's Gospel records that Jesus went back to Capernaum from Nazareth. There, he continued to astonish the people with his teaching. He spoke with authority. In the Capernaum synagogue, Jesus expelled a demonic spirit from a man who could identify Jesus as "the Holy One of God" (Lk 4:34). These types of incidents clearly indicate that Jesus had full human knowledge that he was God's Anointed One and that those of the spirit world, too, could identify his heavenly origins.

Jesus and Jewish Feasts

Passover, Pentecost, and Tabernacles were major Jewish feasts. Hanukkah was another Jewish feast that Jesus participated in during his lifetime.

Passover (Pesach) was the most important Jewish feast because it celebrated the Chosen People's liberation from slavery in Egypt. The Feast of Passover involved the ritual slaughter of the paschal lamb and the eating of a Seder meal in the holy city of Jerusalem to commemorate the Exodus.

Jesus's Last Supper was set around a Passover meal in Jerusalem. Putting together the accounts in the synoptic Gospels and the Gospel of John, it can be

---

Sh'ma The Hebrew name for "hear." It is the first word of the most important Jewish prayer, which is recited daily in the morning and at night: "Hear, O Israel, the Lord is our God, the Lord is one. And as for you, you shall love the Lord your God with all your heart, with all your soul, and with all your strength."

calculated that Jesus was about thirty-three years old when he celebrated the Last Supper. How so? Luke 3:23 reports that "when Jesus began his ministry he was about thirty years of age," and John's Gospel mentions that Jesus celebrated three Passovers during his public ministry (see John 2:13; 6:4; 13:1).

Pesach, *more commonly known as* Passover, *retells the story of the Exodus of the Hebrew people from Egypt.* Passover *refers to the angel of death who "passed over" the houses of Hebrews that were marked with the blood from a lamb.*

Recall that Pentecost was a feast held fifty days after Passover and was originally the spring grain harvest festival. From Jesus's time through today, Jews celebrate Pentecost as *Shavuot*, a day commemorating when God gave the Torah to all of Israel (though there is no mention of this occasion in Scripture). There is a likely reference of Jesus marking this festival. In the story of Jesus's healing of a man on the Sabbath, the Gospel of John reports that it occurred on "a feast of the Jews, and Jesus went up to Jerusalem" (Jn 5:1). The fiftieth day after Passover would fall on the Sabbath.

Tabernacles, or Booths, was a fall harvest celebration. Pilgrims to Jerusalem built huts out of branches to recall the time that Jews spent in the wilderness. They approached the Temple in a procession, waving branches while praising God. This feast is described in the Old Testament, including in Exodus 23:16. John 7 tells about Jesus participating in this feast. As with other Jewish feasts that took on new meaning with Jesus's involvement (e.g., associating Passover with the Last Supper and Pentecost with the coming of the Holy Spirit), on the high day of the Feast of Tabernacles, Jesus describes himself as "living water." He said, "Let anyone who thirsts come to me and drink" (Jn 7:37).

Hanukkah, or the Feast of the Dedication, was not a major Jewish feast during Jesus's time—nor is it today, despite its publicity around Christmas. It is celebrated to commemorate the Temple's rededication in 164 BC after it was profaned by foreign ruler Antiochus IV. Jesus was accused of blasphemy

when he was in Jerusalem for the Feast of the Dedication. Some people gathered around him and asked him to tell them in plain language whether he was the Messiah. Jesus answered, "I told you and you do not believe. The works I do in my Father's name testify to me" (Jn 10:25).

Clearly Jesus participated fully in his family, local community, and Jewish worship as ways to fulfill his divine mission as God's Son. As a faithful Jewish boy raised in the traditions of Israel and obedient to its laws, he continued, as mentioned earlier, to advance in "wisdom and age and favor before God and man" (Lk 2:52).

SECTION Assessment

Comprehension

1. What does the name Jesus mean?

2. Name at least two occasions Jesus went to the Temple.

3. What were three purposes of the synagogue?

4. Share examples from the Gospels of Jesus's participation in the following feasts: Passover, Pentecost, Tabernacles, and Hanukkah.

Reflection

5. What makes a place sacred? Share an example of a place that fits your definition of sacredness.

EVENTS IN THE LIFE OF JESUS

The historical accounts from Roman, Jewish, and Greek sources (see Chapter 1, Section 3) verify there was an actual person named Jesus who was put to death under Pontius Pilate during the reign of Emperor Tiberius. These sources confirm that some Jewish leaders had a hand in the Death of Jesus. These sources also indicate that Jesus had committed followers who believed him to be the Messiah, a lawgiver, and the founder of a new way of life.

Likewise, the New Testament—especially the four Gospels—offers historical evidence that Jesus existed. Inspired by the Holy Spirit, the Gospels were written from a faith perspective and are not biographies in the modern sense of the word; nevertheless, they contain many elements that can be found in other ancient biographies. Most ancient biographies were not exhaustive studies. For one thing, the length of the scrolls on which documents were written prevented long, detailed accounts of a person's life. Ancient biographers were not much interested in telling about the childhood or the physical appearance of a person. Instead, they tended to focus on key events in a person's life, especially how a person died.

Retelling certain key events like this was seen as a way of shedding light on the character of the person. This pattern and orientation can also be seen in the Gospels. Certainly, the evangelists who wrote the Gospels wanted their readers to take as historical fact the episodes, events, and teachings they chose to present in their writings about Jesus.

Importance of the Gospels for Knowing Jesus

The living transmission of the gospel message can be traced directly to the Word of God made flesh. Sacred Scripture and Sacred Tradition each make "present and fruitful in the Church the mystery of Christ" (*CCC*, 80). The

Matthew and Mark

gospel message was preserved by the Apostles, who were called by Jesus from previous occupations and various family lives to follow him. They listened to his preaching. They observed him interact with other people, many of whom were destitute and despised. In private times with him, they heard more about his identity and learned more about his mission. They eventually witnessed his fate as a condemned criminal. They watched the events surrounding his Crucifixion. Moreover, they saw him *after* his Death, risen in power and glory.

This final experience of the Risen Jesus transformed the Apostles from frightened cowards into bold proclaimers of the Gospel. They were so convinced of the truth of their message that they surrendered their own lives in preaching that God has sent his Son (see Galatians 4:4; *CCC*, 422–424). The testimony of the Apostles is preserved in the four Gospels and the epistles of the New Testament, written within a few generations of Jesus's public ministry. These are an accurate, normative, and inspired source of knowledge about Jesus Christ. Knowledge of Scripture is essential for anyone who wants to have a relationship with Jesus Christ. The Gospels "are our principal source for the life and teachings of the Incarnate Word, our Savior" (*Dei Verbum*, 18, quoted in *CCC*, 125). Mining Scripture for historical data and examining other writings preserved from first-century Palestine, when and where Jesus lived, can also help to create a basic biography of his life.

Luke and John

Brief Account of the Life of Jesus

There is historical evidence primarily taken from the Gospels that a real man named Jesus, who has been the subject of the faith of many followers in the years since, did exist. Christ's whole earthly life is worthy of great study because it is in "his words and deeds, his silences and sufferings, indeed his manner of being and speaking" (*CCC*, 516) that God is revealed. Review this information about key events in the life of Jesus:

1 Jesus's Jewish name was given to Mary by the angel Gabriel at the time of the Annunciation: "Then the angel said to her, 'Do not be afraid, Mary, for you have found favor with God. Behold, you will conceive in your womb and bear a son, and you shall name him Jesus'" (Lk 1:30–31). The name Jesus was conferred on the eighth day after his birth, the day of his circumcision.

2 Jesus's hometown was Nazareth, a small, somewhat obscure town in Galilee. However, because of a census ordered by the Roman government that required all Jews to return to their ancestral homes, Jesus's birth took place in Bethlehem, the place of origin of Joseph, his foster father. Jesus's mother's name was Mary. The date of Jesus's birth is cited between 4 and 6 BC, when King Herod the Great ruled in Palestine under Roman Emperor Caesar Augustus.∞

3 After being baptized by the prophet John the Baptist, likely between AD 27 and 30, Jesus began his own public ministry. According to the Gospel of John, Jesus celebrated three Passovers in Jerusalem after he began his public ministry, indicating a total duration of three years. His ministry was often spent in the countryside, where he preached a message of repentance for sins, the coming of God's Kingdom, and the need for all people to believe in him and his teachings. He taught clearly:

> This is the time of fulfillment. The kingdom of God is at hand. Repent, and believe in the gospel. (Mk 1:15)

∞ Note

In the sixth century, a Roman monk and mathematician, Dionysius Exiguus, or Dennis the Short, attempted to calculate an exact chronology of the Christian faith. Dennis began the new Christian calendar in AD 1. ("AD" is an abbreviation for *anno domini*, meaning "in the year of the Lord.") He based his chronology on the date of the Annunciation, which he took as the date of the Incarnation and placed on March 25. By implication, this means that Jesus would have been born nine months later, on December 25.

To complicate the calculations, King Herod the Great, who the Gospels mention was alive at the time of Jesus's birth, died in 4 BC. Since Herod's command to kill all the infants of Bethlehem and its vicinity two years old and under (see Matthew 2:16) occurred no more than two years after Christ's birth, this could push the date of his birth to the year 5 or 6 BC if it happened at the end of Herod's life.

Pope Benedict XVI admitted in his 2012 book *Jesus of Nazareth: The Infancy Narratives* that Dennis the Short "made a mistake in his calculations by several years." However, the exact year of Jesus's birth, while an interesting exercise in historical study, is not what is important about the event. What is important is the entrance into the world of the Savior of the human race.

4 Jesus's manner of preaching and his actions led some people to think of him as a great prophet. For example, he demanded that people make a clear choice to turn away from sin, accept God's love, and believe in him. But not everyone had a positive response to Jesus. Some of his relatives said about him, "He is out of his mind" (Mk 3:21).

Further, some of Jesus's words and actions threatened and angered both the Jewish religious leaders and, subsequently, the Roman officials. He associated with public sinners such as prostitutes and tax collectors. Some of his enemies condemned his actions as the work of the devil.

5 Eventually, the Jewish religious leaders handed Jesus over to the Roman officials for arrest. One of his Twelve Apostles turned him over. Other than St. John, the beloved disciple who remained at the foot of the Cross, the Apostles abandoned him. In religious court, Jesus was found guilty of blasphemy. The accusation: he had claimed to be God's Son. The Jewish leaders handed Jesus over to Pontius Pilate, the Roman prefect for the region, then to King Herod, and then back to Pilate, who, after having Jesus scourged, sentenced him to the cruelest form of capital punishment: crucifixion. This death penalty was carried out in either AD 30 or 33. The crime was ultimately written and posted on the Cross on which he died. It read, "This is Jesus, the King of the Jews" (Mt 27:37). In other words, Jesus was accused and convicted under Roman law of sedition against Emperor Tiberius.

It is important to remember that even non-Christians would acknowledge, based on historical evidence from the Gospels, that Jesus lived, preached, and died at the hands of the Roman government approximately two thousand years ago.

SECTION Assessment

Comprehension

1. Name one reason there weren't many details in ancient biographies as we are used to today.

2. What was Jesus's hometown?

3. What is the basis for the understanding that Jesus's public ministry lasted for three years?

4. What crime was Jesus accused and convicted of under Roman law?

Reflection

5. What do you consider to be the most significant event in the life of Jesus? Why?

6. What is one event in the life of Jesus you would like to know more about? Why?

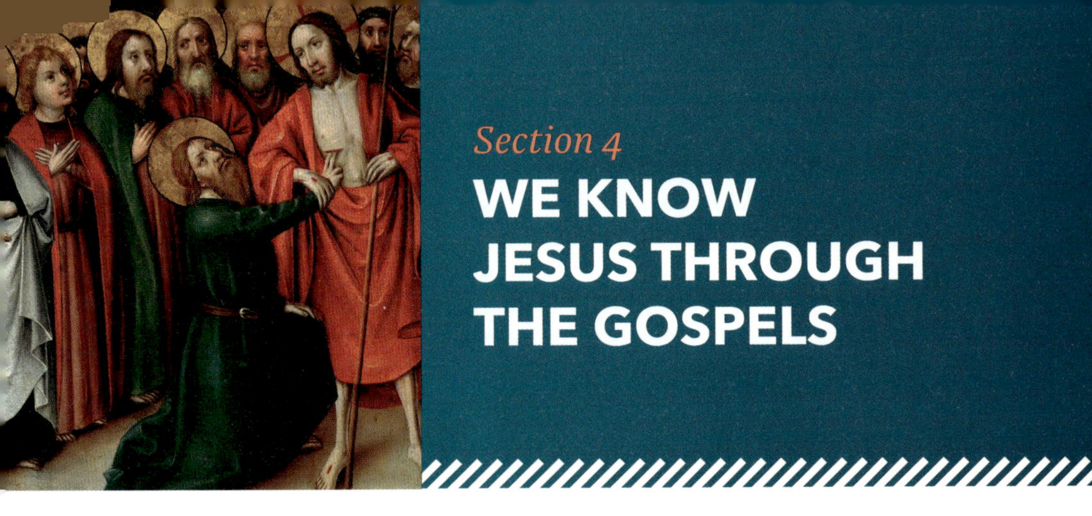

A prophetic exchange occurred between Jesus and St. Thomas after the previously absent Thomas probed the wounds of the Risen Jesus a week after he appeared to the other Apostles. Thomas said to Jesus, "My Lord and my God!" (Jn 20:28), echoing the first verse of the Gospel, "and the Word was God" (Jn 1:1). Jesus was more than the miracle worker, the riveting teacher, and the disrupter of the status quo that the Apostles and other disciples had gotten to know in his time with them. He is God, and for Thomas, encountering and actually touching Jesus's risen body was necessary for him to come to believe.

The prophetic aspect of the conversation came next. Jesus said to Thomas, "Have you come to believe because you have seen me? Blessed are those who have not seen and have believed" (Jn 20:29). All believers who have lived since Jesus spoke these words—including those today—are the "blessed" he describes. We do not see and touch the Risen Jesus as Thomas did. We cannot walk and converse with Jesus as he goes about his earthly ministry as Thomas did. Yet people in every age have come to hear Jesus, witness his miracles, and believe in him as the Second Divine Person of the Blessed Trinity through the testimony of the Gospels.

There Are Four Gospel Accounts

The four Gospels revolve around the one Person of Jesus Christ. These four— the Gospels of Matthew, Mark, Luke, and John—are the most important part of the New Testament canon. They are

- Authentic testimonies of faith in Jesus Christ

- Inspired writings

- Written sources

- Expressions of the Church's faith in Jesus

Why *four* Gospels? Simply, they were each written for a different audience. Think of it this way: Imagine your mother, sister, best friend, and favorite teacher all writing a letter of recommendation to a prospective employer on your behalf. Each would be describing the real you, but each would have a unique perspective. Now imagine that they were not writing to a prospective employer but to a relative in another state whom you had never met. Each of the letters describing your various qualities would be slanted in a different way, depending on the person receiving the letter.

Something similar happened in the writing of the Gospels. All four Gospels are divinely inspired truth, but the perspectives are different because they were composed by different people writing in different times and for people who lived in different places. Further, each Gospel was written to and for a local church and was tailored to meet the needs of that community. All four Gospels present the Good News of Jesus, but they adapt their presentation to the religious needs of their intended audiences.

The evangelists Mark and John writing the Gospels.

It is also important to understand that there were three stages involved in the writing of the Gospels:

> **The first stage** of the formation of the Gospels was the public life and teaching of Jesus in the years he was on earth. The first stage spans not only Jesus's earthly ministry but also his Death and Resurrection "until the day He was taken up" (*Dei Verbum*, 19) to heaven.

> **The second stage** of formation of the Gospels encompassed the years when the Good News was shared by the preaching of the Apostles and, likely, many other people in union with them. This period of about twenty-five to thirty years after the Death, Resurrection, and Ascension of Jesus is known as the *oral tradition*.

> **The third stage** was the period in which the Gospels were written.

The Gospels were eventually written down for a few specific reasons. Some of the early disciples believed the world would end and Jesus would return before they died. When they realized this might not take place, they understood the need to preserve the apostolic testimony in writing. Also, distortions to the oral tradition were occurring. It was important to keep an authentic record of who Jesus was and of the Good News he preached. Additionally, a written text of Jesus's teaching and a source for use at liturgy was needed. The writings of St. Justin Martyr from around the year 155 verify that "the memoirs of the apostles and the writings of the prophets are read [at liturgy], as much as time permits."[2]

Though there are four gospel accounts, "through all the words of Sacred Scripture, God speaks only one single Word, his one Utterance in whom he expresses himself completely" (*CCC*, 102). That one Word is the Jesus Christ, the same Word that was identified in the first verse of John's Gospel and the same Word that St. Thomas identified as "my Lord and my God." Through the Gospels, Christians throughout all generations have been blessed to know the Lord Jesus Christ.

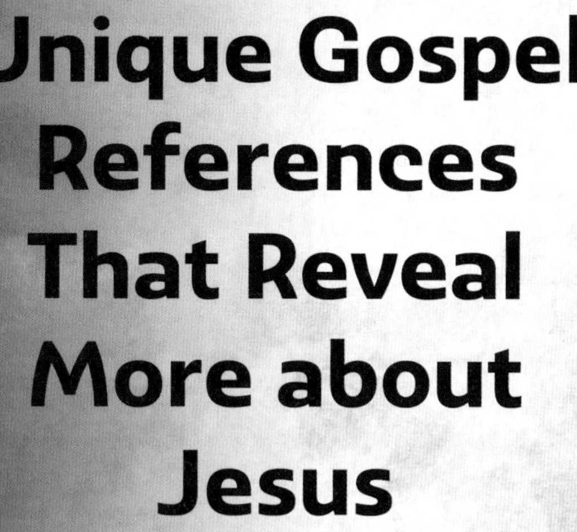

Unique Gospel References That Reveal More about Jesus

Focus Question: What can we learn about God from the human nature of Jesus?

Jesus grew up in the first century as a faithful Jew. His preaching attracted many, and his words were unforgettable. These words were revered by the Apostles and other disciples and handed on. Here are four unique gospel references traced to the words of Jesus.

1. "Abba"

Abba is an Aramaic word for "Father" or, more familiarly, "Dad." Many other religions invoke God as Father. For example, the Jewish people call God "Father" to convey that he is the Creator of the world. Jesus used the term *Abba* to reveal that "God is Father in an unheard-of sense: he is Father not only in being Creator; he is eternally Father in relation to his only Son, who is eternally Son only in relation to his Father" (*CCC*, 240). Jesus can call God "Abba" because he is the Son of God. Another remarkable aspect of Jesus's "Abba" reference is that he invited others to refer to God as "Father" as well. In fact, no one but Christians can rightly call God "Abba."

2. "Amen"

Amen is a Hebrew word borrowed by those (like Jesus) who spoke Aramaic. The word translates as "certainly" and was always used at the end of an oath, blessing, curse, or saying to indicate a person's agreement. "So be it" or "Yes, I agree" captures the sense of the word.

Jesus, however, used the word *amen* differently. He used it to introduce, not end, his own words: "Amen, I say . . ." This phrase was so unique that the gospel writers retained it for the written accounts. It was used fifty times in the synoptic Gospels and twenty-five times in John's Gospel. Jesus seems to have said "Amen, amen" to convey a sense of authority, as in "Hear ye, hear ye." In the Gospel of John, he says, for example, "Amen, amen, I say to you, whatever you ask the Father in my name he will give you" (Jn 16:23). Jesus demanded that affirmation be given to what he said before he said it. He demanded such affirmation because what he was about to say was from the lips of the Son of God.

3. The Parables

There were many creative teachers among the Jewish rabbis of Jesus's day. But the forty-one gospel stories called parables are particularly distinctive when compared with other literature of Judaism, the writings of the Essenes, rabbinic literature, or the writings of St. Paul. A parable is a story that uses easily understood symbols and life occurrences and ends with a surprising lesson.

Consider two of the most famous parables: the good Samaritan (Lk 10:25–37) and the prodigal son (Lk 15:11–32). Each contains everyday people and events that Jesus's listeners would have found familiar:

GOOD SAMARITAN	PRODIGAL SON
Levite	Jealous Older Son
Priest	Father
Samaritan	Wasteful Younger Son
Crime Victim	Pig Farm
Jericho	Home

Jesus intended for his parables to teach with an unexpected twist at the end. Think about how surprising it must have been for Jesus's first-time listeners to hear, in the parable of the good Samaritan, that only an "enemy" of the victim would help him, or to fathom that a father would welcome home a prodigal son who had squandered his entire inheritance.

The parables of Jesus were memorable and unique, and they contained important points about the Kingdom of God that Jesus came to teach. The parables didn't magically appear one day. They were not simply the creation of one or more authors of the Gospels. Rather, they were the product of a remarkable teacher, Jesus.

4. Forgiveness of Sins

Jesus told people their sins were forgiven. He forgave sins himself. According to Jewish authorities, this was a crime of blasphemy. After Jesus forgave the sins of a paralytic who was brought to him for healing, some of the Jewish scribes are quoted as saying, "He is blaspheming. Who but God alone can forgive sins?" (Mk 2:7).

Jesus obviously did not back away from his ministry of forgiving sins. He could forgive sins as a man because he is the Son of God. If he had stopped telling people that their sins were forgiven, he would not have been arrested, transferred to the Romans, and put to death. Connecting the events of Jesus's Passion and Death with the controversial words he spoke provides evidence for their authenticity.

Comprehension

1.   How did Jesus use the term *Abba* in a unique way?
2.   Why did Jesus use "Amen" at the beginning of a statement?
3.   What authority did Jesus's forgiving of sins convey?

Reflection

Name another parable of Jesus. List the ordinary elements Jesus uses. Name the surprising twist at the end. What makes it surprising?

Reading, Studying, and Praying to Know Christ

The gospel understandings of Jesus, though slightly different in their telling, reach the same conclusion: Jesus is God in the flesh, the Second Divine Person

ABBREVIATION	NAME	DATE
DRB	Douay–Rheims Bible	1582, 1609, 1610
DRB	Douay–Rheims Bible Challoner Revision	1749–1752
CB	Confraternity Bible	1941
Knox	Knox Bible	1950
KLNT	Kleist–Lilly New Testament	1956
RSV–CE	Revised Standard Version Catholic Edition	1965–66
JB	Jerusalem Bible	1966
NAB	New American Bible	1970
TLB–CE	The Living Bible Catholic Edition	1971
NJB	New Jerusalem Bible	1985
CCB	Christian Community Bible	1988
NRSV–CE	New Revised Standard Version Catholic Edition	1993
GNT–CE	Good News Translation Catholic Edition	1993
RSV–2CE	Revised Standard Version, Second Catholic Edition	2006
CTS–NCB	CTS New Catholic Bible	2007
NABRE	New American Bible Revised Edition	2011/1986 (OT/NT)
NLT-CE	New Living Translation Catholic Edition	2015
ESV-CE	English Standard Version Catholic Edition	2017
NCB	St. Joseph New Catholic Bible	2019
RNJB	Revised New Jerusalem Bible	2019

of the Blessed Trinity. But how can we be sure? Making the question even more difficult to answer is what St. Paul called "a stumbling block to Jews and foolishness to Gentiles" (1 Cor 1:23). **Paul was referring to the fact that God not only entered human flesh but was sentenced to death and crucified.** As Pope John Paul II said in *Crossing the Threshold of Hope*, "This radical Christian claim has no parallel in any other religious belief."[3] This was certainly part of the dilemma faced by St. Thomas when he could not believe that the crucified Christ had actually risen from the dead. Before coming face to face with the Risen Jesus, Thomas had told the other disciples, "Unless I see the mark of the nails in his hands and put my finger into the nailmarks and put my hand into his side, I will not believe" (Jn 20:25).

Reading, studying, and praying with Sacred Scripture, especially the Gospels, can help us understand some basic elements of Christology, including those related to Jesus's identity.[∞] For example, consider a very brief passage from Luke 4:16–24 from the start of Jesus's public ministry. (Also read another version of the same event in Matthew 13:54–58.) Note that it reveals

∞ Note

Sacred Scripture is an inspired text and "must be read and interpreted in the light of the same Spirit by whom it was written" (*Dei Verbum*, 12, para. 3, quoted in *CCC*, 111). Recall from an earlier course the three criteria for interpreting Scripture in accordance with the Spirit:

1. Read specific passages with the content and unity of the entire Bible in mind.
2. Read the Scripture within *"the living Tradition of the whole Church"* (*CCC*, 113).
3. Pay attention to the analogy of faith. This is the unity of truths among themselves and the entire plan of Revelation.

Also, according to an ancient tradition, the *Catechism of the Catholic Church* (115–119) explains that Scripture can be read in two senses, the literal and the spiritual. The literal sense is what the words mean at the surface level, how they were understood at the time, and how things actually happened. The spiritual sense refers not only to the text of Scripture itself "but also the realities and events about which it speaks" (117).

some of the things about Jesus unpacked in more depth throughout the rest of the Gospels:

> He came to Nazareth, where he had grown up, and went according to his custom into the synagogue on the sabbath day. He stood up to read and was handed a scroll of the prophet Isaiah. (Lk 4:16–17)

This passage reveals that:

1. Jesus came from Nazareth.
2. He customarily prayed in the synagogue on the Jewish day of rest—the Sabbath.
3. Jesus could read.
4. Further, Jesus could read Hebrew, since the Scriptures used in Jewish prayer and worship were written in that language.

God's Revelation of his Son, Jesus Christ, is only one-half of the equation. Once he is revealed, our knowledge of him demands a personal response. The next four chapters of this textbook explore this side of the equation, focusing first on the Christian disciple *par excellence*, Mary, the Mother of God.

Catholic migrants from Eritrea and Ethiopia pray before Mass in their makeshift church near Calais, France.

SECTION Assessment

Comprehension

1. What are four characteristics of the Gospels?

2. Why are there four Gospels?

3. What are the three stages of formation of the Gospels?

4. Why were the Gospels originally written down?

5. What was the stumbling block to faith that St. Paul described?

Reflection

6. How do you fit the definition of "blessed" that Jesus spoke of in his conversation with St. Thomas?

7. How do you understand the Church teaching that Jesus Christ is the "one single Word" of Sacred Scripture?

CHAPTER 4 REVIEW

Section Reviews

Focus Question

What can we learn about God from the human nature of Jesus?

Complete one of the following:

- Archbishop Fulton J. Sheen, a popular twentieth-century television evangelist, said, "Christ's coming into the world was not like that of a sightseer to a strange city, but rather like that of an artist visiting his own studio or an author paging the books he himself has written, for in becoming incarnate, the divine Word was tabernacling himself in his own creation." Pope Benedict XVI wrote, "Jesus was a surprise, the likes of whom no one expected." Write a news account of Christ coming into the world and what it meant for humanity.

- Read the following Scripture passages about the women who appear in Jesus's genealogy in the Gospel of Matthew. Write something you found interesting about each person.

    o Tamar: Genesis 38:6–30

    o Rahab: Joshua 2:1–4

    o Ruth: Book of Ruth

    o Bathsheba: 2 Samuel 11:1–27

- Report on the methods of carpentry in the time of Jesus. What jobs did carpenters do? What products did they make? What raw materials were available for carpenters in the Galilean area? What tools were typically used by carpenters?

Introduction

God Enters History in the Person of Jesus Christ

Review

The Incarnation occurred in an exact place and time. The Second Divine Person of the Blessed Trinity entered human history as a real man. Positioning

Jesus in the time and place of history can help us understand his very real humanity while also knowing that he is divine.

Assignment

Imagine that you can ask Jesus one question about his life growing up in Nazareth. What would it be? Explore this question and Jesus's answer to you in writing.

Section 1

The Cultural and Historical Context of Jesus's Life

Review

The Church has preserved accurate information about the life of Jesus with full authenticity through the ages. Sacred Scripture and Sacred Tradition share inspired details of Jesus's life that came from those who had direct personal contact with him. Historical details present in the Gospels provide a basic biographical sketch of Christ.

Assignment

Name two people who have shared with you something about the life of Jesus. Tell one thing you learned about Jesus from each person.

Section 2

Jesus Was Formed in the Jewish Faith and Tradition

Review

Jesus's name means "YHWH saves." The Jewish traditions and religion he practiced helped him to learn about his identity as the Son of God. Raised in a Jewish family, he worshipped in the Temple and synagogue and celebrated Jewish feasts. These elements of his life—in a particular time and place—also contributed to his human identity.

Assignment

What are some other words to describe Jesus, and what do they mean? Look up and list the name and meaning of titles for Jesus found in Matthew 1:23, John 1:1–5, Mark 8:27–33, and Mark 13:26.

Section 3
Events in the Life of Jesus

Review

All the events of Jesus's life, including his family history, birth, language, preaching, and practice of religion played a part in his identity and mission as the Son of God. These events are transmitted to us today through Sacred Scripture and Sacred Tradition. Using these sources helps to provide a basic biography of Jesus's life.

Assignment

The years of Jesus's life described in this section are often called the "hidden years." Why so? Why is understanding the historical and human background of Jesus helpful in understanding his divine mission?

Section 4
We Know Jesus through the Gospels

Review

The four gospel accounts are the most important part of the New Testament. There are four Gospels because they were each written for a different audience. However, Jesus is the single Word of all Scripture. Reading, studying, and praying with the Gospels can help us understand the basic elements of Christology.

Assignment

Though there are no physical descriptions of Jesus in the Gospels, that has not stopped artists from drawing their own portraits of him over the centuries. Picture Jesus in your own imagination. Sketch out on a piece of paper or in your journal what you think he looks like.

Chapter Projects

Choose and complete at least one of the following projects to assess your understanding of the material in this chapter.

⚙ 1. Make a Mosaic Jesse Tree

Research and write a short background on the history of the Jesse tree, dating back to the Middle Ages. Then create your own mosaic Jesse tree. Use either colored tissue paper or tiles for the tree design. Specifically, decorate ten pieces of tissue paper or tiles to represent the following people in Jesus's genealogy:

- Adam
- Abraham
- Jacob
- Rahab
- Ruth
- David
- Solomon
- Joseph
- Mary
- Jesus

⚙ 2. Create a Timeline of Human History

Create your own timeline that represents the beginning of the earth through today. Include these people and events on your timeline:

- First humans
- Abraham
- King David
- Jesus
- Two significant people or events in ancient history (3500 BC–AD 500)
- Two significant people or events in the Middle Ages (AD 500–1500)
- Two significant people or events in early modern history (AD 1500–1900)
- Two significant people or events in modern history (AD 1900–present)

Include a combination of political, religious, literary, and scientific events and people. Add a scale with equivalency between years and inches on the timeline. Using shading around the timeline or a prominent symbol, add an element that conveys God's presence through all of creation.

⚙ 3. Research the Meaning of and Re-create Christian Symbols

In a notebook, draw each of the following symbols (one page for each symbol). Then write two to three paragraphs on the history and meaning of each symbol and if and where it is used today.

I.N.R.I.

INRI

JESUS CHRIST THE CONQUEROR

CHI-RHO

IHS

LAMB

⚙ 4. Survey Differences in the Gospels

The first three Gospels are called synoptic Gospels. *Synoptic* is a Greek word that means "seen together." As mentioned in the subsection "There Are Four Gospel Accounts" in Chapter 4, Section 4, the four Gospels were written for different audiences and also have different emphases on theological themes. Do some research on the differences between the four Gospels using the introductory notes and other Catholic biblical commentary included in the *New American Bible Revised Edition*. Record your findings in a chart like the one below.

GOSPEL	AUTHOR BACKGROUND	AUDIENCE	MAIN THEOLOGICAL THEMES
Matthew			
Mark			
Luke			
John			

⚙ *5. Compose Different Ways to Share the Good News*

Mark, Matthew, Luke, and John each wrote what could be called a memoir of the life of Jesus. However, their Gospels are not exactly the same. Why? When you write for different audiences, the style of your writing and what you choose to include in your writing is bound to differ. For example, note the differences between Mark 7:1–5 and Matthew 15:1–2. (Read a Catholic biblical commentary to discover the reasons for the differences.) Imagine you have been asked to explain who Jesus Christ is to two different groups—the first, a group of high school juniors in a public school social studies class; the other, a first-grade Catholic religious education class. Write a summary for each audience. Use at least two gospel references in your summaries.

Faithful Disciple
St. Luke the Evangelist

St. Luke was a masterful writer who composed a purposeful and detailed account of the Gospel of Jesus. A Gentile and a Greek native of Antioch, Luke begins his Gospel with a literary prologue popular in Hellenistic circles:

> Since many have undertaken to compile a narrative of the events that have been fulfilled among us, just as those who were eyewitnesses from the beginning and ministers of the word have handed them down to us, I too have decided, after investigating everything accurately anew, to write it down in an orderly sequence for you, most excellent Theophilus, so that you may realize the certainty of the teachings you have received. (Lk 1:1–4)

This prologue is revealing. Luke acknowledges the tradition of other writers (e.g., the authors of the Gospels of Mark and Matthew that came before his) but has set out to provide a more thorough presentation, one that is primarily addressed to Gentile believers. Luke is also the only evangelist to write a "part 2" of his Gospel—the Acts of the Apostles. Acts is written in the same style as Luke's Gospel and uses a similar prologue, addressed again to Theophilus. "Theophilus" is a Greek name for "friend of the Lord." Theophilus is meant to represent all readers of Luke's Gospel.

Luke's Gospel is hailed for its historical accuracy and solid literary presentation. Academic study reveals that Luke's Gospel and the Acts of the Apostles refer to thirty-two countries, fifty-four cities, and nine islands without making a single geographical error.

St. Luke the Evangelist

Luke's writing focuses on Mary, the Mother of Jesus, more than the other Gospels do. He tells the story of Mary's Annunciation; her *Magnificat*, a timeless prayer of praise; and her visit to Elizabeth, the mother of St. John the Baptist. Luke is also the only gospel writer who tells the story of the disappearance of the boy Jesus and his being found in the Temple. It is also Luke's Gospel that shares the parable of the good Samaritan and the story of the rich man and poor Lazarus.

Because of its focus on the faith of Gentiles, women, and the poor, Luke's Gospel is often called the "Gospel of the poor." Prayer is also emphasized more in the Gospel of Luke than in the other Gospels.

St. Luke was multitalented beyond his writing. Some scholars suggest that he was a slave who was trained as a physician. The practice of giving enslaved people medical training was common in the ancient world. Luke was known for being an artisan and was revered (according to tradition) as the first to create an icon of the Blessed Virgin Mary. Luke was also a companion of St. Paul the Apostle after AD 51. The Acts of the Apostles gives a detailed account of Paul's missionary journeys.

Ancient tradition suggests that St. Luke died at the age of eighty-four in Boeotia, a city in Greece. His feast day is October 18. The symbol for St. Luke the Evangelist is the ox, the animal of Jewish sacrifice.

Comprehension

1. How does Luke's prologue reveal his Greek ethnic background?
2. Name two stories unique to Luke.
3. Why is Luke's Gospel sometimes called the "Gospel of the poor"?

Application

Share the context of references to St. Luke in Philemon 1:24, Colossians 4:14, and 2 Timothy 4:11. What do these passages tell you about Luke's identity?

Prayer

The Jesus Prayer, also known as "Prayer of the Heart," goes back to the fifth century. A faith-filled prayer, it invokes the power of the name of Jesus and begs for his mercy. Emphasizing the humility of the one praying, the Jesus Prayer should be recited repeatedly as a form of meditation. Many Eastern Catholics pray the Jesus Prayer throughout the day to fulfill St. Paul's instruction to "pray without ceasing" (1 Thes 5:17). In the simple prayer, we proclaim that

- Jesus is God (Lord).
- Jesus is the Savior.
- Jesus is the Son of God.
- Jesus is merciful.

Jesus Prayer

Lord Jesus Christ, Son of God, have mercy on me, a sinner.

5

Jesus's Own Mother Leads Us to Him

The Angelus

➤Jean-François Millet

Born in the small village of Gruchy in northwest France in 1814, Jean-François Millet was recognized by family members, neighbors, and the local parish priest for his artistic talent. Gruchy was a farming village, and Jean-François, like everyone else, worked the fields each day. He enjoyed farming, but his pastor and his parents took effort to educate him in Greek, Latin, and British literature. Finally, at his father's insistence, he went to the larger town of Cherbourg to study art full-time. Later he continued his studies in Paris. However, Jean-François missed farming. He returned to live in the country and remained there until his death in 1875.

The rustic farm scenes Jean-François produced attracted attention. A rich American art collector commissioned Jean-François to paint a scene of the recent potato famine. He obliged with a painting of a man and woman in their work clothes, standing in a field with their heads bent in prayer. A pitchfork rests nearby. Potatoes are scattered on the ground. On the horizon are what appear to be three factory chimneys.

When the painting was ready, the collector reneged on the deal and failed to purchase it. Jean-François was panicked at first but then had the idea to modify the painting by adding a church tower in the distance. He also changed its title from *Prayer for the Potato Crop* to *The Angelus*. The painting was completed in 1859.

The title of the painting refers to a Catholic prayer recited three times a day—at 6 a.m., noon, and 6 p.m. *Angelus* is Latin for the first words of the gospel passage detailing the angel Gabriel's greeting to Mary at the Annunciation. Saying the prayer at dawn, noon, and dusk is meant to break up a person's day and remind them of God's presence in their daily work. Traditionally, the *Angelus* was announced by the ringing of church bells. Jean-François recalled, "The idea for *The Angelus* came to me because I remembered that my grandmother, hearing the church bells ringing while we were working in the fields, always made us stop work to say the *Angelus* prayer for the poor departed."

Today it resides in the Musée d'Orsay in Paris. It is said that Jean-François posed the following question to his agent, the first person who saw *The Angelus*: "Can you hear the bells?"

If you would like to research more about the use of bells in church history, see Chapter 5 Review, Chapter Project 1.

How does Mary lead us to her Son, Jesus?

Chapter Overview

Introduction

Mary Is an Image of Her Son

Section 1

Mary Is the Mother of God

Section 2

The Life of Mary from Scripture

Section 3

The Church Teaches about Mary

Section 4

Honoring Mary with Prayer and Devotion

MARY IS AN IMAGE OF HER SON

Growing in friendship with Jesus is made easier because of Mary. Mary, the Mother of Jesus, desires that all people have a close relationship with her Son. She provides many graces to help us with this goal.

Catholics are sometimes criticized for the attention they give to Mary. Some people mistakenly assert that Catholics put Mary ahead of Jesus or that Catholics worship Mary. Both of these statements are certainly untrue. Catholics do not worship Mary (or the saints). Worshipping anyone, or anything, besides God is **idolatry**. Nor do Catholics put love for Mary or the saints ahead of love for God.

While he was dying on the Cross, Jesus saw Mary standing nearby and told his beloved disciple, "Behold, your mother" (Jn 19:27). Jesus wants all people to know Mary and to love her. In turn, she only wants us to know Jesus more deeply. No one should worry about loving Mary more than they love Jesus or that they love her too much. Rather, we are invited to draw close to Mary and bring our concerns to her because it is Christ's will that we become more like her, intimately connected to him in love and friendship.

Mary Is the Disciple Par Excellence

Pope Paul VI described Mary as the "most authentic form of perfect imitation of Christ." The Second Vatican Council recounted St. Ambrose's teaching that Mary is "a type of the Church in the order of faith, charity, and

---

idolatry The worship of idols. Idolatry is an offense against the First Commandment, in which God says that we are to have "no other gods besides me." A form of idolatry prevalent today is secularism, in which people claim to be free to create their own destiny. Idolatry is always a grave sin.

perfect union with Christ" (*Lumen Gentium*, 63). She is the ultimate witness for her Son, Jesus. She is his disciple par excellence.

In Mary, one of the great mysteries of faith is revealed. When God chose Mary to be the mother of his Son, leading to her greatest title, "Mother of God," he made an irrevocable commitment to involve human beings in all that he does. In Mary we can see clearly that God chooses to accomplish his plan of salvation through human beings, rather than apart from them. This means that, like Mary, who said yes to God's surprising and seemingly impossible request to be the Mother of God, we too must say yes to whatever role God has in mind for us in our life. This yes is a daily response to what God asks of us. Our consent to what God desires leads us on our own unique path of Christian discipleship.

Mary Is an Advocate

Recall from the lesson on the Holy Spirit (see the subsection "What Is the Holy Spirit Like" in Chapter 3, Section 3) that an advocate is someone who "argues for a cause" or "pleads on another's behalf." When they were on earth, Mary and all the saints cooperated with God to do good work on behalf of others. From heaven, Mary continues to take on this role, pleading on behalf of humankind to her Son through the Holy Spirit and, ultimately, to God the Father for others who are in need on earth and in Purgatory. According to twentieth-century martyr St. Maximilian Kolbe, grace flows from the Father to the Son and through the Holy Spirit and Mary to humanity. However, he also said that the human reaction to this grace flows in the inverse direction—to Mary first, and then to the Son and Father by way of the Holy Spirit. This places Mary first in line to hear our pleadings and to advocate for us to God.

At the wedding at Cana (see John 2:1–12 and the subsection "Mary's Request at the Wedding at Cana" in Chapter 5, Section 2), Mary saw the need for more wine and asked Jesus to do something about it. In the same way, she now sees people's needs and makes requests to her Son on their behalf. The fact that Mary advocates and intercedes for us does not distance us from Christ. Think of it this way: If you asked a sibling to intercede for you and make a request to your parents on your behalf, doing so would not damage the relationship you have with your sibling or your parents. In fact, it could strengthen both relationships.

When we call upon Mary to be our advocate, we are testifying to God's overwhelming love for all humanity. God loves us so much that he allows us to

"The mother of Jesus said to him, 'They have no wine.' And Jesus said to her, 'Woman, how does your concern affect me. My hour has not yet come'" (Jn 2:3–4).

have a share in his work. Wholly gifted by God's grace, Mary was able to give a free response of affirmation to the special vocation God intended for her. Similarly, we are called to accept God's grace and respond to his love. Honoring Mary is appropriate because she has already done what we are struggling to do today.

Because Christ was to be conceived in her, Mary was transformed into an effective image of Christ. When we cooperate with the Holy Spirit within us, we too will be transformed into an effective image of Christ. We will grow closer to Jesus.

SECTION Assessment

Comprehension

1. How does the term *advocate* describe Mary?

2. How was the wedding at Cana an occasion when Mary fulfilled the role of advocate?

3. Why shouldn't Catholics be concerned about claims that they "love Mary too much" or "put Mary ahead of Jesus"?

Reflection

4. What do you find remarkable about God including Mary in his work of salvation?

MARY IS THE MOTHER OF GOD

The most important title for Mary, "Mother of God," was not something first proclaimed by Apostles, Church Fathers, or popes. St. Elizabeth addressed Mary as "the mother of my Lord" (Lk 1:43) while Mary was pregnant with Jesus. The word for "Lord" quoted in Scripture in its Hebrew and Aramaic form is *Adonai*. Because Jews so revered the sacred name of God,∞ they refrained from writing or speaking it and used *Adonai* instead. When Elizabeth greeted Mary, she was clearly identifying her as the Mother of God even before she gave birth to Jesus.

But how can a creature be mother of the Creator? This is a question the Church considered during its first four centuries, in connection with answering at the Council of Ephesus the Christological question of whether Jesus is really God (see the subsection "Church Councils Respond to Other Heresies" in Chapter 1, Section 4). Another way of asking the question is, "Can a woman be the mother of a Divine Person?" Remember that Jesus is one Divine Person with a human nature and a divine nature. He is the Second Divine Person of the Blessed Trinity, one Divine Person among Three Divine Persons of the one God. Suffice to say, if the answer to the question is "Yes, Mary is the Mother of a Divine Person," then it can also be said that she is truly the Mother of God.

Fr. Raymond J. de Souza, a Catholic apologist, answers the question by comparing Mary's motherhood to that of other human mothers. He writes,

---

∞ Note

YHWH, or "I AM."

A mother is a woman who conceives in her womb the body of her child and later gives birth to that same child. Everyone knows that. Yet she does not create the soul of the child—God creates it. But she bears both the body and soul of the child in her womb: she bears the whole person. No child can say to his mother, "You are only the mother of my body, not my soul, because God created my soul, not you."[1]

De Souza goes on to remind us that a human mother does not create her child's body either! In fact, she creates nothing of her child. God creates the child's soul within his or her body at conception. A mother nurtures her child while pregnant and eventually gives birth to that child. And when she does, she is mother of the *whole person*, that is, the material body and spiritual soul that make up her son or daughter. Connecting this example with Mary, we can follow this five-step progression of statements to come to a better understanding of how Mary is the Mother of God:

1.   Jesus is one of the Three Divine Persons of the Blessed Trinity.

2.   As the Second Divine Person of the Blessed Trinity, Jesus is God.

3.   Mary is the Mother of Jesus.

4.   Because Mary is the Mother of Jesus, she is the Mother of the Second Divine Person of the Blessed Trinity.

5.   Mary, therefore, is the Mother of God.[2]

Understanding how Jesus is *one Divine Person with two natures* helps us to understand more about how Mary truly is the Mother of God (see the subsection "Church Councils Respond to Other Heresies" in Chapter 1, Section 4). Additionally, Jesus's words to his beloved disciple from the Cross tell us clearly that he offers his mother to all of us. The Mother of God is our mother too. God, the Creator, has given one of his creatures a monumental role in helping all of us to return to him.

Tracing the Title and Meaning of Mary as Mother of God

The title "Mother of God" for Mary is familiar to those who pray the Hail Mary. The final part of that prayer includes the invocation, "Holy Mary,

Mother of God, pray for us sinners." This part of the prayer was added around the time of the Council of Trent in the sixteenth century. The *Catechism of the Council of Trent* also includes a statement about the title "Mother of God." The timing is interesting for two reasons. First, the council itself was in great part a response to the Protestant Reformation that began with the protest of Martin Luther. One of the minor criticisms of the early Protestants was that the first part of the Hail Mary prayer, which is a combination of two gospel passages, had no petition. A Dutch Jesuit priest, Peter Canisius, is credited with adding the petition to fill out the Hail Mary prayer. Second, while Protestant reformers such as Luther, John Calvin, and Ulrich Zwingli criticized the Church in several of its beliefs and disciplines, all acknowledged Mary as the Mother of God. Luther wrote, "Not only was Mary the Mother of him who is born, but of him who, before the world, was eternally born of the Father, from a mother in time and at the same time man and God."[3]

Mary was understood to be and referred to as the Mother of God from the earliest days of the Church. As mentioned, St. Elizabeth's address to Mary as "the mother of my Lord" was an affirmation of Mary's most important title. Likewise, the angel's greeting to Mary in Luke 1:28 ("Hail, favored one!") is further evidence from Scripture of Mary's role in God's work of salvation. In the Latin translation of the New Testament, "Hail, favored one!" is rendered as "Hail, full of grace."∞ **The Church came to understand that if Mary is full of grace, then she can also mediate grace.** Mary can share with others what she herself has been given.

There are also several recorded references to Mary as Mother of God outside of Scripture in the early centuries of the Church. St. Irenaeus, in opposition to Gnosticism in AD 190, wrote that "the Virgin Mary . . . being obedient to God's word, received from an angel glad tidings that she should bear *God*" (emphasis added).[4] St. Hippolytus of Rome in the third century was the first to use the title *Theotokos*, or "God-bearer," for Mary in connection with hotly debated Christological arguments that centered on how Christ is both divine and human. The Councils of Ephesus and Chalcedon subsequently taught

∞ Note

Theologian Scott Hahn points out that the Greek word for the phrase "full of grace" (*kecharitōmenē*) appears only this one time in all of Sacred Scripture, an indication of how special Mary is in all of salvation history.

that Jesus Christ is one Divine Person subsisting in two natures, divine and human. St. Cyril of Alexandria wrote, "When (the Word) took his most chaste body, animated by an intelligent soul, from the Holy Virgin, and came forth a Man, he did not cease to be God nor did he reject the dignity of his own preeminence; for in this, as I said, no change is known."[5]

In later centuries, many other saints have been devoted to Mary as Mother. St. Anselm (1093–1109) said that "it is impossible to save one's soul without devotion to Mary and without her protection." St. Louis-Marie de Montfort (1673–1713), who pioneered a retreat leading to consecration to Mary, pointed out that "all true children of God have God for their Father and Mary for their Mother; anyone who does not have Mary for their Mother does not have God for their Father." St. Thérèse of Lisieux (1873–1897) said, "What a joy to remember that Mary is our Mother. She is more Mother than Queen."

Mary's role as Mother of God has strong implications for understanding the meaning of the Incarnation. Mary conceived and brought forth in human nature the all-powerful Son of God who exists in all eternity, with no beginning or end. She did not conceive the divine nature of her Son, but she is Mother of God in the sense that, from her own flesh and blood she gave the Son of God a human nature like hers.

Like all human mothers, Mary did a lot more than carry a child in her womb and give birth to her Son. She took care of his physical needs—she nursed him, clothed him, and taught him how to feed and care for himself. Mary also nurtured Jesus's spiritual, mental, and emotional development just as any other mother does for her child. The difference between Mary

A statue of St. Louis Marie de Montfort at the Church of the Assumption in Thailand. St. Louis had a deep devotion to the Blessed Virgin Mary and wrote a thirty-three-day retreat of prayers and devotions leading to Catholics consecrating themselves to Jesus through Mary.

and all other mothers is that the child Jesus, whom she conceived by the Holy Spirit, "was none other than the Father's eternal Son, the second person of the Holy Trinity" (*CCC*, 495).

Mother of the Church

"Mother of God" is the highest among Mary's titles.∞ Because she is Mother of God, Mary is also the Mother of the Church that Christ established to be his own body. As the Mother of the Church, Mary has a particular role and

> **∞ Note**
>
> The Church, from her earliest days, has given Mary titles that describe her unique role in the Church. Some of these titles are Advocate, Exemplar, Helper, Benefactress, and Mediatrix. Most of the titles associated with devotion to Mary are found in the Litany of the Blessed Virgin, also known as the Litany of Loreto. A litany is a prayer that includes a series of petitions and requests. The Litany of the Blessed Virgin was first prayed in Loreto, Italy, in the mid-sixteenth century. It was approved by Pope Sixtus V in 1587. More information about three of the titles from the Litany of Loreto follows.
>
> *Cause of Our Joy.* This title has two meanings. First, since Christ, the bearer of the Good News of salvation, came to the world through Mary, the Church came to understand that she is the cause or source of this great joy. Also, prior to the Incarnation, the world was plagued by the disobedience of Adam and Eve, or Original Sin. Mary's obedience to God turned the tide and reshaped the world to great joy. Devotion to Mary under this title is especially popular in France and Canada ("Notre Dame de Liesse").
>
> *Gate of Heaven.* Mary never points to herself, only to her Son. The title "Gate of Heaven" reminds the Church of Mary's role in leading the faithful to her Son, the source of eternal life. Pope John XXIII wrote a prayer entitled "To Our Lady, the Gate of Heaven," reminding the Church to "teach our hearts to desire the things of Heaven."
>
> *Queen of Peace.* This invocation was added to the Litany of the Blessed Virgin Mary by Pope Benedict XV in 1917, during World War I (1914–18). Years later, in a prayer dedicated to the Queen of Peace, Pope John XXIII reminded the Church to pray to Mary under this title for two special graces: peace of mind and the spirit of peace in families, parishes, and throughout the Church.

responsibility. Just as she nurtured Jesus and helped him to grow in wisdom, so too she cooperates with him in caring for and guiding the Church. Pope Paul VI once said of Mary that she "carries on in heaven her maternal role with regard to the members of Christ, cooperating in the birth and development of divine life in the souls of the redeemed."

According to the *Catechism of the Catholic Church*, "Mary's role in the Church is inseparable from her union with Christ and flows directly from it" (964). Mary's motherhood is a gift that Christ makes personally to the Church as a whole and to every individual personally. By giving Mary to the Church as Mother, Jesus expects Catholics to learn to imitate her fidelity, obedience, compassion, love, and prayerfulness. **Mary is a perfect model of faith and holiness.**

The Church is also called "Mother" because the Church follows Mary's example. Though there is not a wealth of information about the life of Mary in Scripture, the Church studies and prays over what is prophesied about Mary from the Old Testament and what is known about her life from the New Testament.

SECTION Assessment

Comprehension

1. Why did the Jews use *Adonai* to name God?

2. What does it mean to say that a mother is a mother of the *whole person* she gives birth to?

3. What is ironic about Luther and the other Protestant reformers believing that Mary is the Mother of God?

4. Who was the first person to use the title *Theotokos* to describe Mary?

5. Paraphrase the five-step progression of statements of how Mary is the Mother of God in one clearly written paragraph.

6. Finish this sentence: "Mary's role in the Church is inseparable from __________ ."

Reflection

7. St. Thérèse of Lisieux said Mary "is more Mother than Queen." What do you think she meant by this statement?

8. Choose one of the following qualities of Mary and tell how she inspires you to practice the quality in your life: fidelity, obedience, compassion, love, prayerfulness.

THE LIFE OF MARY FROM SCRIPTURE

There is no information about Mary's ancestors or childhood in Scripture. An apocryphal gospel called the Protoevangelium of James includes information on Mary's parents, naming them Joachim and Anne. Both Joachim and Anne are recognized as saints by the Church. Several other early Church Fathers and saints also named Joachim and Anne as Mary's parents. Some of these writers included the detail that Mary's birth came when her parents were in advanced age and after many years of prayer for a child (see the Faithful Disciples profile "St. Joachim and St. Anne" in Chapter 5).

At the time of the Annunciation (see Luke 1:26–27), Mary lived in Nazareth. The place of her birth is unknown. Mary's early life can certainly be imagined from what is known about her surroundings and the period when she lived. Mary's Hebrew name translates to "Miryam." It is *almost* certain that Mary's ancestors were from the family of King David. The Letter to the Romans begins with a description of Jesus who "descended from David according to the flesh" (1:3). However, because the genealogies of Jesus listed in both Matthew 1:1–17 and Luke 3:23–38 trace to Joseph, Jesus's foster father, rather than Mary, her ancestral connection with King David is not definite.

Even more about Mary can be learned from the Old Testament. As with the ancestors of Jesus and the messages of the prophets who predicted his coming, several women from the Old Testament foretold the life and mission of Mary. A survey of both the Old and New Testaments provides a good sampling of evidence of Mary's significance as Mother of God and Mother of the Church.

Old Testament Women Who Foreshadowed Mary's Mission

Many women from the Old Testament pointed toward Mary's mission as the Mother of God. First, there was Eve (see also the subsection "Waiting for the Messiah" in Chapter 1, Introduction). After her disobedience, leading to Original Sin, Eve received a promise that her posterity would eventually achieve a great and lasting victory over sin and evil. In this **Protoevangelium** of the coming of the Messiah and Redeemer, God tells Satan,

> I will put enmity between you and the woman,
>> and between your offspring and hers;
> They will strike at your head,
>> while you strike at their heel. (Gn 3:15)

There is some debate as to whether "hers" in the passage refers to Mary or Eve, but it does reveal that a descendant of Eve (who is Mary's Son, Jesus) brings about the redemption of the world. The "offspring" mentioned is clearly a reference to Jesus. This battle between good and evil is played out again in Revelation 12:1–18, when Satan (described as a dragon) pursues "the woman who had given birth to the male child" (v. 13) and the woman is able to keep him at bay. Mary is the New Eve who undid what the first Eve had done.

After Eve, several other women from the Old Testament prepared for the mission of Mary by living in hope of the fulfillment of the promise of salvation. With faith, Sarah, the wife of Abraham, gave birth to a son in her old age. Hannah, the mother of the prophet Samuel, listened to the message of the Lord whispering to her and consecrated her son to his service.

Mary, unlike Eve, refrained from sin. She is the New Eve. She gave her Son to the world. Her offspring—Jesus Christ—attained final victory over Eve's tempter, the evil one.

Protoevangelium A term that means "the first gospel," which is found in Genesis 3:15, where God reveals he will send a Savior to redeem the world from its sins.

Mary Is the New Eve

Focus Question: How does Mary lead us to her Son, Jesus?

Just as Jesus is described as the "last Adam" or "New Adam" (e.g., see Romans 5:19), similar associations have been made between Eve and Mary. For example, in the second century, St. Irenaeus, the bishop who was the last known living connection with the Apostles, wrote,

> In accordance with this design, Mary the Virgin is found obedient, saying, "Behold the handmaid of the Lord; be it unto me according to your word" (Lk 1:38). But Eve was disobedient, for she did not obey when as yet she was a . . . virgin having become disobedient, was made the cause of death, both to herself and to the entire human race; so did Mary, having a man betrothed [to her], and being nevertheless a virgin, by yielding obedience, become the cause of salvation, both to herself and the whole human race.[6]

Thirty years before St. Irenaeus, apologist St. Justin Martyr recorded a dialogue he had with a Jewish man named Trypho, in which he compared Mary with Eve:

> For Eve, who was a virgin and undefiled, having conceived the word of the serpent, brought forth disobedience and death. But the Virgin Mary received faith and joy, when the angel Gabriel announced the good tidings to her that the Spirit of the Lord would come upon her,

and the power of the Highest would overshadow her. (*Dialogue with Trypho*)

While Scripture itself is not explicit in calling Mary the "New Eve," there are several distinct comparisons between Mary and Eve in the following Scripture passages:

Eve	Mary
• Eve was created without sin (Gn 2:25; 3:6–7).	• Mary was born full of grace and without sin (Lk 1:28).
• Virgin (Gn 2:25)	• Virgin (Lk 1:27, 34)
• Tempted by the serpent, who was the fallen angel, Satan (Gn 3:1–7).	• Visited by the angel Gabriel (Lk 1:26).
• Disobedience led to Original Sin and death, through her husband Adam (Gn 3:12, 17–19).	• Obedience led to salvation through her Son, Jesus Christ (Lk 1:38).
• Eve became "mother of all the living" (Gn 3:20).	• Jesus presented Mary to the beloved disciple as the new "mother of all the living" (Jn 19:26–27).

Pope John Paul II also described Mary as the New Eve because of her obedience to God. "God puts the destiny of all mankind in a young woman's hands," he wrote. "Mary's 'yes' is the premise for fulfilling the plan which God in his love had prepared for the world's salvation."[7] The *Catechism of the Catholic Church* summarizes how Mary was a descendant of Eve yet stands out from Eve and the other women who came before her: "Throughout the Old Covenant the mission of many holy women *prepared* for that of Mary. At the very beginning there was Eve. . . . After a long period of waiting the times are fulfilled in [Mary], the exalted Daughter of Sion, and the new plan of salvation is established" (489).

St. Paul made the comparison between Adam and Christ in 1 Corinthians 15:45–46: "So, too, it is written, 'The first man, Adam, became a living being,' the last Adam a life-giving spirit. But the spiritual was not first; rather the natural and then the spiritual." In a similar way, Mary has come to be known as the "New Eve." She is the woman who "gave birth to a son, a male child, destined to rule all the nations with an iron rod" (Rv 12:5) while fighting off Satan. Whereas Eve had succumbed to the tempter, Mary triumphed over him.

Comprehension

1. What are two similarities between Eve and Mary?
2. What is a significant difference between the two?
3. According to Pope John Paul II, what is significant about Mary's yes?

Reflection

If Eve had not sinned, would there have been a need for Mary, the New Eve, in God's plan? Explain your answer.

Ruth, a Gentile who was left a widow by her Jewish husband, followed her mother-in-law home to Bethlehem and was given in marriage to another Jewish man, Boaz. Ruth became the great-grandmother of King David, the royal ancestor of Jesus and Mary.

The Annunciation

Mary is first introduced by name in the New Testament at the occasion of the Annunciation, or announcement of the birth of Jesus (see Luke 1:26–38). She is greeted by the angel Gabriel with the words, "Hail, favored one!" (v. 28).

Mary must have been frightened by the angel's visit. As you can imagine, what the angel said—that Mary was to conceive a special child without having sexual relations with Joseph—was too much for Mary to fully understand. But Mary was open to doing God's will, whatever that might mean. Without hesitating, Mary responded, "Behold, I am the handmaid of the Lord. May it be done to me according to your word" (Lk 1:38). This last phrase, "May it be done to me," is known in Latin as *fiat*.

Mary's fiat was an empty humbling of her own will while granting it to God. This is the same thing Jesus did in emptying himself to become human.

Pope John Paul II wrote, "There is a complete harmony with the words of the Son, who, according to the Letter to the Hebrews, says to the Father as he comes into the world: 'Sacrifices and offering you have not desired, but a body you have prepared for me. . . . Lo, I have come to do your will, O God' (Heb 10:5–7)" (*Redemptoris Mater*, 13).

Annunciation of Mary

Luke's description of the Annunciation concludes by reporting that the angel left Mary, but God did not leave her. Within Mary's womb, a baby was soon conceived. This child was the Son of God. There were certainly many other times throughout the rest of her life when Mary had to repeat her fiat to God as she attempted to understand more of the mystery of his plan.

Mary's Visit to Elizabeth and the Magnificat

After the Annunciation, Mary immediately set off to visit her relative Elizabeth in the village of Ein Karem in Judea, at least a week's journey on foot from Nazareth.∞ On Mary's arrival, Elizabeth said, "Most blessed are you among women, and blessed is the fruit of your womb." She also asked, "And how does this happen to me, that the mother of my Lord should come to me?"

∞ Note

The distance from Nazareth to Ein Karem is about eighty-one miles in a straight line. Traveling the distance by footpath was probably at least one hundred miles. Also, the difference in elevation between Nazareth and Ein Karem is 1,336 feet, so Mary had to walk quite a distance uphill. The mountainous path had many hidden crevices and was known to have bandits along the way. Though not mentioned in Scripture, it is reasonable to assume St. Joseph traveled with Mary on this treacherous trip.

The Visitation

(Lk 1:42, 43). Elizabeth's words are similar to those uttered by King David when the Ark of the Covenant containing the tablets with the commandments was brought to Jerusalem: "How can the ark of the Lord come to me?" (2 Sm 6:9). Comparing these two passages, it is clear that God's living presence was in the ark and in Mary.

Woven into the account of the Visitation in Luke 1:46–55 is Mary's canticle, called by its Latin name, the *Magnificat*, for its first three words ("My soul proclaims"). In this canticle, Mary shares her role in God's plan, which she describes as "his handmaid's lowliness." In fact, God's Son is born into such lowliness. Her message is that God loves the humble and the poor and that he exalts those who typically go unnoticed.

The Visitation and the *Magnificat* teach valuable lessons. It would have been natural for Mary to have been anxious and wary of people's reactions to her pregnancy outside of marriage. But Mary held on to the angel's promise. God had a plan, and she had to trust him. Her example shows that, even in challenging situations, it's best to put the needs of others before our own needs and concerns. It's also important to recognize that God is always close to us and has freely chosen to associate our efforts with the work of his grace.

Mary's Experiences of Jesus's Birth and His Childhood

The Gospels record several remarkable events related to Jesus's birth and his childhood. Not surprisingly, most of these events involve Mary. First is the mystery of Jesus's virginal conception. The Old Testament foretold the virginal conception to fulfill God's promise given to the prophet Isaiah: "Therefore the Lord himself will give you a sign; the young woman, pregnant and about to bear a son, shall name him Emmanuel" (Is 7:14). The *Catechism of the Catholic Church* explains the virginal conception as "a divine work that surpasses all human understanding and possibility" (497). Mary was "ever-virgin," meaning she remained a virgin throughout her life. (See the subsection "Perpetual Virginity" in Chapter 5, Section 3, for more clarification of this Church teaching.)

Much of Mary's experience of motherhood involved both physical and spiritual poverty, beginning with the birth of Jesus, when Mary could not give birth at home. Because of a census, she had to travel to her husband's ancestral home, Bethlehem, where she gave birth to Jesus in a stable. Mary was prayerful and reflective about all that was happening to her. Shepherds from the fields received a message that a Savior was born (see Luke 2:8–14). When they told Mary what they heard, she "kept all these things, reflecting on them in her heart" (Lk 2:19). Likewise, when she and Joseph presented the Infant Jesus to the religious leaders at the Temple in Jerusalem, Simeon, a "righteous and devout" man, warned her of the suffering she would experience as Jesus's mother, saying, "You yourself a sword will pierce" (Lk 2:25, 35).∞ This prediction came to pass when Mary witnessed the Death of Jesus from below his Cross (see the subsection "Mary at the Foot of the Cross" in Chapter 5, Section 2).

According to Matthew's Gospel, after Jesus's birth, Jesus, Mary, and Joseph were forced to flee to Egypt to escape King Herod's decree calling for the slaughter of all infant boys born in the Bethlehem vicinity. Egypt was a traditional place for Jewish people to flee when facing danger in Palestine.≈

∞ Note

Typically, a Jewish couple would present a year-old lamb at the time of their child's presentation, but because they were poor, Mary and Joseph offered "a pair of turtledoves or two young pigeons" (Lk 2:24) as a substitute, as Jewish law allowed.

≈ Note

For example, when King Solomon tried to have Jeroboam, the king of the Northern Kingdom of Israel, killed, Jeroboam fled to Egypt (see 1 Kings 11:40).

Primarily, however, the lesson of the trip of the Holy Family to Egypt and back again to Nazareth when the danger was over was to emulate the Exodus experience of Israel.∞

When Jesus was twelve years old, he and his parents went to Jerusalem for the Passover. Afterward, he "remained behind in Jerusalem, but his parents did not know it" (Lk 2:43). After three days, Mary and Joseph found Jesus in the Temple, his "Father's house" (Lk 2:49). Imagine a mother's worry when her child is missing for three days. When he was found, Mary said to him, "Son, why have you done this to us? Your father and I have been looking for you with great anxiety" (Lk 2:48). You may be familiar with Jesus's response to his mother: he was only doing the will of his Father in heaven. Like Jesus, Mary herself had been doing the Father's will her entire life, especially from the time of the Annunciation. Following his Father's will would be something Jesus would do all the way to his Death on the Cross.

Mary's Request at the Wedding at Cana

Mary had a unique role in Jesus's first miracle at the wedding at Cana (see John 2:1–12). Mary realized that the hosts of the wedding celebration faced embarrassment as the supply of wine was running low. She asked Jesus to take care of the problem, though it doesn't appear that she had a miracle in mind, for at the same time she asked the servers to help find a solution under Jesus's leadership. Jesus responded, "Woman, how does your concern affect me? My hour has not yet come" (v. 4).

The "hour" Jesus referred to was his Passion, Death, and Resurrection. Nevertheless, due to his mother's persistence, Jesus acted. While Mary may have been thinking only of the immediate situation—the lack of wine and the embarrassing results—Jesus had other concerns in mind. When he solved the problem by turning water into wine, he was revealing God's power and plan for the world. The miracle fulfilled Old Testament prophecies of flowing wine that would accompany the coming of the Messiah and salvation for the elect

---

∞ Note

Matthew wrote primarily for Jewish converts to Christianity, who would have especially appreciated the connection between the Holy Family's escape to Egypt and the Exodus.

(see Joel 4:18). The water used in this miracle is also understood as a symbol of the waters that purify those who are baptized. The wine and the feast itself signify the institution of the Eucharist, which brings the Church into communion with Christ. And, of course, Jesus's attendance at the wedding is a sign of his presence in the Sacrament of Matrimony. His presence in Cana at a wedding is "the confirmation of the goodness of marriage and the proclamation that thenceforth marriage will be an efficacious sign of Christ's presence" (*CCC*, 1613).

Mary is mentioned three times in the telling of this miracle. Her influence on this occasion cannot be overlooked. Just as she interceded on behalf of the hosts at the wedding celebration, she intercedes for all who call on her. Also interesting about this occasion is the fact that it is the last time there is recorded dialogue between Mary and Jesus in any of the Gospels.

Mary at the Foot of the Cross

The Church has often connected the Cana event with Mary's presence at the foot of the Cross as Jesus neared death. Note the similarity in the way the words *woman* and *hour* are used in each account:

> "Woman, how does your concern affect me? My hour has not yet come." (Jn 2:4)

> When Jesus saw his mother and the disciple there whom he loved, he said to his mother, "Woman, behold, your son." Then he said to the disciple, "Behold, your mother." And from that hour the disciple took her into his home. (Jn 19:26–27)

"Standing by the cross of Jesus were his mother and his mother's sister, Mary the wife of Clopas, and Mary of Magdala" (Jn 19:25).

Unlike at Cana, Jesus's hour *had* come as he hung on the Cross. And now that the world's redemption from sin was at hand, Mary truly became the New Eve. Jesus's use of *woman* to describe his mother also parallels the use of *woman* in the Protoevangelium (Gn 3:15) to describe the one who will "strike at the head" of Satan.

The words of Jesus from the Cross to his mother confirm that Mary cooperated with Jesus at every step of his work of redemption, from his conception to his Death: "Mary's role in the Church is inseparable from her union with Christ and flows directly from it" (*CCC*, 964).

Mary in the Upper Room

We see the first evidence of Mary's role in the Church when the Apostles were waiting in the Upper Room in Jerusalem for the coming of the Holy Spirit at Pentecost. They were there "together with some women, and Mary the mother of Jesus" (Acts 1:14). Though a very simple reference, it shows that Mary was already fulfilling her role as Mother of the Church by praying with, and for, the Church that Jesus had founded.

The Pentecost account is the last New Testament reference to Mary by name. However, the Book of Revelation refers to a "woman clothed with the sun, with the moon under her feet, and on her head a crown of twelve stars" (12:1). The author of this inspired apocalyptic text most likely intended for *woman* to refer directly to Mary and to the Church as a whole. The woman referred to in this passage does not exclude Mary, for she does represent the Church as Jesus commissioned.

"If there is no Church without Pentecost, without the Mother of Jesus there is no Pentecost either, since she lived in a singular way what the Church experiences each day under the action of the Holy Spirit" (Pope Benedict XVI).

SECTION Assessment

Comprehension

1. How is Mary's response, "May it be done to me according to your word," connected to the Annunciation?

2. How did the Visitation of Mary to Elizabeth parallel King David's reception of the Ark of the Covenant?

3. What is the main theme of the *Magnificat*?

4. Name one example from Scripture when Mary was prayerful and reflective.

Vocabulary

5. Why is the passage from Genesis 3:15 known as the *Protoevangelium*?

Reflection

6. What is a lesson for your life that you can learn from Mary's request to Jesus at the wedding at Cana?

7. How do Jesus's words on the Cross, "Behold your mother," apply to the Church today?

8. How can the Scripture passages associated with Mary named in this section help you to answer the question, "Why do Catholics honor Mary?"

THE CHURCH TEACHES ABOUT MARY

Because Mary is the Mother of the Church, the Church loves her as a child loves his or her mother. In the earliest centuries of its history, the Church defined several truths about Mary, most often while defending against heresies being promulgated against her Son. Three truths about Mary are these:

1. Mary's role in God's work of salvation was present from the time of her Immaculate Conception.

2. Mary's purity remained throughout the course of her life.

3. Mary's Immaculate Conception does not make her God, but it does make her like God in a very important way. Like the Holy Spirit, she was conceived purely in love.

Recall that St. Maximilian Kolbe called Mary the "created Immaculate Conception," whereas the Holy Spirit is the "uncreated Immaculate Conception," who was conceived from the love between God the Father and God the Son, making him the Third Divine Person of the Blessed Trinity (see Chapter 3, Section 4). Mary cooperated with the Holy Spirit through her entire life. She is perpetually a virgin—a Church teaching that elicited several questions in the past as it still does today.

When Jesus gave his mother to the Church while she stood at the foot of the Cross, he pronounced and magnified her role. After his Ascension, she supported the growth of the Church with her prayers. She called on "the gift of the Spirit, who had already overshadowed her in the Annunciation" (*Lumen Gentium*, 59).

More details of the Church's teachings about Mary are explained in the following subsections.

Immaculate Conception

From the first moment of her conception in the womb of her mother, Mary was preserved from Original Sin. This is known as the **Immaculate Conception**. This also means that from the first moment of her existence, Mary was full of grace.∞ Besides being free from Original Sin, Mary never committed a personal sin. She lived a blameless life. Pope John Paul II wrote that Mary's election "is more powerful than any experience of evil and sin" (*Redemptoris Mater*, 5). God the Father blessed Mary more than any other person who has ever lived or will ever live.

Mary was full of grace from the time of her Immaculate Conception to her Assumption into heaven.

∞ Note

Pope Pius IX said that the unique phrase "full of grace" (see the subsection "Tracing the Title and Meaning of Mary as Mother of God" in Chapter 5, Section 1) indicates that "the Blessed Virgin was, through grace, entirely free from every stain of sin, and from all corruption of body, soul and mind; that she was always united with God and joined to him by an eternal covenant" (*Ineffabilis Deus*, 1854).

Immaculate Conception The belief that Mary was conceived in her mother's womb without the stain of Original Sin that all other human beings inherit. This teaching was declared infallible by Pope Pius IX in 1854.

Mary, Queen of Heaven and Earth, is featured above the Lady Chapel at the Basilica of the Sacred Heart at Notre Dame, Indiana.

These special gifts come to Mary because of her Son, Jesus, who has also redeemed her "in a more exalted fashion" (*Lumen Gentium*, 53, 59, quoted in *CCC*, 492). None of this is to say that Mary's special role in God's plan of salvation prevents us or anyone else from sharing in his graces. Rather, when God chose Mary to be the Mother of God, he made an irrevocable commitment to involve *all* human beings in everything that he does. In the person of Mary, all of humanity is chosen to be an eternal part of God's plan.

The Immaculate Conception is the sign and the promise that everything that can separate humans from God has become powerless. Mary's freedom from sin is the promise that, one day, all of God's People will be freed from the tendency toward sin and from its lasting effects, though in this life the reality of sin and the struggle with **concupiscence** and temptation remain, as does the possibility of losing the life of grace.

How did the Church's belief in the Immaculate Conception

---

concupiscence The disordered nature of human appetites or desires, one of the temporal consequences of Original Sin. The state of concupiscence remains even after Baptism and produces an inclination to sin.

become dogma? The process took place over centuries. From the earliest days, written testimony exists that the Church believed that Mary was free from Original Sin. In the East, the Feast of the Immaculate Conception was originally called the "Conception of St. Anne," meaning that Anne, the mother of Mary, had conceived her. As the centuries went on, religious communities such as the Franciscans and Carmelites developed special devotions to the Immaculate Conception. In the fifteenth century, Pope Sixtus IV allowed the entire Church to celebrate the Immaculate Conception, but he did not declare the teaching a dogma. Finally, in 1854, Pope Pius IX declared belief in the Immaculate Conception to be a dogma of the Church.

Interestingly, the Lady who appeared to St. Bernadette Soubirous at Lourdes, France, in 1858 eventually identified herself by saying, "I am the Immaculate Conception." Many believed this was Mary giving her approval to the Church's official recognition of her purity from sin.

Perpetual Virginity

Mary's perpetual virginity—that is, her virginity for life—is one of the most defined of all Church dogmas. It was taught originally by the Church Fathers, including Tertullian, St. Ambrose, and St. Augustine. At the Second Council of Constantinople in AD 533, Pope Martin I officially gave Mary the title "ever-virgin." In Latin, the council decreed that Mary was a virgin *ante partum, in partu, et post partum*, that is, "before, during, and after Christ's birth." The Gospels of Matthew (1:18) and Luke (1:34–35; 3:23) are clear that Jesus was born of a virgin and that his conception occurred without a human father. Those who disagree with Church teaching on this subject usually focus on Mary's virginity *after* the birth of Jesus.

This question arises out of passages in the New Testament (e.g., Mt 13:55–56; Mk 6:1–6) that refer to "brothers and sisters" of Jesus. The Church has always taught that these passages refer to close relations of Jesus, perhaps cousins or even close neighbors, but not to other children of Mary. There are many scriptural studies of these texts that reveal the same results. For example, neither Hebrew nor the Western Aramaic language that Jesus spoke had a special word meaning "cousin." The word available to them—*ah*—was used for various types of relations. The patriarchal family dominated Jesus's world. His society considered the oldest living male the patriarch, or father. In such a family structure, cousins typically referred to themselves as brothers and sisters.

Scripture itself gives more support to the Church's teaching. For example, two of the men Matthew's Gospel names as brothers of Jesus—James and Joses—could not have been the sons of Mary, Jesus's mother, because Matthew 27:56 and Mark 15:40 mention them as sons of "another Mary." This Mary was one of the women who witnessed Jesus's Crucifixion and who later went to anoint him on the morning he rose from the dead.

Also, consider this: if Jesus had blood brothers, why would he entrust his mother to John, the beloved disciple, and not to one of his biological siblings (see John 19:26–27)? James, named as "brother of the Lord," was the leader of the church in Jerusalem and martyred in AD 62 (see Galatians 1:19), meaning he was still living at the time of Jesus's Death. If James were really Mary's natural child, would it have not made more sense for him, rather than one of the disciples, to take responsibility for his mother?

Beyond this scriptural evidence, Mary's perpetual virginity is logical in other ways. Her virginity is a sign of the world to come when Jesus taught that we will neither marry nor be given in marriage, but be like angels instead (see Matthew 22:30). Her virginity is also a symbol of the Church, which is the virgin bride of Christ. St. Ambrose wrote, "Fittingly is Mary espoused, but Virgin because she prefigures the Church which is undefiled yet wed. A Virgin of the Spirit, a Virgin brings forth without travail."[8] Mary's soul *and* body were entirely consecrated to God. Her perpetual virginity is a sign of her eternal bond with God: Father, Son, and Holy Spirit.

Assumption

After her earthly life ended, Mary was immediately taken, body and soul, into the loving and joyful presence of God. This is known as the **Assumption of Mary**. The Second Vatican Council teaches: "Finally the Immaculate Virgin, preserved from all stain of original sin, when the course of her earthly life was finished, was taken up body and soul into heavenly glory, and exalted by the Lord as Queen over all things, so that she might be the more fully conformed

---

Assumption of Mary The dogmatic teaching of the Church that when the earthly life of Mary was completed, she was taken body and soul into the presence of God. Mary was granted this grace because she is the sinless Mother of God.

Pope Pius XII declared formally that Mary was assumed into heaven on November 1, 1950.

to her Son, the Lord of lords and conqueror of sin and death" (*Lumen Gentium*, 59, quoted in *CCC*, 966). Note that *Lumen Gentium* does not speak of Mary's death. The Church does not define whether Mary died a physical death before her Assumption or was assumed into heaven without dying a physical death. The *Catechism of the Catholic Church* teaches that "the Assumption of the Blessed Virgin is a singular participation in her Son's Resurrection and an anticipation of the resurrection of other Christians" (966).

As with the dogma of the Immaculate Conception, belief in the Assumption was popular and prevalent well before it was officially declared. According to a famous story told from the fifth-century Council of Chalcedon, the Eastern Roman emperor asked St. Juvenal, the bishop of Jerusalem, to have the relics of Mary's body brought to Constantinople. The bishop is said to have responded, "Mary died in the presence of the Apostles, but her tomb, when opened later on the request of St. Thomas, was found empty and thus the Apostles concluded that the body was taken up to heaven."

A feast to honor the Assumption on August 15 was celebrated in the Holy Land as early as the sixth century, in what a bishop of that era described as a celebration on the anniversary of Mary's "falling asleep." The Eastern Church named the feast the "Falling Asleep of the Mother of God." In 1950, Pope Pius XII officially declared the Assumption of Mary a dogma of faith, saying that Mary's body and soul "were united as she was taken to heaven to be with her Son, Jesus, the Son of God."

Mary's Assumption into heaven body and soul is the sign of the Church's eschatological hope. *Eschatological* refers to a study of the final events in the history of the world. To associate Mary's Assumption with eschatological hope means that the Church can envision that all the faithful will rise to heaven, body and soul, at the end of time. Mary's rising in body, in particular, brings much hope. "It is very commonly accepted that the life of the human person continues in a spiritual fashion after death" (*CCC*, 996). Mary's Assumption in soul *and* body reminds us that our bodies, too, will rise after death. This is why the bodies of those who are dying and the bodies of those who have died should be treated with respect and love.

Mary's Assumption is also a reminder that even though the evil in the world has not run its course, there is foolproof evidence that God's final triumph over evil has already been accomplished.

Apparitions

Apparitions of Mary have been reported in every century of the Church's life; however, not all, or even a majority, have been officially recognized by the Church. An apparition is, first of all, a gift of grace—an extraordinary appearance on earth of Jesus, the saints, or angels. This makes apparitions a miraculous occurrence. Why does God send apparitions? Usually, these special manifestations are necessary to turn the world around from its indifference to the Lord and to bring the Good News of Jesus more fully alive.

Marian apparitions give rise to new titles for Mary and can help the Church live more fully by Christ's Revelation in a certain period of history. This intercession is sometimes sought through a pilgrimage to the apparition site. In addition to the approved apparition of Our Lady to St. Bernadette at Lourdes (see Chapter 3, Section 4), three Marian apparitions and accompanying titles for Mary are introduced in the subsections that follow.

Our Lady of Guadalupe

Consistent with her life on earth, Mary's appearance in 1531 near Mexico City to a poor peasant, Juan Diego, had the purpose of bringing people closer to her Son. The Spanish missionaries who had previously come to Mexico had little success in bringing the native people to the faith, in part because of the resentment the Mexicans felt toward the Spanish conquistadors who made them slaves and destroyed some of their native religious sites. One of these sites was a temple of the mother goddess Tonantzin at Tepeyac outside Mexico City.

The Basilica of Our Lady of Guadalupe in Mexico City was built in 1709 near the hill at Tepeyac. It houses the cloak of St. Juan Diego with the image of Our Lady. Several million visitors come to the basilica each year, especially around Our Lady of Guadalupe's feast day on December 12.

Then, on December 9, 1531, Juan Diego saw an apparition of a young woman at the Hill of Tepeyac. The woman spoke to Juan Diego in his own language, Nahuatl, telling him to build a church at the site in her honor. Juan Diego took the message to Juan de Zumárraga, the Spanish archbishop of Mexico City. The archbishop told Juan Diego to return to the hill and ask the Lady for a miraculous sign. A series of miracles followed. First, Juan Diego's uncle, who had been seriously ill, was cured. Next, the Lady told Juan Diego to go to the top of the hill and collect flowers. Juan Diego found Castilian roses, which were not native to Mexico or even in season. The Lady arranged the flowers on Juan Diego's peasant cloak, or tilma. When, on December 12, he returned to the archbishop and opened his cloak, the flowers fell to the floor and an image of the Virgin Mary was imprinted on the tilma.

The tilma with Mary's image remains preserved and on display at the Basilica of Our Lady of Guadalupe, the most visited Marian shrine in the world. The famous image itself is drawn from the vision of Mary at the Apocalypse described in Revelation 12:1. The blue-green color of the image was also a color familiar in the indigenous religions of the native people of the time and representative of their gods of matrimony and motherhood.

Mary's appearance to St. Juan Diego (canonized in 2002) bore much fruit. Within a few short years, nearly six million native Mexicans were baptized into the Church. Under the title of Our Lady of Guadalupe, Mary remains the patroness of Mexico and all of the Americas.

Our Lady of Fatima

In one of her most famous apparitions, Mary appeared six times to three young children—Lucia and her cousins Francisco and his sister Jacinta—between May 13 and October 13, 1917, in the small village of Fatima, Portugal. Mary's appearances and message coincided with World War I and the Communist revolution in Russia, which began in October 1917 and introduced decades of oppressive and atheistic rule in Russia and Eastern Europe.

According to an account written by Lucia, who was nine years old at the time, on May 13, a Lady appeared who was "all in white, more brilliant than the sun." She told the children not to be afraid and that "I come from heaven." What did Mary want of these children and those with whom they shared her message? She asked them to pray and devote themselves to the Blessed Trinity and to recite the Rosary every day to help bring peace to the world and an end to the war.

Mary appeared to the children again on June 13 and July 13. On August 13, the children were kidnapped and jailed by the mayor of Vila Nova de Ourém, the district where Fatima was located. The mayor was an atheist. He threatened the children with death unless they promised to renounce everything they had claimed. They refused and were kept in jail for a night. According to witnesses, the children converted other prisoners to the Catholic faith while there.

When Mary unexpectedly appeared to the children on August 19, she told them that because of the mayor's behavior, a miracle she promised for all to see would not be as spectacular as her original intention. However, the miracle on October 13, 1917, was still memorable. Nearly seventy thousand pilgrims were in Fatima that day. Among them were reporters from the secular newspapers, hoping to find evidence to discount the children's accounts of Mary's apparitions. What the people saw was the sun appearing as a disk that gave off various colors, spinning like a fireball and looking like it would fall to the earth. The people were in panic, thinking the world was about to end. Then, suddenly, the sun stopped spinning and returned to its place in the sky. The ground, previously muddy and wet from hours of rain, was dry, as were the clothes of the people. A headline in a secular newspaper read, "The Sun Danced." The story told of the sun "falling from the sky."

On the day of this miracle, Mary also appeared to the children. Our Lady of Fatima told the children, "I am the Lady of the Rosary."

Pope John Paul II on a visit to Fatima, Portugal.

The younger children, Francisco and Jacinta, died within three years of Mary's appearances. Lucia entered the Carmelite convent and took the name Sr. Maria Lucia of the Immaculate Heart of Mary. She died on February 13, 2005, at the age of ninety-seven.

Our Lady of Fatima asked for devotion to her Immaculate Heart along with prayer and sacrifice. Prior to his pontificate, Pope Benedict XVI endorsed Mary's promise that "my Immaculate Heart will triumph" and added,

> The Evil One has power in this world, as we see and experience continually; he has power because our human freedom continually lets itself be led away from God. But since God himself took a human heart and has thus steered human freedom towards what is good, the freedom to choose evil no longer has the last word. From that time forth, the word that prevails is this: "In this world you will have tribulation, but take heart, I have overcome the world" (Jn 16:33). The message of Fatima invites us to trust in this promise. (Address, June 26, 2000)

Our Lady of Champion

In early October 1859, fifty-eight years before her last appearance at Fatima, Mary appeared near Champion, Wisconsin, to a young Belgian immigrant named Adele Brise. Adele described the woman who appeared to her as "dazzling white." On October 9, a few days after Mary's first appearance, Adele saw the apparition again while walking to Mass in the town of Bay Settlement. On the way home, the woman spoke to Adele, who recounted Mary's words:

> I am the Queen of Heaven who prays for the conversion of sinners and I wish you to do the same. You received Holy Communion this morning and that is well. But you must do more. Make a general confession and offer Communion for the conversion of sinners. Gather the children in this wild country and teach them what they should know for salvation. Teach them their catechism, how to sign themselves with the Sign of the Cross, and how to approach the sacraments; that is what I wish you to do. Go and fear nothing, I will help you.

Adele Brise helped to found a Catholic school for the area. She also visited people's homes to instruct children in the faith as Mary had asked. In 1871, the local shrine dedicated to Our Lady was preserved from fires that plagued the region and included the Great Chicago Fire. With the faithful gathered near the shrine asking for the intercession of Our Lady of Good Help, the fire stopped when it reached the perimeter.

Our Lady's appearances to Adele Brise in Wisconsin are especially noteworthy as the first and only apparition of Mary in the United States approved by the Church. In declaring the authenticity of the apparitions in 2010, Bishop David Ricken of Green Bay encouraged "the faithful to frequent this holy place as a place of solace and prayer."

Catholics celebrate the appearance of Mary to Adele Brise, a young Belgian immigrant woman, in October 1859 in Champion, Wisconsin.

Why does Mary continue to appear in the world? The answer is the same for all that she does: to bring her children closer to her Son. In today's time of prevalent unbelief, Mary's appearance in a supernatural way reminds us that God does exist and that Jesus Christ continues to offer his love to us for our salvation.

SECTION Assessment

Comprehension

1. When did Mary's role in God's work of salvation begin?

2. What is the meaning of the Latin phrase *ante partum, in partu, et post partum* regarding Mary's virginity?

3. What evidence does the Church provide that Mary had no other children but Jesus?

4. How is Mary's Assumption into heaven an eschatological sign?

5. What is unique about the apparition of Our Lady of Good Help?

Vocabulary

6. Briefly explain how the Church's belief in the *Immaculate Conception* became dogma.

7. What does the Church teach about Mary's death related to the Assumption of Mary?

8. Define *apparitions* as associated with Mary.

Reflection

9. Name a question you have about one of the Church teachings about Mary covered in this section.

10. Why do you think that Jesus taught that there will be no marriage in heaven?

HONORING MARY WITH PRAYER AND DEVOTION

From her earliest days, the Church has honored Mary as the spiritual mother of all humanity and as a powerful intercessor who can help lead people to Christ. Because she is these things, we can and should pray to Mary. The origin of the verb "to pray" is *orare* in Latin, which means "to plead." We plead with Mary as our intercessor to help "all her children, wherever they may be and whatever their condition, to find in Christ the path to the Father's house" (*Redemptoris Mater*, 47).

A prayer fragment preserved from the third or fourth century underscores this devotion. It reads, "Mother of God [hear] my supplications: suffer us not [to be] in adversity but deliver us from danger." When Mary was officially declared to be *Theotokos*, Mother of God, at the Council of Ephesus (431), other titles and images for her role in the life of the Church also came to the fore. She is "invoked in the Church under the titles of Advocate, Helper, Benefactress, and Mediatrix" (*CCC*, 969).

St. Bernard of Clairvaux (d. 1153) gave voice to the popular theology of his day when he said that while Christ might be thought of as the floodwaters of grace, Mary is the aqueduct that brings those waters to people in manageable amounts. During this period, devotion to Mary continued to grow, and many Catholics came to believe that the best way to approach Jesus was through Mary. The role of Mary in the Church became a prominent topic in Catholic theology.

In the twentieth century, the Church issued several official teachings about veneration of Mary and Mary's role in the Church, especially her role as Mediatrix, an intercessor in the salvific redemption offered by her Son,

Jesus.∞ All of these teachings acknowledged the words of St. Paul from Sacred Scripture: "There is . . . one mediator between God and the human race, Christ Jesus, himself human, who gave himself as ransom for all" (1 Tm 2:5–6). But, the Church explained, acknowledging this exclusive role of Christ does not require diminishing Mary's role as Mediatrix in her Son's work. In fact, God himself takes delight in Mary's role and encourages it. The Second Vatican Council taught that

> all the saving influences of the Blessed Virgin on humankind originate . . . from divine pleasure. They flow forth from the superabundance of the merits of Christ, rest on his mediation, depend entirely on it, and draw all their power from it. In no way do they impede the union of the faithful with Christ. Rather, they foster this union. (Adapted from *Lumen Gentium*, 60)

The Second Vatican Council concluded that the title Mediatrix would be placed alongside several of Mary's other titles, such as Intercessor and Advocate. **The Council emphasized that Mary's mediation is a participation in Christ's mediation and does not exist apart from it.** Mary does not have the power to answer prayers on her own, for example. The Council taught further:

> No creature could ever be counted as equal with the Incarnate Word and Redeemer. Just as the priesthood of Christ is shared in various ways both by the ministers and the faithful, and as the one goodness of God is really communicated in different ways to his creatures, so also the unique mediation of the Redeemer does not exclude but rather gives rise to a manifold cooperation which is but a sharing in this one source.
>
> The Church does not hesitate to profess this subordinate role of Mary . . . so that encouraged by this material help [the faithful] may the more intimately adhere to the Mediator and Redeemer. (*Lumen Gentium*, 62)

Pope John Paul II also emphasized that there is no good reason *not* to call on Mary as Intercessor, Advocate, and Mediatrix because she "'precedes' us all at

∞ Note

Mediatrix is the feminine form of *Mediator*.

the head of a long line of witnesses of faith in one Lord, the Son of God, who was conceived in her virginal womb by the power of the Holy Spirit" (*Redemptoris Mater*, 30).

Ways to Honor Mary

Today, many people honor Mary by consecrating themselves to Jesus through her. **When you consecrate yourself to Jesus through Mary, you make a promise to her that you will allow her to fulfill her motherly task and conform you to Christ.** It means surrendering your will to hers and giving her permission to take your prayers and actions and distribute them where they are most needed and in ways that bring you closer to her Son. Many saints have suggested consecration to Jesus through Mary, most famously St. Louis Marie de Montfort (see the subsection "Tracing the Title and Meaning of Mary as Mother of God" in Chapter 5, Section 1), but also more recently St. Maximilian Kolbe, St. Teresa of Calcutta, and St. John Paul II.∞

There are many prayers and devotions you can do each day for Mary. A simple one is to converse with her regularly and remind her to care for you in a motherly way. In *Marialis Cultus*, Pope Paul VI discusses two widespread devotions that honor Mary and are sources of grace: the *Angelus* and the Rosary. Both are recommended for universal practice. They are described in the next subsections.

The Angelus

Recently, all of the 43,000 students and 4,500 staff members in the Catholic schools of the Diocese of Parramatta in Australia stopped at noon each day to do the same thing: pray the *Angelus*. The reinstatement of this traditional Church prayer to honor the angel Gabriel's announcement that Mary would be the mother of the Savior was called for by Bishop Anthony Fisher, who said that praying the *Angelus* would be an important "interruption" to the day. "While the *Angelus* will only take a few minutes to pray each day, it is an

---

∞ Note

A popular book by Fr. Michael Gaitley, MIC, *33 Days to Morning Glory: A Do-It-Yourself Retreat for Marian Consecration* (Stockbridge, MA: Marian Press, 2001), offers insights into Mary through the lenses of these saints.

important reminder that there is more to life, much more, than the toil of everyday routines," Bishop Fisher said.

The name of the *Angelus* is Latin for "the angel," the first words of the opening verse. The *Angelus* consists of three recitations of the Hail Mary accompanied by three introductory verses, a concluding verse, and prayer. While many Catholic schools all over the world continue to recite the *Angelus* at

Children hold figures of the child Jesus while praying the Angelus at the Vatican on the Feast of the Immaculate Conception.

noon, the prayer is also said at dawn (6:00 a.m.) and dusk (6:00 p.m.). **This simple and short prayer is a reminder that God is present to us.** It gives us the opportunity to reply yes to God in the same way that Mary first offered her fiat at the Annunciation and on many occasions before and afterward.

For much of the twentieth century, Catholic church bells would ring at dawn, noon, and dusk to remind Catholics that it was time to stop and pray. The form of the *Angelus* is simple:

V.   The Angel of the Lord declared unto Mary.

R.   And she conceived of the Holy Spirit.
Hail Mary . . .

V.   Behold the handmaid of the Lord.

R.   Be it done unto me according to your word.
Hail Mary . . .

V.   And the Word was made flesh.

R.   And dwelt among us.
Hail Mary . . .

V.   Pray for us, O holy Mother of God.

R.   That we may be made worthy of the promises of Christ.

Let us pray: Pour forth, we beseech you, O Lord, thy grace into our hearts; that we, to whom the Incarnation of Christ, thy Son, was made known by the message of an angel, may by his Passion and Cross be brought to the glory of his Resurrection. Through the same Christ, our Lord. Amen.

Pope St. Paul VI on a visit to Fatima, Portugal.

During the Easter season, the *Regina Caeli* ("Queen of Heaven"; see the sub-section "Prayer" in the Chapter 5 Review) is substituted for the *Angelus*.

The *Angelus* has a long history, evolving from a practice in the twelfth century when St. Anthony of Padua encouraged his fellow Franciscans to recite three Hail Marys a day. Pope Paul VI wrote that "the *Angelus* retains an unaltered and intact freshness" with essential elements that make it timeless: a simple structure, a scriptural basis, a special liturgical rhythm that sanctifies different hours of the day, its historical origin, and its focus on the great Christian mystery of the Incarnation of Jesus Christ.

Pope Paul VI and succeeding popes have worked to restore the practice of the *Angelus* by publicly praying it themselves. For example, on Sundays at noon, Pope Francis continues the tradition by reciting the *Angelus* from a balcony window over St. Peter's Square along with the many visitors who gather below.

The Rosary

The Rosary is the most popular devotional prayer in honor of Mary. However, like the *Angelus*, it is really a prayer that is Christological in nature, meaning that it encourages meditation on key events in the life of Jesus. The Rosary developed out of the practice of medieval monks who used to recite all 150 psalms. Because many monks did not know all the psalms by heart and could not read, they substituted other prayers, usually 150 Hail Marys or Our

Fathers. The devotion soon became popular among the laity. To help people remember how many prayers they had recited, beads were introduced.

Pope Pius V established the original fifteen mysteries of the Rosary in the sixteenth century. Pope John Paul II proposed a fourth set of mysteries, called the Luminous Mysteries or "Mysteries of Light," in 2002. The mysteries of the Rosary are organized into four groups of five meditations. The first set of meditations, the joyful mysteries, focus on certain joyful events in the life of Jesus and Mary. The second set of meditations, the luminous mysteries, take up Christ's public ministry between his Baptism and his Passion. These mysteries were added in order "to bring out fully the Christological depth of the Rosary," according to Pope John Paul II. The third set of meditations, the sorrowful mysteries, are centered on Jesus's Passion and Death. Finally, the glorious mysteries focus on Jesus's Resurrection, Ascension, and the coming of the Holy Spirit. They conclude with meditations on Mary's Assumption to heaven and her title as Queen of Heaven.

The Rosary is a powerful and well-practiced prayer. Can you imagine nearly one hundred thousand people gathering to pray the Rosary? This happened regularly in several sports stadiums across the United States in the 1950s and 1960s as part of the Family Rosary Crusade, introduced by Fr. Patrick Peyton, CSC, known as the "Rosary priest."

Fr. Patrick Peyton leads the praying of the Rosary in Knock, Ireland.

In 1938, Fr. Peyton contracted tuberculosis, often a fatal disease at the time. After his recovery, which he credited to Mary's intercession, he promised Mary that he would devote his life to spreading this devotion and letting everyone know the graces available to those who turn to her with confidence and love. After being ordained in 1941, he traveled around the globe, speaking in pulpits, preaching on radio and television, and gathering people in large outdoor stadiums to pray the Rosary. Fr. Peyton's successors at Holy Cross Family Ministries continue to promote the Rosary. In 2007, fifty thousand people gathered at the famous Rose Bowl in Pasadena, California, to recite the Rosary. The cause for Fr. Peyton's sainthood is now being considered. Even more recently, praying the Rosary in public squares of major cities has been occurring regularly in Ireland, Canada, Italy, France, Great Britain, India, Australia, Croatia, and many other places, often on the **First Saturday** of each month.

In the words of Pope John Paul II, the Rosary is a simple meditative prayer in which "the main episodes in the life of Jesus Christ pass before the eyes of those who pray it."[9] Pope Paul VI wrote, "As a Gospel prayer, centered on the mystery of the redemptive Incarnation, the Rosary is a prayer with a clearly Christological orientation. Its most characteristic element, in fact, the litany-like succession of Hail Marys, becomes in itself an unceasing praise of Christ" (*Marialis Cultus*, 46). Pope Francis added, "This simple prayer helps us to contemplate all that God in his love has done for us and for our salvation, and allows us to understand that our life is united to that of Christ."[10]

No matter which Marian prayer or devotion you choose, know that Mary is herself "the perfect pray-er." You can pray with, and to, Mary. "The prayer of the Church is sustained by the prayer of Mary and united with it in hope" (*CCC*, 2679).

First Saturday A devotion requested by Mary of the children of Fatima for the reparation of sins. To complete the First Saturday devotion, Catholics must do all of the following on the First Saturday of the month for five consecutive months: (1) go to Confession (may be eight days before or after First Saturday); (2) receive Holy Communion (can be at a Saturday evening vigil Mass); (3) pray five decades of the Rosary; (4) keep Our Lady company for fifteen minutes. This can be done by meditating on one or more of the mysteries of the Rosary.

SECTION Assessment

Comprehension

1. Name an example from Mary's life when she cooperated in the role of Mediatrix with her Son.

2. What is the great Christian mystery that is the focus of the *Angelus*?

3. What is the name of the prayer that replaces the *Angelus* during the Easter season, and what does the title mean?

4. List in sequence the four sets of mysteries of the Rosary.

5. What did Pope John Paul II mean when he said that "the main episodes in the life of Jesus Christ pass before the eyes of those who pray" the Rosary?

Vocabulary

6. What is significant about the *First Saturday* of the month in the Catholic Church?

Reflection

7. Why do you think people would gather in a football stadium to pray the Rosary? Would you? Explain why or why not.

8. How would you respond to a person who says "Catholics pray to Mary"?

Section Reviews

Focus Question

How does Mary lead us to her Son, Jesus?

Complete one of the following:

- The Church calendar is filled with special holy days and celebrations to honor Mary. Three Marian feasts are holy days of obligation. List the names and dates of these feasts. Then list three other Marian feasts and their dates.

- Analyze the lyrics of two Marian liturgical hymns. (You can search for Marian hymns in the index of a liturgical hymnal.) Name the hymns you have chosen. Answer the following:

    - How do the lyrics speak of Mary's faith?

    - How do the lyrics point to faith in Jesus?

- Pope Paul VI wrote, "Mary is held up as an example to the faithful for the way in which in her own particular life she fully and responsibly accepted the word of God and did it. . . . She is worthy of imitation because she was the first and most perfect of Christ's disciples." Write about two examples from Mary's life that you would like to emulate.

Introduction

Mary Is an Image of Her Son

Review

We don't have to worry about loving Mary too much. Jesus said to his beloved disciple—and all of us—"Behold, your mother" (Jn 19:27). Mary is the most perfect imitation of Christ and the disciple par excellence. She lets us know that God is pleased to work out his plan of salvation with the help of humans. Mary is also an advocate for us with her Son. God's graces flow from the Father to the Son to us through her and our response to these graces returns inversely, through her to the Son and the Father by way of the Holy Spirit.

Assignment

Print these two sentences: "Mary is the disciple *par excellence*" and "Mary is an advocate." Below each sentence, write two additional sentences that clarify their meaning.

Section 1

Mary Is the Mother of God

Review

Of all titles for Mary, "Mother of God" is the highest. Mary can be called Mother of God because from her own flesh and blood she gave the Son of God a human nature like hers. Mary is also Mother of the Church. She continues to care for and guide the Church. All Catholics are called to learn from her and follow her example of fidelity, obedience, compassion, love, and prayerfulness. Mary is known by countless other titles as well.

Assignment

Mary was a teenager when she conceived and gave birth to Jesus. What are three questions you would most like to ask her about the experience?

Section 2

The Life of Mary from Scripture

Review

Most of the evidence for Mary's life comes from Sacred Scripture, including the Old Testament, which depicts several women who prepared for Mary's mission as Mother of God. In fact, Mary is referred to as the "New Eve" who undid what the first Eve had done (disobeyed God and brought Original Sin into the world). Among the mentions of events in Mary's life from the New Testament are the Annunciation, Visitation, Nativity, wedding at Cana, and Mary at the foot of the Cross.

Assignment

The *Magnificat* (Lk 1:46–55) describes in Mary's own words her willing-ness to give her entire being to God. Read a Scripture commentary on the

Magnificat. Write a three-to-five-paragraph essay that explains its origins, including references to Old Testament passages.

Section 3
The Church Teaches about Mary

Review

While fighting heresies against Jesus, the early Church simultaneously defined important teachings about Mary. The Church taught about the Immaculate Conception, Mary's perpetual virginity, her Assumption to heaven, and her apparitions, which reveal many other titles and teachings about her.

Assignment

Read paragraphs 496–507 of the *Catechism of the Catholic Church.* How does the Church respond to the claim that Mary's virginity is the product of legend or theological constructs not claiming to be history?

Section 4
Honoring Mary with Prayer and Devotion

Review

Mary is a powerful intercessor and advocate for grace. As Mediatrix, she participates in Christ's work as the one Mediator between God and the human race. Practicing devotions to her is a way to honor her and receive graces through her intercession. Two such devotions are the *Angelus*, which focuses on the Incarnation of Christ, and the Rosary, a meditative prayer in which, according to Pope John Paul II, "the main episodes in the life of Jesus Christ pass before the eyes of those who pray it."

Assignment

What is a Marian devotion that you have come to know through a local parish or diocese?

Chapter Projects

Choose and complete at least one of the following projects to assess your understanding of the material in this chapter.

⚙ 1. Research the Use of Bells in the Catholic Church

Bells have a purpose both outside and inside a church. Outside, bells are used to call people to prayer. Inside, bells are used to highlight certain aspects of the liturgy. Complete all four of the following assignments about church bells:

- List three examples of bells being used by the Chosen People in the Old Testament.

- Share the history of bells used at Mass. What is their purpose? When are they rung?

- Research bell towers built for Catholic churches. What is the oldest Catholic church bell tower in the world? When was it built?

- Draw one Catholic church bell tower in your area and write an overview of its history, or photograph three Catholic bell towers in your area and write overviews of their history.

⚙ 2. Write Your Own Litany to Honor Mary

A litany is a poetic prayer that contains a series of repeating invocations; it is said in petition for a blessing or another specific need. The Litany of Loreto (see note in subsection "Mother of the Church" in Chapter 5, Section 1) is one example. The Catholic Church has five litanies approved for public worship to be led by a priest or deacon. They are litanies to the Sacred Heart of Jesus, the Precious Blood of Jesus, the saints, the Blessed Mother, and St. Joseph. There are many other litanies for private prayer. For your own litany to Mary, include at least twenty invocations. Consider these other suggestions:

- Begin with a lead statement using a title or description of Mary. Use a combination of traditional titles, titles gleaned from Scripture, and your own original descriptive titles for her.

- Follow each lead statement with the repeated response, "Pray for us."
- *Optional*: Hand-print your litany in creative script.

⚙ *3. Interpret a Marian Poem*

Thomas Merton (1915–1968) was a Trappist monk who came to worldwide attention with the release of his autobiography, *The Seven Storey Mountain*, in 1948. He remained a prolific writer for the rest of his life, penning many books and articles about prayer and social-justice issues. Merton also wrote twenty-seven poems about Mary, addressing several aspects of her life. For example, in the first two stanzas of "The Blessed Virgin Mary Compared to a Window," Merton describes the sinless quality of Mary present from her Immaculate Conception:

> Because my will is simple as a window
> And knows no pride of original earth,
> It is my life to die, like a glass, by light:
> Slain in the strong rays of the bridegroom sun.
>
> Because my love is simple as a window
> And knows no shame of original dust,
> I longed all night (when I was visible) for dawn my death,
> When I would marry day, my Holy Spirit:
> And die by transubstantiation into the light.

Choose this complete poem or one of Merton's other poems on Mary. Rehearse reading the poem with the goal of communicating its meaning to a live audience. Share the reading in a live classroom presentation or record it in a format approved by your teacher. Include a three-minute oral summary of the poem at the end of your presentation that shares its year of origin and the meaning of its Marian theme.

⚙ *4. Report on the Lourdes Apparition*

Mary appeared to St. Bernadette Soubirous, a fourteen-year-old girl, near Lourdes, France, on several occasions in 1858. Mary identified herself to St. Bernadette as "the Immaculate Conception." Research more about this apparition of Mary and the life of St. Bernadette. Follow the directions below to complete each part of the assignment.

- Write an essay that (1) details the history of Mary's appearances to St. Bernadette, (2) tells about the life of St. Bernadette, and (3) reports on the Church's process of approval for the apparition.

- Watch all or part of the 1943 motion picture *The Song of Bernadette*. Report on the popular reviews of the film from the time when it was first released.

- Survey your family members or classmates on their prayer needs. Enter at least five of their petitions under your own name and email address at the official Our Lady of Lourdes website. Keep a printed copy of the petitions to turn in with the project.

- More than seven thousand healings have occurred at Lourdes since Mary appeared to St. Bernadette. In 2018, the Church approved a seventieth miracle from Lourdes when wheelchair-bound Sr. Bernadette Moriau was able to walk after attending a blessing ceremony at Lourdes. Report on a recent healing at Lourdes that is under investigation.

⚙ 5. Explore the Mysteries of the Rosary through Scripture

For each set of Rosary mysteries—joyful, luminous, sorrowful, and glorious—select a Scripture passage to accompany each mystery. (Some suggestions are included below.) Record the scriptural Rosary in a paper scrapbook or an online file.

Find an image (e.g., photos from online sources or from a print magazine) to accompany each passage. Include some of your own photos or drawings in the mix of images.

FIRST JOYFUL MYSTERY	The Annunciation	Luke 1:38
SECOND JOYFUL MYSTERY	The Visitation	

CHAPTER 5 REVIEW

THIRD JOYFUL MYSTERY	The Birth of Jesus	
FOURTH JOYFUL MYSTERY	The Presentation of Jesus in the Temple	
FIFTH JOYFUL MYSTERY	The Finding of Jesus in the Temple	
FIRST LUMINOUS MYSTERY	The Baptism of Christ	
SECOND LUMINOUS MYSTERY	The Wedding Feast at Cana	John 2:5
THIRD LUMINOUS MYSTERY	Jesus's Proclamation of the Coming of the Kingdom of God	
FOURTH LUMINOUS MYSTERY	The Transfiguration	
FIFTH LUMINOUS MYSTERY	The Institution of the Eucharist	
FIRST SORROWFUL MYSTERY	The Agony in the Garden	

SECOND SORROWFUL MYSTERY	The Scourging at the Pillar	Isaiah 53:5
THIRD SORROWFUL MYSTERY	The Crowning with Thorns	
FOURTH SORROWFUL MYSTERY	The Carrying of the Cross	
FIFTH SORROWFUL MYSTERY	The Crucifixion	
FIRST GLORIOUS MYSTERY	The Resurrection of Jesus	
SECOND GLORIOUS MYSTERY	The Ascension of Jesus	
THIRD GLORIOUS MYSTERY	The Descent of the Holy Spirit	
FOURTH GLORIOUS MYSTERY	The Assumption of Mary into Heaven	Revelation 12:1
FIFTH GLORIOUS MYSTERY	The Coronation of Mary as Queen of Heaven	

Faithful Disciples
St. Joachim and St. Anne

While it is true that there is no verifiable evidence about the names and lives of the parents of Mary, by tradition the Church has always considered Mary's parents to be St. Joachim and St. Anne. According to traditional sources, St. Anne was born in Bethlehem. She married Joachim, a livestock owner from Nazareth, later in life. Anne was unable to bear children. Because he was childless, Joachim was refused the opportunity to make his offering at the Temple under the pretext that men without offspring were unworthy. Joachim was heartbroken and went off to the desert to pray. When he didn't return home, Anne prayed to God to take away her sterility, promising that she would dedicate her child to his service. The prayers of the couple were heard, and an angel promised them a child. Their child was a daughter they named Miryam, or Mary. The story is similar to that of Hannah, the mother of the prophet Samuel (see 1 Samuel 1:2–2:21), who had also been childless into old age.

You might wonder why the Church would venerate two saints whose identities cannot be verified. The reason is simple. Mary, the Mother of God, was born of human parents. Whoever her parents were and wherever they were born and

St. Joachim and St. Anne

lived, they are certainly worthy of honor because they raised Mary to be prayerful and faithful to God, willing to commit her entire being to following his will.

St. Joachim and St. Anne share July 26 as their feast day. St. Anne is the patron saint of mothers, grandmothers, and pregnant women, especially those in labor. St. Joachim is the patron saint of fathers and grandfathers.

Comprehension

1. What are the sources of the Church's information about Sts. Anne and Joachim?
2. Why would the Church venerate two saints without any verifiable information about their lives?

Application

Read 1 Samuel 1:9–28. Draw comparisons between St. Anne's and Hannah's stories.

Prayer

Regina Caeli is Latin for "Queen of Heaven." This antiphon addressed to Mary ends the Night Prayer of the Church's Divine Office during the Easter season while also taking the place of the *Angelus* during that same season. Authorship of the prayer is unknown; its history dates to a collection found in the thirteenth century. It was originally prayed by Franciscans as part of the Divine Office at that time.

Regina Caeli

Queen of Heaven, rejoice, alleluia.
The Son you merited to bear, alleluia.
has risen as he said, alleluia.
Pray to God for us, alleluia.
Rejoice and be glad, O Virgin Mary, alleluia.
For the Lord has truly risen, alleluia.
Let us pray:
O God, who through the Resurrection
of your Son, our Lord Jesus Christ,
did vouchsafe to give joy to the world;
grant, we beseech you, that through
his mother, the Virgin Mary, we may
obtain the joys of everlasting life.
Through Christ our Lord.
Amen.

Jesus Calls Us to Faith

Adeste Fideles

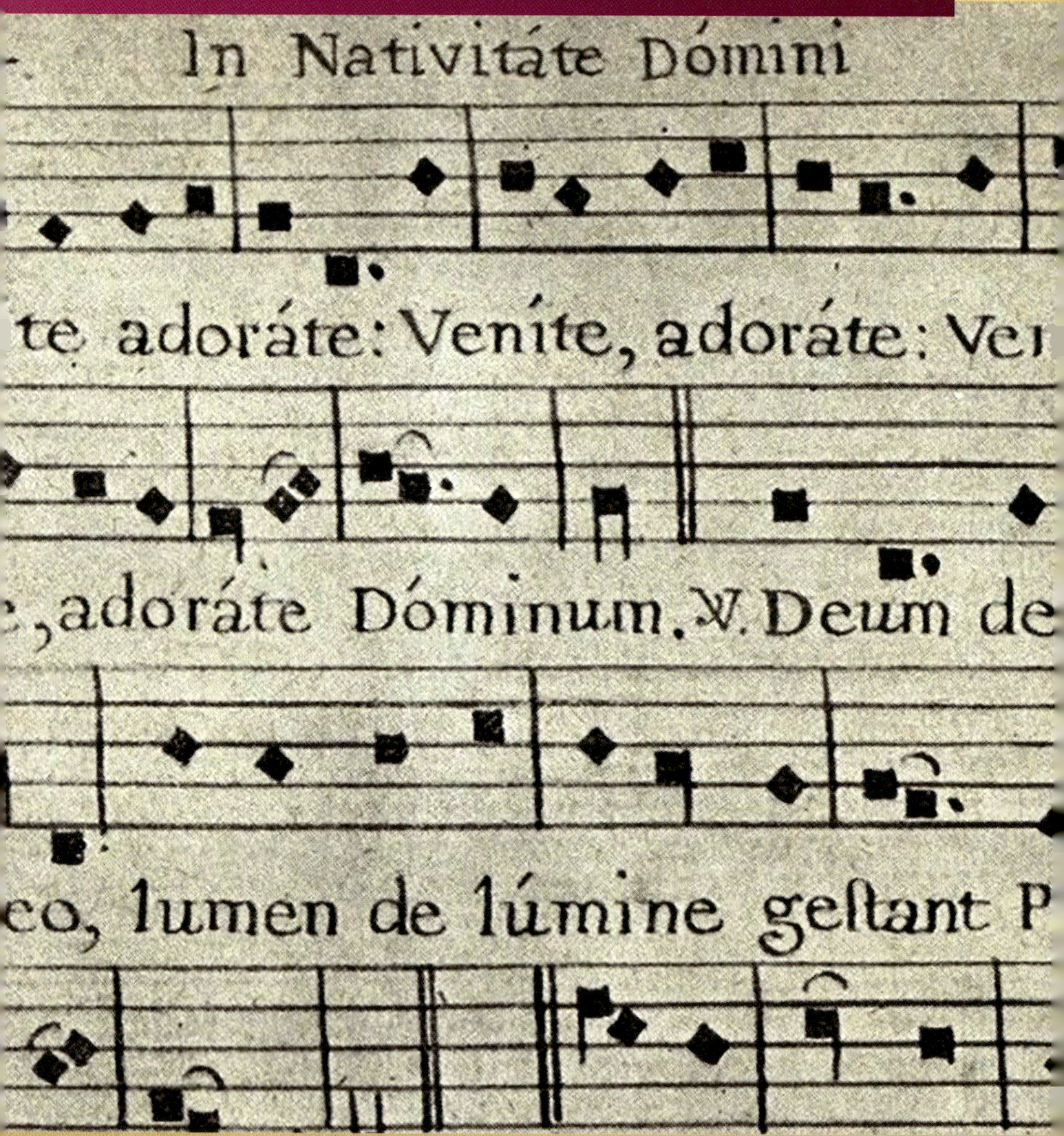

John Francis Wade

If you were asked to choose a church hymn with lyrics that spoke of faith, there is a good chance you would name the Christmas carol "O Come, All Ye Faithful," also known by its Latin name, *Adeste Fideles*. The original lyrics of the hymn are variously traced to St. Bonaventure in the thirteenth century, King John of Portugal, or Cistercian monks in the seventeenth century. In the eighteenth century a French Catholic priest wrote an additional three verses in Latin. Likewise, the music has been attributed to several composers, including English organist John Reading Sr.; his son, John Jr.; the famous composer George Frideric Handel; and Marcos da Fonseca Portugal, a Portuguese musician. All of these citations are dated in the seventeenth and eighteenth centuries. However, an older manuscript of the hymn was discovered in Oxford, England, though the exact date and name of the composer are not legible. (The image of this earliest text is pictured here.)

In today's church hymnals, "O Come, All Ye Faithful" is usually credited to an English Catholic, John Francis Wade (1711–1786), who lived in exile in France after the Jacobite uprising in 1745 was crushed. The aim of the revolt had been to restore a Catholic king—Charles Edward Stuart—to the throne of England. Some scholars suggest that "O Come, All Ye Faithful" was a song to call faithful Catholics of the Jacobite rebellion to come and support Charles Edward Stuart.

More popularly, the hymn is sung by Catholics and other Christians at Christmas. By the eighteenth century, *Adeste Fideles* was popular in Germany and France. At that time it was known as "The Midnight Mass" because it was sung by monks as part of a Christmas Eve procession. It's easy to understand why the hymn is popular around Christmas. The first verse speaks of coming in joy and triumph to Bethlehem to worship the newborn King. The second verse sends our joy all the way to God the Father in heaven. The third verse emphasizes that the "Word of the Father" has now come to the world in the flesh of Jesus Incarnate. These are the central verses sung by Christians ever since the song was first made widely available.

If you would like to rehearse and perform "O Come, All Ye Faithful" in Latin, see Chapter 6 Review, Chapter Project 1.

How does a Catholic's faith mirror the life of Jesus Christ?

Chapter Overview

Introduction
The Necessity of Faith

Section 1
Faith Is a Virtue

Section 2
I Believe: Faith Is Personal

Section 3
We Believe: Faith Is Communal

Section 4
Faith Leads Us to the Church

THE NECESSITY OF FAITH

If we look at Sacred Scripture and examine the words and actions of saints, popes, theologians, and martyrs as preserved in Sacred Tradition, we know the vital connection between having faith and living a Christian life. Mary, the disciple par excellence (see the subsection "Mary Is the Disciple Par Excellence" in Chapter 5, Introduction), had more faith than any other person who has ever lived and was able to reap the rewards of her faith, ultimately being assumed into heaven (see the subsection "Assumption" in Chapter 5, Section 3). St. Alphonsus Liguori relates that Mary

> saw her Son in the crib of Bethlehem, and believed him the Creator of the world. She saw him fly from Herod, and yet believed him the King of kings. She saw him born and believed him eternal. She saw him poor and in need of food, and believed him the Lord of the universe. She saw him lying on straw, and believed him to be omnipotent. She observed that he did not speak, and she believed him infinite wisdom. She heard him weep, and believed him the joy of Paradise. In fine, she saw him in death, despised and crucified, and, although faith wavered in others, Mary remained firm in the belief that he was God.[1]

Jesus himself taught and demonstrated that with faith, what might be deemed impossible is possible. For example:

- Matthew's Gospel (14:22–33) tells of Jesus "walking on the sea" in the midst of a storm. Peter says to Jesus, "Lord, if it is you, command me to come to you on the water." Jesus directs Peter to "come" and **Peter is able "to walk on the water toward Jesus.** But when the storm intensifies, Peter becomes fearful and Jesus has to save him. Jesus connects Peter's troubles to little faith: "Why did you doubt?" Jesus says to him.

- Also in Matthew's Gospel, Jesus says that **"if you have faith the size of a mustard seed, you will say to this mountain, 'Move from here to there,' and it will move. Nothing will be impossible for you" (17:20).** Early Church Fathers and Doctors of the Church interpreted Jesus's words as referring not to the "empty show" (St. Jerome) of moving a literal mountain but rather to moving the suffering and evil of a person "to the abyss" (Origen). In other words, through faith a disciple conquers the world of suffering and evil.

Jesus's actions were impacted by the faith—or lack of faith—of others. When he returned home to Nazareth, some of his neighbors "took offense at him . . . so he was not able to perform any mighty deed there, apart from curing a few sick people by laying his hands on them. He was amazed at their lack of faith" (Mk 6:3, 5–6).∞

Faith Is One Way to Know God

Faith is a term with multiple meanings. In common use, faith has to do with trust and belief. Faith is a gift that comes from God and one that also invites us to respond to the gift. You might think of it this way: Imagine receiving a gift from a grandparent with a new laptop inside for you to use at school and help with your studies. The gift is wrapped beautifully with shiny paper and a colorful bow. The package looks too nice to open. But open it you must if you are to get the benefits of the laptop for your studies. Faith is like that. The gift from God is great indeed, but we must unwrap it—in other words, respond to it—in order to use it.

Faith is one way for us to know God. When we hand over our intellect and will to God, he rewards us by revealing himself to us through different means. St. Paul referred to our human response to God's Revelation as "the obedience

∞ Note

Matthew 13:58 reports that Jesus did not work "many mighty deeds" in Nazareth because of the "lack of faith." In any case, "curing a few sick people" is hardly a trivial deed!

of faith" (Rom 1:5). One characteristic of faith is that we must believe what we don't see, which primarily entails what will happen to us after we die. In *Brothers Karamazov*, the masterpiece novel by Russian Fyodor Dostoyevsky (1821–1881), a monk called Elder Zosima encounters a woman who tells him she suffers from a lack of faith, not in God but in her future life after death. "The thought of life beyond the grave distracts me to anguish, to terror," she says. Elder Zosima admits that there is no "proving" life beyond the grave to her, other than encouraging her to love her neighbors more actively and deeply: "In as far as you advance in love you will grow surer of the reality of God and of the immortality of your soul."[2] Something similar is true about faith in God: we know him more clearly when we love our neighbors more actively and deeply.

St. Augustine of Hippo pointed out that humans believe in *many* things they cannot see; for example, we all believe in the love shown to us by a friend or family member even though we can't literally "see" love. Augustine explains, "No will can be seen by the eyes of the body." Rather, he continues, "you will see acts, and hear words, but concerning [the love of] your friends [for you], that which cannot be seen and heard you will believe." In other words, we come to greater faith through evidence. In the Christian sense, evidence for our faith comes through our natural reason that recognizes God's presence in everyday occurrences, from Sacred Scripture and Sacred Tradition, and through the witness of great saints and martyrs who have gone before us. Through these tangible things that we *can* see we come to faith in what we *can't* see.

Once a heretic who opposed Christianity—through the prayers of his mother, St. Monica—St. Augustine of Hippo was baptized by St. Ambrose and went on to become a bishop and one of the Church's great theologians.

SECTION Assessment

Comprehension

1. What is a common definition of faith?

2. Rather than moving a literal mountain, how did early Church Fathers interpret Jesus's words from Matthew 17:20?

3. What did Elder Zosima from *Brothers Karamazov* suggest that a person do to become more sure of his or her faith?

Reflection

4. Which of the examples of Mary's faith do you find most inspiring? Explain why.

5. Share an example of something you believe in but cannot see. How does this example of faith compare to a belief in God?

FAITH IS A VIRTUE

You cannot have a life with God without faith. You cannot be open to the truth of the Father's Revelation of his Son, Jesus, without Christian faith. Faith is both a gift of God and a human act in which God invites you to respond to the whole truth that he has revealed. The Holy Spirit offers grace not only to believe what the Father has revealed but also to accept the Father's Revelation and to give your entire life to Jesus Christ, who is Lord and Savior.

Furthermore, the theological definition of faith is deeper than the basic definition of the term. **In a religious sense, faith is a person's positive response to God's Revelation.** God comes to us in many ways as previously discussed—for example, through nature, through our relationships, and most especially through the Divine Person Jesus Christ. We can think of each of these efforts as God's invitation to us to believe in him. Our response to the invitation is faith. As the *Catechism of the Catholic Church* explains, "By faith, man completely submits his intellect and his will to God. With his whole being man gives his assent to God the revealer" (143). By being enrolled in this course, it is presumed that you (or someone who cares about you) have some openness to accepting this invitation.

It is also important to understand that faith is one of the **theological virtues**, along with hope and charity. Theological virtues are gifts that are infused into the soul. We cannot earn the gift of faith. Once infused into

---

theological virtues Three foundational virtues that are infused by God into the souls of the faithful: faith (belief in and personal knowledge of God), hope (trust in God's salvation and his bestowal of the graces needed to attain it), and charity (love of God and love of neighbor as oneself).

the soul, faith gives us certain capabilities. Faith draws us closer to God and enables us to live in relationship with the Blessed Trinity.

Faith Has Essential Elements

You've been challenged to be open to the gift of faith. Doing so makes it possible to recognize and accept that Jesus Christ is the Incarnate Son of God, the Messiah, and the Lord. Being cognizant of the gift of faith in itself is sometimes difficult. The world is filled with distractions and invitations to follow secular trends and to ignore even the most obvious graces of the Holy Spirit. **Accepting the gift of faith takes effort. It is more than a spiritual exercise; it is a task of the intellect as well.** You must take time to study and learn about basic core Catholic beliefs like the Blessed Trinity, the Incarnation, the Paschal Mystery, Mary, and judgment. You must also understand how essential elements of the theological virtue of faith contribute to your acceptance or rejection of these beliefs. Consider:

Faith is a gift, but your response must be free.

No one can be forced to embrace faith. Thus, faith is also a free human act in which the heart and mind cooperate with God's gift of grace.

Faith is reasonable.

Faith is not a blind action but a reasonable one, because you are able to perceive the beauty of God's actions, especially those saving actions that Jesus performed: his teaching, miracles, Passion, Death, and Resurrection. Other external proofs, or signs— such as the miracles of the saints, prophecies, the growth and holiness of the Church, and the great good that the Church has accomplished since her founding by Jesus Christ almost two thousand years ago—provide more evidence that supports faith.

Faith is certain.

The certainty of faith resides in the truthfulness of God the Father, who revealed that you believe in him through his Son, Jesus, and who is made manifest to you through the unerring light of the Holy Spirit. This certainty also lies in the fact that what the Catholic Church teaches is true. Jesus Christ has given to his Church the fullness of the Holy Spirit and a share in his own infallibility so that the Church's Magisterium always teaches the truth and never falls into error.

Faith grows with understanding.

Growing in faith is a lifelong task. You can nurture your faith through reading Scripture, praying, participating in the sacraments, reading books about the lives of the saints and other Catholic books on spirituality, and learning from faithful and well-informed Catholics. As you grow in your knowledge of God, your faith will deepen and become stronger.

Faith and science do not conflict.

The truth of God's Revelation does not contradict the truth of science. The God who made things discoverable by human reason is the same God who reveals himself and offers the gift of faith. The truths that can be discovered in the natural world cannot contradict the truths that God reveals (see *CCC*, 159).

Faith is an act of the Church.

Faith is an act that is done within the community of faith—that is, the Church. Faith is both personal and communal (see Sections 2 and 3). Each person must make his or her own personal act of faith, but that act is not of the person's own making. You make a personal act of faith in what the community of the Church believes, and so you become yourself a member of the Church.

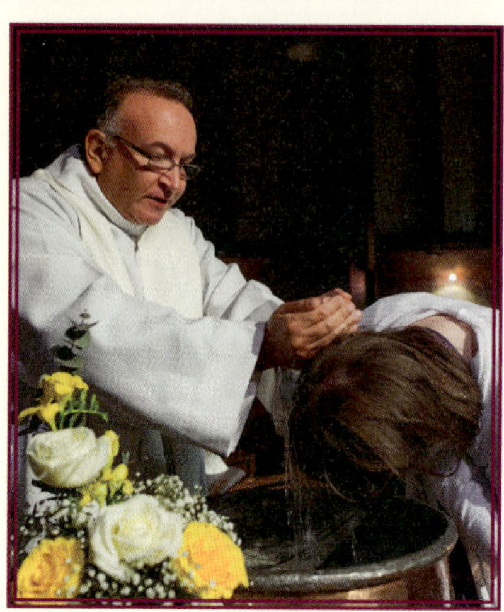

Faith brings you to relationship with the Blessed Trinity.

The act of faith allows you to establish a personal relationship with Jesus, the Son of God, through the Holy Spirit, so that Jesus's Father becomes your Father. Through faith, you come to live within the communion of love of the Blessed Trinity.

In a certain sense, faith is your lifeline to God. It is a gift that enables you to respond to God's Word and unites you personally with him: Father, Son, and Holy Spirit. Faith is an essential gift, necessary for salvation: "Believing in Jesus Christ and the One who sent him for our salvation is necessary for obtaining that salvation" (*CCC*, 161).

How Is Faith Shared?

How do Catholics "receive" faith? In the Sacrament of Baptism, the Blessed Trinity gives the baptized person sanctifying grace, the grace of justification. One of the results of this gift is that the person is then able to believe in God, hope in him, and love him through the theological virtues. Faith is typically first proclaimed in the Christian home, called the **domestic church**. This is the place where children witness parents praying, worshipping God, and loving one another. This is the place where children experience lives of holiness along with acts of self-denial. Children, too, participate in these actions and receive the sacraments.

The "obedience of faith" that St. Paul wrote of (see Romans 1:5; 16:26) and the other theological virtues of hope and love lead to the moral virtues and the virtue of **religion** by which we render to God his due in justice. The virtue of religion enables us to revere and love the loving God. The word *religion* derives from a Latin word that means "to bind together." To fail to develop the virtue of religion in our life is to thwart an essential part of our spiritual nature, a nature that seeks out and responds in love to God.

Centered uniquely on the belief in Jesus Christ as Lord and Savior, religion gives us a framework to collect our beliefs in God and put them into practice. The virtue of religion requires that we worship God with others as well as individually. All people are called to participate in the fullness of faith present in the Catholic Church. However, the Church recognizes in other religions the presence of God "who is unknown yet near since he gives life and breath and all things and wants all men to be saved" (*CCC*, 843). For example, Judaism is held in special honor by the Church because the Jews received the first covenant from God. The Church teaches positively that "all salvation comes from Christ the Head through the Church which is his Body" (*CCC*, 846). Catholics are able to give themselves totally to God in Jesus Christ and to accept him and his message as it comes through the Church founded by Christ. Indeed, it is in and through the Catholic Church that we profess publicly that Jesus is the Son of God.

In summary, God reveals himself to us. Faith is our response to God's Revelation. Faith is necessary for our salvation. The faith life of the Church gives life to, supports, and nourishes the life of the individual Christian. A requirement of membership in the Catholic Church is for all members to extend to

---

domestic church A name for the Christian family. In the family, parents and children exercise their priesthood of the baptized by worshipping God, receiving the sacraments, and witnessing to Christ and the Church by living as faithful disciples.

religion A set of beliefs and practices followed by those committed to the service and worship of God (*CCC*, Glossary).

the entire world God's invitation to believe in, accept, and dedicate their lives to Jesus Christ. This is done by word and example. When we accept and live out the gift of faith, we are on the path to eternal life through Jesus Christ. Remember Jesus's message to the ten lepers he cleansed and made whole: "Stand up and go; your faith has saved you" (Lk 17:19).

SECTION Assessment

Comprehension

1. Where does the certainty of faith reside?

2. Why is the act of faith a reasonable, not a blind, act?

Vocabulary

3. What are the *theological virtues* and how do we acquire them?

4. What are some ways that a Christian receives faith within the domestic church?

5. How is *religion* different from faith?

Reflection

6. Tell about a person in whom you have great faith. How strong is your faith in this person? How has your faith in this person ever been tested or threatened?

I BELIEVE: FAITH IS PERSONAL

Pope John Paul II wrote that faith is "contact with the mystery of God" (*Redemptoris Mater*, 17). Because faith is a free gift from God and one that demands our response, faith is personal. It is our personal decision whether or not to surrender ourselves to the mystery of God that has been revealed to us. **When we do make a conscious decision to trust and believe, our faith is deepened. This personal response to God's mystery must occur before we can act in communion with others in the Church, the Body of Christ.** God must touch us with the gift of faith, and only then will we experience the fullness of faith, which is unity with Christ, the head of the Body.

To believe in Christ "means 'to abandon oneself' to the truth of the word of the living God, knowing and humbly recognizing 'how unsearchable are his judgments and how inscrutable his ways' (Rom 11:33)" (*Redemptoris Mater*, 14). The gift of personal faith can come in many ways. It may begin with a life-changing event, or it may begin with the commitment of parents to raise their children in ways that are shaped by Jesus. Faith may come in a moment or be part of a longer process in which we gradually take ownership of all that has been given to us. In either case, believing is not something that happens once and for all time.

Since God never takes away our freedom, we are always free to stop allowing Christ to shape our lives. We can separate ourselves from the Body of Christ either through a deliberate decision or by gradually developing habits that move us further and further from Christ. For this reason, we must nourish our faith if we are to remain committed to what we believe. Faith must be sustained by prayer, study, reflection, and regular reception of the sacraments. And faith needs to be exercised by our loving action. Our faith is only made visible when we practice Christian virtues—that is, attitudes and habits that lead us to do what God desires. There are many different moral virtues, which we can acquire with the help of God's grace. Three examples of personal faith lived through virtue follow.

The Virtue of Courage as a Sign of Personal Faith

Courage is equated with fortitude; it is "the moral virtue that ensures firmness in difficulties and constancy in the pursuit of good" (*CCC*, 1808). **This virtue enables us to face trials and persecutions, resist temptations, and conquer fears, even the fear of death.** The virtue of courage was exhibited in a dramatic way by José Sánchez del Río, a fourteen-year-old boy who lived in the early twentieth century.

José Sánchez del Río was born in 1913 in Sahuayo, Mexico. In 1926, the Cristero War began in Mexico in response to the persecution of the Catholic Church by the Mexican government. The federal government was seizing Church property, closing Catholic schools and convents, and exiling or executing Catholic priests. Many Mexican citizens organized soldiers, the Cristeros, to fight against these persecutions, under the banner of "Viva Cristo Rey" ("Long Live Christ the King"). ∞

Young José, only fourteen years old, wanted to join in the fight to defend the Church. His mother was opposed to this idea, telling him he was too young. "Mama," he said to her, "do not let me lose the opportunity to gain heaven so easily and so soon." He joined the Cristeros as a flagbearer. On February 5, 1928, José was taken prisoner with other Cristeros. The

José Sánchez del Río

In 1926, the Church went underground in Mexico. Bishops closed the churches. A wave of protest among Catholics (95 percent of Mexican citizens were Catholic) erupted into the Cristero War or Cristero Rebellion. Nearly fifty thousand soldiers fought for the Church against federal troops.

government soldiers forced him to watch his compatriots being hanged. José offered encouragement to one man, telling him, "You will be in heaven before me. Prepare a place for me. Tell Christ the King I shall be with him soon."

Imprisoned, José prayed the Rosary and wrote letters to his parents. On February 10, the prison guards tortured him by shearing the skin off his feet and then making him walk on salt through the town to the cemetery. José was in pain but would not give in to their demands that he renounce his faith. Instead he shouted, "Long live Christ the King! Long live Our Lady of Guadalupe!" At the cemetery, he was given one more chance to deny Christ, but he would not. He was then shot to death in front of his parents.

On October 16, 2016, Pope Francis canonized José Sánchez del Río. In 2021, Cardinal Francisco Robles Ortega dedicated a statue of the new saint in Guadalajara, Mexico. The cardinal commented, "There are many young men and women today who are not finding what to do with their lives. They don't know what they are in this world for. They are not discovering what they came into this world for and they live an existential void," which only "produces a deeper void." He encouraged young people to look to the powerful witness of José Sánchez del Río.[3]

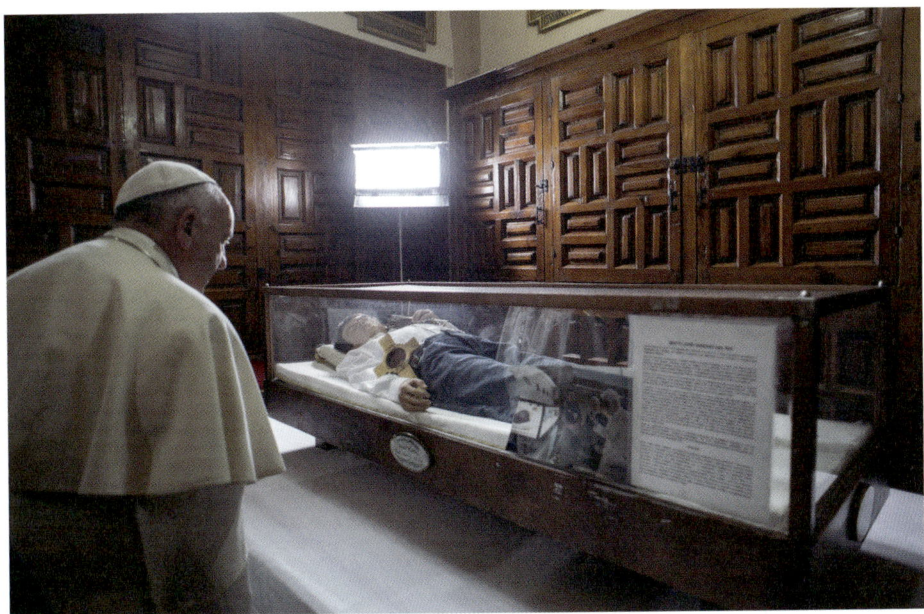

Pope Francis prays before the remains of child-martyr Jose Sanchez del Rio, in Morelia's Cathedral, Mexico, in 2016.

The Latin root of courage is *cor*, which means "heart." With this virtue of the Holy Spirit, we can "take heart" and be encouraged even when facing our greatest fears. Asking for an increase in this gift can lead the way to doing brave and meaningful things in our lives, much like St. José Sánchez del Río, who lived only a century ago.

St. Josemaría Escrivá

The Virtue of Poverty as a Sign of Personal Faith

In the Sermon on the Mount, Jesus called the poor in spirit blessed in the very first Beatitude (see the subsection "Moral Teaching" in the Appendix). Poverty can itself be a virtue because it allows us to trust God for all of our needs. St. Josemaría Escrivá, who founded Opus Dei in 1928, an organization to promote holiness among laypeople and priests, differentiated between the vow of poverty taken by religious and the virtue of poverty as it is to be lived out by "an ordinary Christian." Of the latter, he said that we should *all* desire to be in communion with those who are poor, "sharing their way of life, their joys and happiness, working with them, loving the world and all the good things that exist in it; using all created things to solve the problems of human life and to establish a spiritual and material environment which will foster personal and social development."[4]

One way to practice the virtue of poverty as St. Josemaría describes is to identify with and include those who feel marginalized. There are several positive developments among young people related to this virtue. For example, a recent study showed a consistent decline in bullying in schools between 2014 and 2022; 88.5 percent of students reported feeling safe at school, and 79 percent reported a sense of belonging at school.[5] Those who are the outcasts of any group, including a school student body, fit in the category of "poor in spirit."

Consider this piece of evidence: in recent years, teenagers who may be described as neurotypical[6] have discovered the rewards for themselves in reaching out to those who are neurodivergent (people whose brains work differently than the neurotypical) or have other physical, mental, or emotional differences. Often this connection is forged at school, including Catholic schools. Though only a small percentage of Catholic schools have the resources to accept students with special needs,[∞] the number of schools and dioceses sponsoring inclusive academic and social programs is increasing by the year. The benefits have been striking. Adam Hank, a special-needs student in San Diego, went to Catholic elementary school and Catholic high school. His principal at All Hallows Academy, Mary Skeen, said that "all our virtues have been impacted by Adam's presence on campus," explaining that his being there allowed other students to demonstrate compassion and respect, among other virtues. **Adam, who served on student council and played on the basketball team, said he liked the school "because everyone was nice to me."**[7]

According to St. Josemaría, "We *live* poverty . . . by thinking of others and using things in such a way that there will be something to offer others." There is evidence that all school-age students—not only those in Catholic schools or of high school age—are doing better in identifying with those with special needs, the lonely, and the challenged, and making them feel welcomed.

The Virtue of Prayer as a Sign of Personal Faith

Prayer is an action of the virtue of religion. The *Catechism of the Catholic Church* defines prayer as "the elevation of the mind and heart to God in praise of his glory" (Glossary). When we pray, we acknowledge God's goodness and power

∞ Note

The National Catholic Board on Full Inclusion reported that 2 percent of Catholic schools include students with intellectual disabilities. The National Catholic Education Association estimates that 6.9 percent of Catholic schools have students with a diagnosed disability or learning difference. However, the NCEA also thinks its own statistic is a low estimate. "We also know that there's a lot of children with learning differences that may not be diagnosed or may not be reported," said NCEA president Lincoln Snyder (Katie Yoder, "Why It's Important to Welcome Kids with Disabilities at Catholic Schools," *Our Sunday Visitor*, August 4, 2023).

along with our own needs and dependence on him. This is what makes prayer a "virtue," for it implies our deep reverence for God in our daily lives.

An intense daily prayer life was the catalyst that led Goyo Hidalgo, a Spanish native living a carefree and often sinful existence in Los Angeles, to, first, renew his practice of Catholicism, which had been slipping away, and, second, to eventually enter the seminary and become an ordained priest in 2016. His journey "from prodigal to priest" was grounded in prayer before the Blessed Sacrament in a small chapel located in a Catholic bookstore run by Paulist sisters:

> The process was very ordinary. It was just me, nothing to hide, nothing to prove, no need to impress. It was just me with a naked soul and a wounded heart. And there, in that intimacy, in the voluntary surrounding and peaceful stage of my life, I fell in love with God again. Wounds started to heal, trust flowed effortlessly, and I felt the love of God, just like when I was a child. Now I wanted to love him back and I wasn't sure how or where to start. Prayer seemed the logical thing to do.[8]

Prayer in the chapel was at first very forced for Goyo Hidalgo. He tried reciting prayers he remembered from his childhood. But he soon "progressed" to simply "talking to God," recalling that a basic Catholic definition of prayer is "conversation with God." He kept the conversation going outside of the chapel too: "I was sure that just talking to God was not enough, or even considered a prayer, but I just couldn't stop it. I talked to him on my way to work, when walking my dog, at home, and at the gym."[9]

Personal prayer is something that all of us should practice, often. When you pray, you may feel guilty that too much of your prayer falls into the "gimme" category—that is, "God, give me this," "God, give me that." These are defined as *prayers of petition*. We should try to balance prayers of petition with *prayers of blessing*. In blessing prayer, there is a dialogue, a loving exchange that acknowledges the very existence, being, and goodness of the other. The *Catechism* says, "Because God blesses the human heart, it can in return bless him who is the source of every blessing" (2645).

Truthfully, our prayer lives often do need to deepen and grow in new ways. But that is not a reason to keep us from constantly talking with God as we develop those new ways. Remember, Jesus taught about a persistent person who knocked on the door of a friend's house at midnight, looking for three loaves of bread. Jesus pointed out that if the friend in the house "does not get up to give him the loaves because of their friendship, he will get up to give him whatever he needs because of his persistence" (Lk 11:8). Jesus went on to say, "And I tell you, ask and you will receive; seek and you will find; knock and the door will be opened to you. For everyone who asks, receives; and the one who seeks, finds; and to the one who knocks, the door will be opened" (Lk 11:9–10). So, while you should expand your prayer form to other expressions, do not feel guilty about petitioning God for all that you need. Just by asking, you are offering concrete evidence to God, yourself, and others of your personal faith.

SECTION Assessment

Comprehension

1. What makes our faith personal?

2. What are two ways personal faith might come to us?

3. How is personal faith witnessed?

4. Explain how fortitude is equated with courage.

5. What did St. José Sánchez del Río mean when he told his mother he did not want to "lose the opportunity to gain heaven so easily and so soon"?

6. What is the purpose of Opus Dei?

7. How does the *Catechism of the Catholic Church* define prayer?

Reflection

8. What do you fear about boldly practicing your faith?

9. How have you benefited by interacting with someone who is neurodivergent or has another special need?

10. How do you pray more often, with prayers of petition or prayers of blessing? Why do you think this is so?

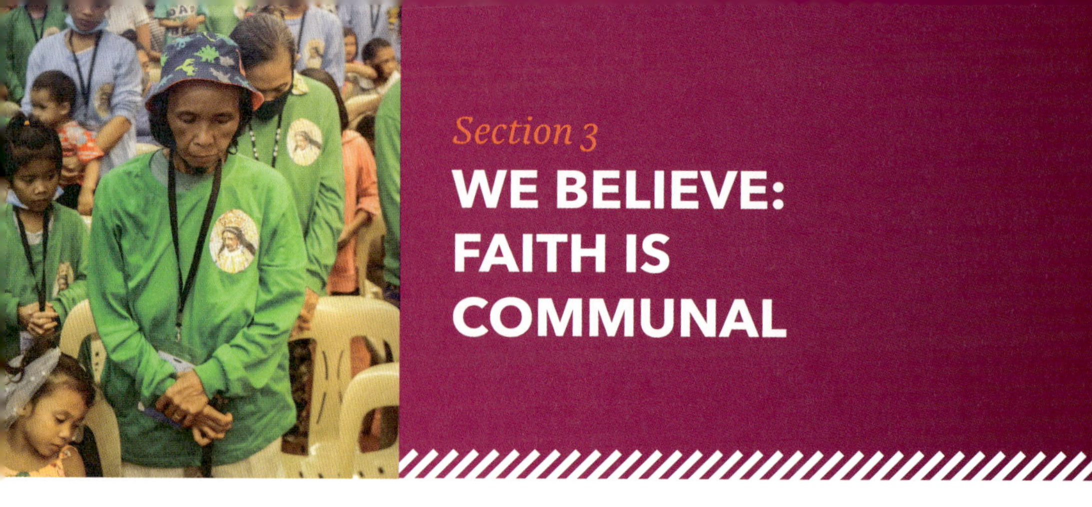

WE BELIEVE: FAITH IS COMMUNAL

As important as our own personal faith is, no one acting alone can be the Body of Christ. Each one of us is only a single member of that Body, the Church. A true believer in Christ must join with others. Our faith must be communal as well as personal. We must believe in Christ not only as individuals but also as groups—families, groups of friends, parishes, dioceses, and the worldwide Church at large. In other words, we cannot really answer God's call to faith unless we are part of groups that are shaped by Christ and supported by his Church.

It is not easy to surrender our lives to Christ in faith as individuals; it is even more difficult to do so as members of communities in which the many different individuals have different concepts of what it means to surrender to Christ and believe in him. Nevertheless, the Church believes that we can be united in faith. As Jesus said, "For where two or three are gathered together in my name, there am I in the midst of them" (Mt 18:20). Catholics who trust that they receive an abundance of God's grace in cultivating their personal relationship with him may likewise assume that they will be even more abundantly blessed in their communal relationship with God when they are joined by others.

The formal structures of the Church help both individuals and communities of believers to establish, express, and maintain their faith lives. The formal structures of the Church that are defined and protected by the Magisterium—including creeds, doctrines, rituals, and outreach—make our communal relationship with Christ visible and tangible to the world. Unless we commit ourselves individually to the formal structures of faith, we might find that we are picking and choosing our faith in ways that no longer shape us and challenge us as Jesus intends. If we reject the formal structures of faith, we will probably end up only selecting those aspects that demand the least of us and that are most in keeping with the secular culture in which we live. On the other hand, when we work within the formal structures of the Church, the Body of Christ, we provide dramatic witness to the world of Christ living and in action. Three examples follow.

The Virtue of Courage as a Sign of Communal Faith

The one faith in Christ that the Church confesses is present in many cultures, peoples, and nations throughout the world. It is transmitted by one Baptism and is "grounded in the conviction that all people have only one God and Father" (*CCC*, 172). **St. Irenaeus of Lyons pointed out the beauty of the Church believing, preaching, and handing on the faith with a "unanimous voice, as if possessing only one mouth."**[10] Sometimes, in the history of the Church, the unanimous voice rises in a courageous action of communal faith that can be witnessed by all. That is what occurred in Poland in the second half of the twentieth century.

In 1989 the Round Table Talks between members of the ruling Communist Party and organizers of the Solidarity movement—a labor union with great support of Polish citizens—resulted in a reordering of the Polish government from one that tolerated only limited freedom to a democratic one that allowed complete personal freedom. The Catholic bishops were asked to mediate this meeting as a neutral presence, but their loyalties clearly sided with Solidarity.[11]

Solidarity was born in post–World War II Poland after the Soviet Union overtook the country and implemented Marxism and Communism. The Poles, limited in what they could say about the heavy-handed government, focused

Lech Walsea, a Polish labor union leader who later became president of Poland, partnered with Pope John Paul II to lead a movement that helped overthrow the communist government of Poland. He was awarded the Nobel Peace Prize in 1983.

instead on Polish folklore, legends, traditions, and especially Catholic piety. The Solidarity movement originated by keeping Poland's memories alive. The Catholic Church helped to define the movement; Fr. Józef Tischner was a founder of Solidarity. He emphasized that the work of the movement should be grounded in central concepts such as authenticity, truth telling, fidelity, dialogue, and sacrifice.

The Church was granted *some* freedoms in Poland in the Communist era, as long as the priests and bishops agreed to remain out of politics. To stay clear of government sanctions and punishment, Catholics learned to talk in double-speak. For example, Catholics spoke of "Christ's Crucifixion" to refer to their own suffering; when they spoke "truth in everyday life," they meant "Christ's truth." **But things changed in 1979 when the newly elected Polish pope, John Paul II, made an eight-day pilgrimage to his home country. Nearly thirteen million people were present with the pope on his visit.** Specially chosen Scripture readings for Mass highlighted the theme "Do not be afraid." The experience brought Poles of all ages together. Even non-Catholic Poles like Adam Michnik felt emboldened by the pope's visit. "In June, 1979, I lived through one of those moments in my life that gave me a sense that I was alive for a reason," he said. "I felt absolutely no sense of separation. Alongside me kneeled a Catholic priest, and no one in that square had any intention to divide the people. It was natural that we were all together."[12]

Shortly after the 1989 Round Table Talks, the Solidary Party took control of a democratic government. The Church had remained strong and stead-fast in the years of Communist rule. Ultimately this unified and courageous movement won out, and Communism was obliterated in Poland and through-out much of Europe. Catholics—unified under priests, bishops, and a Polish pope—played a key role.

The Virtue of Poverty as a Sign of Communal Faith

Practicing the virtue of poverty is a task of the entire Church. Beginning with Pope Leo XIII's 1891 encyclical *Rerum Novarum* (*Of Revolutionary Change*), the Church has stressed the responsibility of all Catholics, not just priests and religious, to carry out a common mission of caring for the poor. Caring for the poor is no longer viewed as a work of charity but as a matter of justice. The *Catechism of the Catholic Church* specifically states that part of the vocation of all Catholics is the restructuring of social life in order to obtain justice: "It is the role of the laity 'to animate temporal realities with Christian commitment, by which they show that they are agents of peace and justice'" (2442, quoting John Paul II, *Sollicitudo Rei Socialis* [*On Social Concern*]).

The Church sees that part of her task is to restore the world to the state of equality God intended, especially in the areas of freedom and opportunity. The Church believes that all people should be able to meet their basic needs without undue hardship and that their lives should not be reduced to a day-to-day fight for survival. The Church also holds that all people should be able to participate in the economic life of their nation. Economic policy should not be decided only by those who have wealth, and opportunities for advancement should not go primarily to those who already have the most. Pope John Paul II and other popes since have challenged government to provide a "preferential option for the poor."∞

A particular way that Catholics work together to aid the poor is through an organization called Catholic Relief Services (CRS), the official agency of the United States Conference of Catholic

The Catholic Relief Services Rice Bowl is a Lenten program in which schools, parishes, and dioceses contribute donations to support hunger and poverty both worldwide and locally. Since its inception in 1975, CRS Rice Bowl has raised more than $320 million.

∞ Note

The preferential option for the poor theme highlights the call to treat those who are impoverished in a special way. This preferential option is just common sense. For example, when a child is sick, or weakened and susceptible to serious health risks, the family gives the child special attention and resources until he or she becomes healthy again. The parents make sure the child rests, eats the right foods, and visits a doctor who can prescribe the appropriate medicines. And so it is with the poor in society. Like the sick child, they deserve particular concern because of their vulnerable position. All of us are called to give the poor special attention and offer the resources necessary for human growth.

Bishops in support of ending poverty on an international level. CRS was founded at the end of World War II to provide aid to people recovering and rebuilding in war-torn areas. These days, CRS sponsors local chapters in parishes and dioceses, as well as clubs in Catholic high schools, to advocate for international aid for the poor. A particular focus is developing relationships with local congressional representatives to encourage support for spending bills that send funding to impoverished areas.

At Bishop Luers High School in Fort Wayne, Indiana, the school's CRS club completes an in-class service project each week and an all-school service project twice a year to help the community. Some students in the club recently underwent a refugee simulation offered by CRS to gain a perspective of what it is like to be a refugee; another group made sandwiches for a local homeless shelter. "It's working pretty seamlessly because we already had a lot of the structure in place," said adviser Nicole Rudolph. "This is helping us be able to enrich our structure and bring it to a more Catholic and global point of view."[13]

The Virtue of Prayer as a Sign of Communal Faith

Fr. Goyo Hidalgo appreciated the silence and calm of personal prayer before the Blessed Sacrament. He said he couldn't concentrate in church after Mass because there was too much noise and distraction and too many people around. "I just wanted to be alone. I wanted God all for myself for as long as I needed. I felt as if I wouldn't have enough time to be with God in the short time before they closed the church after Mass."

Fr. Goyo Hidalgo

As evidenced by Fr. Hidalgo's ensuing vocation to the priesthood and our need to offer our own personal pledge of faith to God, there is nothing wrong with praying alone. Yet it is also essential to pray together with other committed believers. In the *liturgy*—especially the Eucharist—all that Christ has done, is doing, and will do is made part of the present moment. The liturgy is the sign of the redemption and transformation of the world that was begun in

Christ and will be completed at the time of his Second Coming. The Church uses the public liturgy to enact the world as God intends it to be.∞ **The liturgy is the place to which we bring the activity of the world so that it may be reshaped by the mystery of Christ and then returned to the world as something new.** In the liturgical life of the Church, all of the basic elements of communal life take on new meaning. Birth and death, eating and drinking, greeting one another, communication in marriage, forgiveness—all are transformed in the presence of Jesus. The liturgical life of the Church helps us to see and understand that transformation; what is more, it gives us the grace to live our new life in Christ in the world.

Public liturgy also touches the lives of people who are not Catholics. The night before the March for Life, the annual rally for the protection of human life from conception through all stages until death, the Church holds a national prayer vigil and Mass at the Basilica of the National Shrine of the Immaculate Conception in Washington, DC. More than six thousand people regularly attend this Mass. In 2023, the national prayer vigil was held for the first time since the US Supreme Court overturned the *Roe v. Wade* decision in its ruling in the case *Dobbs v. Jackson Women's Health Organization.* The Mass highlighted the Church's ongoing public commitment to the spectrum of life issues. A young blind woman with her service dog, a single father with his seven-year-old daughter, and a mother with a toddler who had Down syndrome brought the gifts to the altar during the Offertory. Before the Liturgy of the Eucharist, a prayer for pregnant mothers was shared.

The homily of Bishop Michael Burbidge that night highlighted the words of Pope Francis, who said, "The secret of Christian living is love. Only love fills the empty spaces caused by evil." Bishop Burbidge went on, "Into the empty spaces of our wounded politics, may we communicate the need to let go of partisanship and to do what is right and just."[14]

∞ Note

It is worth noting that the Second Vatican Council's document on the liturgy is called a "constitution." A *constitution* addresses the essence of the Church's identity and understanding of her mission. What the Church does in its liturgy is as important to the Church's identity as her doctrines and dogmas.

Faith, whether celebrated personally or communally, is the correct response to God's Revelation. When you accept the gift of faith and practice it, you are on the road to eternal life.

SECTION Assessment

Comprehension

1. What is another name for the Body of Christ?

2. How is faith first transmitted in the Church?

3. How did Poles use doublespeak to keep their faith alive during Communist rule?

4. Why is it important for Catholics to commit themselves to the formal structures of the Church?

5. Explain the mission of Catholic Relief Services.

Reflection

6. Name a group shaped by Christ and supported by the Church that you participate in or would like to participate in. Explain why.

7. How do you understand the difference between caring for the poor out of charity (love) and caring for the poor out of justice?

FAITH LEADS US TO THE CHURCH

Faith in Jesus Christ should naturally lead the believer to Christ's Church, the Catholic Church, which he founded and in which he lives. Catholics profess in the Nicene or Apostles' Creed at Mass each Sunday: "I believe in one, holy, catholic, and apostolic Church." Why? Because Christ, his Good News of salvation, and all the means he left for us to grow in faith are found in the Church.

The connection between Christ and the Church is richly described in the First Letter to the Corinthians, where St. Paul teaches that the Church is the Body of Christ in the world. Jesus is the head of the Body; the baptized are her members. **Faith in Jesus Christ and the Sacrament of Baptism incorporate a person into the Body of Christ—that is, the Church—by the power of the Holy Spirit.** St. Paul writes,

> As a body is one though it has many parts, and all the parts of the body, though many, are one body, so also Christ. For in one Spirit we were all baptized into one body, whether Jews or Greeks, slaves or free persons, and we were all given to drink of one Spirit. (1 Cor 12:12–13)

This passage emphasizes the dignity of each member of Christ's Body. Catholics are members of the Church, each united with Christ and *each other*. Each member of Christ's Body is important and has a role in bringing Christ into the world. "God is love, and whoever remains in love remains in God and God in him" (1 Jn 4:16). Christ lives in his Church. His love can be found there.

What Are the Marks of the Church?

Focus Question: How does a Catholic's faith mirror the life of Jesus Christ?

At the First Council of Constantinople in AD 381, the words "I believe in one, holy, catholic and apostolic Church" were added to the creed. Those who were gathered at this second ecumenical council (the Council of Nicaea was the first) indicated that a Christian's faith in God—Father, Son, and Holy Spirit—could not be separated from a belief that the Church was "one, holy, catholic and apostolic."

These characteristics are known as the four marks of the Church. The four marks—and how they are manifested throughout the history of the Church in different ways, times, and cultures—demonstrate that the nature of the Catholic Church is an expression of Jesus Christ.

The marks of the Church are essential to the Church and designate her as the true Church. They strengthen Catholics to serve in the Church and to build up the faith. They also attract nonbelievers to the Church. They are described here:

ONE

This mark describes the unity of the Church, a unity rooted in the mystery of the Blessed Trinity. The oneness of the Church is founded on the one God and Father of Jesus Christ. Also, Jesus is the one head of his one Body, the Church, which was founded upon him as the Revelation of the one, true Gospel. Moreover, the Holy Spirit is the one living source of the oneness of the Church. Charity—love— "binds everything together in perfect harmony" (Col 3:14, quoted in *CCC*, 1844).

HOLY

Jesus, who is all-holy, loves the Church as his Bride. United with Christ, the Church is made holy by him. Christ sent the Holy Spirit to give the Church all the means necessary to grow in holiness and bring glory to God. Love is the soul of holiness to which everyone is called (see *CCC*, 826).

CATHOLIC

The Church is catholic, or universal, in two ways. First, the Church is catholic because Christ is present in the Church. Christ is present in the Church in the fullness of his Body, with the fullness of the means of salvation, the fullness of the sacraments, and the fullness of ordained ministry in apostolic succession. Second, the Church is catholic because Christ sends her out on a mission to all people in all places until the end of time. No one is excluded from hearing and responding to the Gospel or from the Church. Through faith and Baptism, everyone can become a member of the Catholic Church.

APOSTOLIC

Christ founded the Church on the Apostles when he poured the Holy Spirit upon them. It is the teaching of the Apostles that the Church faithfully hands on through the successors of the Apostles, the pope and bishops. This is known as apostolic succession.

When Catholics live the marks of the Church, the Church is strong. According to a favorite image of the Church Fathers, the Church is "like the moon, all her light is reflected from the sun." The strength of the Church comes when her members efficiently and lovingly mirror the life of Christ.

Comprehension

1. Who is the source of the oneness of the Church?
2. What is the "soul of holiness" to which everyone is called?
3. Name the two ways that the Church is catholic, or universal.
4. Define *apostolic succession*.

Reflection

Write a short letter to your pastor, godparent, or any close mentor explaining how you will live your faith in God. Include in the letter some of the plans you have for your life.

The Church Is a Foretaste of God's Kingdom

Jesus established the Church to carry on his work in his name after his Ascension to heaven. He founded this community—"the seed and beginning of the Kingdom . . . 'the little flock'" (*CCC*, 764)—to help people of every age find true happiness and joy as well as bring them to eternal salvation. Jesus's founding of the Church was part of God the Father's plan of salvation. Jesus, the Father's "total

Poles kneel and pray during the annual Corpus Christi (Body of Christ) procession from the Wawel Castle to the main square of Kraków.

self-communication," shows us who the Father is. Jesus's words, actions, and very presence ushered in the Kingdom of God. **The Church is a foretaste of the fullness of God's Kingdom, which will come to fruition at the end of time.**

Christ founded the Church on the Apostles. Jesus's questioning of Peter about his true identity set the stage for the Church. Peter said to Jesus, "You are the Messiah, the Son of the living God" (Mt 16:16). Jesus said to Peter in reply,

> Blessed are you, Simon son of Jonah. For flesh and blood has not revealed this to you, but my heavenly Father. And so I say to you, you are Peter, and upon this rock I will build my church, and the gates of the netherworld shall not prevail against it. I will give you the keys to the kingdom of heaven. Whatever you bind on earth shall be bound in heaven; and whatever you loose on earth shall be loosed in heaven. (Mt 16:17–19)

Simon Peter was able to state clearly the identity of Jesus because God revealed it to him. Jesus gave Simon a new name—Peter—meaning "Rock." The *Catechism of the Catholic Church* teaches,

> The Lord Jesus endowed his community with a structure that will remain until the Kingdom is fully achieved. Before all else there is the choice of the Twelve with Peter as their head. Representing the twelve tribes of Israel, they are the foundation stones of the new Jerusalem. The Twelve and the other disciples share in Christ's mission and his power, but also in his lot. By all his actions, Christ prepares and builds his Church. (765)

The Church was born from Christ's Death on the Cross. At Pentecost, when the Risen Lord poured out his Holy Spirit upon the Apostles, the Church "was made manifest to the world" (*CCC*, 1076).

The Union of Christ and His Church

Christ gave to Peter and the other Apostles—and their successors—the responsibility to preach the Gospel down through the ages and to teach the truths of the faith. This gift of teaching authority was given by Christ to the Church and is known as the *Magisterium*, a Latin term for "teacher." A prime task of the Magisterium is to hand on the Deposit of Faith and to see to it that Divine Revelation is accurately, authentically, and completely presented to the people of the world.

In considering the meaning and purpose of the Church's Magisterium, we must also acknowledge that there are different types of magisterial teaching. The *ordinary magisterium* refers to ordinary teachings of popes and bishops that reiterate consistent and long-held Church teachings. These teachings may be transmitted in papal documents and encyclicals or in letters written by bishops. The *extraordinary magisterium* refers to occasions when the pope declares a teaching to be infallible "from the chair" of Peter. The Latin term for "from the chair" is *ex cathedra*. This type of teaching is very rare. The last time a pope issued an ex cathedra teaching was Pope Pius XII's teaching on the Assumption of Mary (see the subsection "Assumption" in Chapter 5, Section 3). Another action of the extraordinary magisterium is found in teachings of the entire body of bishops, in union with the pope, especially in an ecumenical council.

The authority of the Magisterium comes from Jesus; therefore it is accurate to say that the teaching of the Magisterium is connected with Christ himself. "The task of giving an authentic interpretation of the Word of God, whether in its written form or in the form of Tradition . . . has been entrusted to the bishops in communion with the successor of Peter, the Bishop of Rome" (*CCC*, 85).

Small groups meet at the Catholic synod in Rome in October 2023.

Infallible teachings of the Magisterium are not optional; they must be obeyed by Catholics. When the Magisterium "proposes a doctrine 'for belief as being divinely revealed,' and as the teaching of Christ, the definitions 'must be adhered to with the obedience of faith'" (*CCC*, 891, quoting *Dei Verbum*, 10 §2, and *Lumen Gentium*, 25 §2). The Holy Spirit is the guide and guarantor who ensures that the Magisterium always and everywhere teaches and protects the fullness of the Gospel. The Magisterium assures that individual and communally shared faith remains accurate from generation to generation.

The Holy Spirit also unites the Church to Jesus so that he and the Church form one living reality, one Body, of which the Holy Spirit can be said to be the soul—the Church's life-giving principle. **The union of Christ and his Body is not a mere metaphor. It is a living reality.** There is a real and true living personal union between Christ and the Church. This is why any discussion of Divine Revelation and faith must be centered in the Church. The Church comprises all the saints in heaven, the souls in Purgatory, and the faithful living on earth. Christ lives in his Church so completely that "Christ and his Church thus together make up the 'whole Christ' (*Christus totus*). The Church is one with Christ" (see *CCC*, 795). Our participation in the Church is a visible sign of our unseen faith in the Lord Jesus Christ.

SECTION Assessment

Comprehension

1. How does St. Paul describe the connection between Christ and the Church?

2. Who composes the Church?

3. How was St. Peter clearly able to state the identity of Jesus?

4. What is a prime task of the Magisterium?

Reflection

5. As you grow in faith in Christ, explain how you imagine yourself being a more active participant in Christ's Church.

Section Reviews

Focus Question

How does a Catholic's faith mirror the life of Jesus Christ?

Complete one of the following:

- Read Hebrews 11:1–40. Write the essential definition of faith from this passage and five other things the passage teaches you about the meaning of faith.

- The Nicene Creed states that all things were made through Jesus, the Son of God. Name two things that really remind you of Jesus and tell why. (These might be religious items such as a crucifix, a statue of a saint, or rosary beads. Or they might be things found in nature. They could even be human-made inventions that are life-giving or healing.)

- Compose a prayer that expresses your journey of faith in Jesus Christ.

Introduction
The Necessity of Faith

Review

Faith is necessary to live a Christian life. With faith, what is deemed impossible becomes possible. Jesus's own words and actions attest to the necessity of faith. The term *faith* has multiple meanings, but in common use it has to do with trust and belief. It is only tangible through its actions and response. It must be used in order for it to grow. We see examples of faith through the witness of great Christians who have come before us.

Assignment

There are several elements that make up faith (e.g., response, gift). Make a flow chart with the word *faith* at the top and list several other words below that connect with faith.

Section 1
Faith Is a Virtue

Review

Faith is the correct response to God's Revelation; it is an act of the intellect and will. Faith is an unearned gift from God; it is also one of three theological virtues, along with hope and charity. As such, faith is a gift that is infused into our souls at Baptism. There are several essential qualities of faith, including that faith must be free and that faith is both a personal act and a communal act of the Church. Faith is most commonly first proclaimed in the home, the domestic church. When you accept the gift of faith, you are on the road to eternal life.

Assignment

Explain in two or three sentences what these words of St. Catherine of Genoa have to do with faith: "Every little glimpse that can be gained of God exceeds every pain and every joy that one can conceive without it."

Section 2
I Believe: Faith Is Personal

Review

The personal response to faith must occur before we can act in communion with others, especially in the Church, the Body of Christ. Through courageous actions, intense personal prayer, and identifying with those in need, we practice living the faith and begin to make it our own. The impetus for personal faith may come in a life-changing event or, more typically, through a longer process that is often characterized by the example of parents, teachers, and priests.

Assignment

Think of one person who has shared the gift of faith with you. Name three specific things you have done to respond affirmatively to receiving that gift.

Section 3
We Believe: Faith Is Communal

Review

Faith must be communal as well as personal. The formal structures of the Church—defined and protected by the Magisterium—help both individuals and communities like families and parishes establish, express, and maintain their faith lives. If we attempt to go it alone without the help and direction of the Church, we are likely to drift into the influence of secular culture over the more rewarding, and sometimes more challenging, demands of the Church.

Assignment

Using a church bulletin or diocesan website, find an upcoming liturgy, prayer service, Eucharistic Adoration, or other sponsored event that you think might help you grow in your faith. Write as much information as you can about the event and why you think you might want to participate.

Section 4
Faith Leads Us to the Church

Review

Before his Ascension into heaven, Jesus established a community to pass on the faith and to live the faith. This community is the Catholic Church. The pope is the successor of St. Peter. According to St. Paul, the Church is the Body of Christ. This reality emphasizes the vital, life-sustaining connection the Church has with Christ. The four marks of the Church—one, holy, catholic, apostolic—are characteristics of the Church professed in the Nicene Creed.

Assignment

Think about a group you belong to (e.g., team, band, or class at school). Draw comparisons between belonging to that group and belonging to the Church as the Body of Christ. How are the experiences similar? How are they different?

Chapter Projects

Choose and complete at least one of the following projects to assess your understanding of the material in this chapter.

⚙ 1. Sing a Verse of "O Come, All Ye Faithful" in Latin

Practice singing the first verse of *Adeste Fidelis* before recording your performance on video. Set the video with a backdrop of religious or natural images. To familiarize yourself with the correct pronunciation of the words, review this phonetic guide:

Adeste fidelis	Add-es-tay fee-deh-less
Laeti triumphantes	Lay-tee tree-oom-fahn-tes
Venite, venite in Bethlehem	Ven-ee-teh, ven-ee-teh in Bethlehem
Natum videte	Na-toom vee-det-eh
regem angelorum	Reh-jem an-jeh-low-rum
Venite adoremus	Ven-ee-tay ah-door-eh-moos
Venite adoremus	Ven-ee- tay ah-door-eh-moos
Venite adoremus	Ven-ee- tay ah-door-eh-moos
Dominum.	Doh-mee-noom.

Suggestion: Watch a video recording of *Adeste Fidelis* being sung in Latin. Sing along until you have it down!

⚙ 2. Make a List of Fifteen Ways to Improve Your Catholic Faith

Write down fifteen things you can do to improve your faith. Add the following to each item:

- Why you think this item is important and how it will improve your faith.
- How you specifically will do it.

Examples might include praying a daily Rosary, going to Mass every Sunday, and doing an act of mercy.

⚙ 3. Define Church and the Connection between Jesus and the Church

The Second Vatican Council document *Lumen Gentium* (*Dogmatic Constitution on the Church*) answers several questions about Jesus's connection with the Church and the Church as the Body of Christ. Look up the document on the Vatican website (http://www.vatican.va). Use the paragraphs cited below to answer the following questions:

- What is the Church? (paragraph 4)
- Who founded the Church? (paragraph 5)
- In what sense is the Church "the mystical Body of Christ"? (paragraph 7)
- How is the Church like the Word of God who became human? (paragraph 8)

Based on chapter 1 of *Lumen Gentium*, write a clear definition of *Church*. Cite relevant passages.

⚙ 4. Research and Present Various Symbols for Jesus

Using a digital camera, take photos of symbols for Christ in local Catholic churches, schools, cemeteries, and shrines. Research the meaning of each symbol. If possible, interview staff members at the different locations for more information. Create a print or digital poster or book that presents and explains these symbols for Christ. Include an introduction that provides background information about the sites you visited.

⚙ *5. Analyze and Comment on New Testament Passages on Faith*

Locate the following New Testament passages on faith. Transcribe them on lined writing paper. Write two paragraphs on each passage, explaining what it says about faith. Use biblical references from the *New American Bible Revised Edition* to help you to explain the passages. Make sure to account for all elements in each passage.

- Acts 16:31
- Hebrews 11:1
- Hebrews 11:6
- Galatians 5:6
- James 2:26

Faithful Disciple
St. Thérèse of Lisieux

Even as a very young child, St. Thérèse of Lisieux had a sense that prayer was simply a reflection of her friendship with God.

Thérèse was the youngest of five daughters of Louis and Zélie Martin, a faith-filled couple who lived and worked in Alençon, France. There's little doubt that Thérèse, as the baby of the family, was pampered and spoiled. Even her doting mother wrote that Thérèse "flies into frightful tantrums when things don't go just right." But Zélie also saw how intelligent, loving, and good-hearted her youngest child was. Sadly, Zélie died of cancer in August 1877, when Thérèse was only four years old.

Losing her mother wounded Thérèse deeply, but it also shifted her attention to heaven and the Kingdom of God. Prayer, she began to see, was not a series of memorized words to be recited. "You don't have to be kneeling or in church to be praying," Thérèse would often say.

Thérèse felt called to a religious vocation. In 1888, she joined the Carmelites, a religious order devoted to prayer. Soon it was clear that Thérèse had insights and ideas about prayer that shocked many in her community. For instance, Thérèse often fell asleep during the long hours spent in chapel. She reasoned that God loved her while she slept, just as parents love their children just as much asleep as awake.

Thérèse made even the most ordinary events of her day part of her prayer. She called this her "little way to God" and wrote about it in her best-selling autobiography, *Story of a Soul*. St. Thérèse of Lisieux died from tuberculosis

St. Thérèse of Lisieux

at age twenty-four. She was canonized in 1925, only twenty-eight years after her death. She was named a Doctor of the Church in 1997. Her feast day is October 1.

Thérèse's parents, Louis and Zélie Martin, were canonized by Pope Francis in 2015.

Comprehension

1. What was St. Thérèse of Lisieux's early insight about prayer?
2. What religious community did St. Thérèse join?
3. What is an example of an unconventional idea Thérèse had about prayer?

Application

The "little way" St. Thérèse of Lisieux described was really her abandonment to Christ, just as he called for in Mark 8:34–35. Thérèse offered the most common nuisances of each day (e.g., the snoring of other nuns, the symptoms of a common cold) to Jesus. Make a plan to follow the "little way" for one day. Write a prayer naming and offering some things that happened to you to God.

Prayer

The Apostles' Creed is simple, short, logically ordered, and prayerful. It highlights our faith in the essential Christian doctrine of the Blessed Trinity by proclaiming

- The First Divine Person (the almighty and eternal God) and his work of creation

- The Second Divine Person (Jesus Christ, God-made-man) and his marvelous work of redemption

- The Third Divine Person (the Holy Spirit), who is the origin and sanctification that comes to us through Christ's one, holy, catholic, apostolic Church (*CCC*, 190)

Apostles' Creed

I believe in God,
the Father almighty,
Creator of heaven and earth,
and in Jesus Christ, his only Son, our Lord,
who was conceived by the Holy Spirit,
born of the Virgin Mary,
suffered under Pontius Pilate,
was crucified, died, and was buried;
he descended into hell;
on the third day he rose again from the dead;
he ascended into heaven,
and is seated at the right hand of God the Father almighty;
from there he will come to judge the living and the dead.
I believe in the Holy Spirit,
the holy catholic Church,
the communion of saints,
the forgiveness of sins,
the resurrection of the body,
and life everlasting.
Amen.

7

Jesus Calls Disciples

The Penitent Mary Magdalene

➤ Domenikos Theotokopoulos

Painter-philosopher Domenikos Theotokopoulos (1541–1614), self-proclaimed as "El Greco" (The Greek), painted five versions of *The Penitent Mary Magdalene*. The most famous one, housed in the National Museum of Fine Arts in Budapest, Hungary, is pictured here. El Greco completed this painting around 1576–1578.

Mary Magdalene was one of Jesus's closest friends, who was present with him at his Crucifixion (see John 19:25–27) and who discovered the empty tomb on Easter (see John 20:1–18). She has been portrayed in several ways over the centuries, partly because she has been connected with three distinct women in the New Testament. In a sermon in AD 591, Pope Gregory the Great proposed that these three women were all actually Mary Magdalene—the woman who witnessed the Crucifixion and found the empty tomb, the penitent prostitute who dried Jesus's feet with her hair, and the Mary who was the sister of Lazarus and Martha. The Eastern Church always viewed these three women as distinct, but due to Pope Gregory's sermon, in Western art Mary Magdalene was often depicted as a repentant sinner and a penitent prostitute. There is no evidence from the Bible that Mary Magdalene was a prostitute. The key point for us to remember is that Mary Magdalene was the first person to whom Christ appeared after his Resurrection. She is not Mary of Bethany or the sinful woman mentioned in Luke 7:36–50.

In this version of *The Penitent Mary Magdalene*, note the beam of light from the sky, which is meant to show that Mary hears God's voice and is intent on changing her heart and showing sorrow for her sins. The skull represents her mortality, while the ivy climbing up the rocky hill is thought to represent her climb to eternal life, which has been made possible by her penance.

This completed painting is nearly four by six feet in size, a relatively large canvas, and is typical of El Greco paintings in its attention to detail. The other versions of this painting highlight, add, or subtract features of both Mary Magdalene and the setting, including adding roses to her cheeks, elongating her face, and including an alabaster jar instead of the skull.

If you would like to research more about St. Mary Magdalene and why she is called the "Apostle of the Apostles," see Chapter 7 Review, Chapter Project 1.

What does it mean to be an authentic disciple of Jesus Christ?

Chapter Overview

Introduction
Becoming a Disciple (or Not)

Section 1
What Did Jesus Teach about Discipleship?

Section 2
Commitment to Jesus Is Associated with Friendship

Section 3
Disciples Help to Spread the Gospel

Section 4
Jesus Taught His Disciples How to Pray

BECOMING A DISCIPLE (OR NOT)

Faith is a gift that comes from having an encounter with the living God. As mentioned previously, the gift of faith can be opened over time; think of the person baptized as an infant and confirmed as a teenager, who comes to appreciate the gift of faith years after receiving the Sacraments of Initiation, perhaps through intellectual questioning, being inspired by a saint or a person of faith, or through a dramatic spiritual experience. In whatever way a person encounters the living God, there is a concrete connection between opening one's eyes in faith to God and becoming a disciple of Jesus Christ.

The first verses of the Gospel of Mark give a clear example of two sets of brothers who, upon encountering the living God, immediately set out on the path of discipleship. The four—brothers Simon and Andrew, and brothers James and John—were all fishermen. Jesus called to Simon and Andrew, "Come after me, and I will make you fishers of men" (Mk 1:17). They left their nets and followed him. James and John were in a boat mending their nets when Jesus called to them. They left not only their boat but their father Zebedee, who was sitting in it. From a rather obscure invitation to be "fishers of men," the rest of the Gospel tells how these four men and later other Apostles and disciples followed Jesus to Jerusalem, where he was arrested, sentenced to death, and brutally crucified. The word *disciple* means "follower." The Glossary that accompanies the *Catechism of the Catholic Church* defines disciples as "those who accepted Jesus' message to follow him."

On the other hand, there have always been people who were lukewarm to Jesus and his teachings. There have always been people who were once followers of Christ but later ignored or outright rejected him. Recall another incident described in the Gospel of Mark about the rich man who approached Jesus. The man was looking for an answer to one of the most basic human

As with Duccio's Madonna and Child *(see Chapter 1), the gold background of* The Calling of the Apostles Peter and Andrew *hints at the Byzantine style of the work. The figures of Jesus, Peter, and Andrew are painted as if they stood still and modeled for the artist, hinting at the style of the Renaissance era that is to come. Christ is standing on a rocky shore. The gold behind him creates a sense of depth on the horizon. The net of the fishermen is transparent and full of fish, held on to with two hands by Andrew and one hand by Peter. The expressions of Jesus and the two brothers are serious, much like the work of discipleship that would begin after the two left their boat.*

questions. He asked Jesus, "Good teacher, what must I do to inherit eternal life?" (Mk 10:17).

Jesus told the man to keep all of the commandments. The man told Jesus he had always done just that. Then Jesus said to him, "You are lacking in one thing. Go, sell what you have, and give to [the] poor and you will have treasure in heaven; then come, follow me" (Mk 10:21). The man went away from Jesus and did not follow him. In this case, the Gospel says, it was because "he had many possessions" (Mk 10:22).

You probably know people who have walked away from Jesus and their Catholic faith. A recent study on young adults leaving the Catholic Church reported that some people quit identifying as Catholics at the average age of thirteen, even before they stopped attending a Catholic school or parish. Why? Some of the reasons had to do with "a decline of social trust in institutions," "no involvement in religious education or youth ministry," and "dislike for the religion's rules and rigidity." What about those teens who remained in the Church? One of the initiators of the study indicated that teens who experienced a positive community atmosphere at their parish were more likely to remain Catholic and to continue to grow in their encounter with Jesus.[1] The key to the equation of faith is Jesus. Real discipleship has always involved turning away from the norms, what is comfortable, or "what everyone else is doing." A disciple of Jesus is not someone who takes his invitation to follow him, absorbs his lessons, but then retreats to a former way of life.

No one will tell you there won't be challenges in being a disciple. Mary, Jesus's first disciple, suffered by watching her Son's suffering and Death. Recall that many of Jesus's disciples from the first two centuries, including the Apostles who were originally simple fishermen, were martyred. **Today, you will still face challenges in being a true disciple—likely not death, but perhaps wonderment, ridicule, and questioning about why you continue to be an active Catholic when so many your age have chosen not to be.** However, the rewards of faith (e.g., a life based in truth, the opportunity for heaven) are so great that these challenges are worth overcoming. They can also serve as reminders to analyze how you are currently practicing your faith. It is wise to be aware of any signs of why you might be "drifting away" from the faith.

Steps to Becoming a Better Disciple

As you read earlier, the rich man did not follow Jesus because he did not want to give up his wealth. You also read about some reasons young Catholics give today for why they no longer identify with the Church.

It only takes a moment to consider why you *would* want to remain a disciple of Jesus. Here is God's Son, the perfect teacher, who is understanding, patient, and kind. Here is the one who loves perfectly, the one who gave his life for his friends so that they might have abundant eternal life with him. **This friendship Jesus offers you includes a participation in the inner life of the Blessed Trinity. He offers you the chance to live forever in eternal**

happiness. These are the reasons why it is worth it to commit yourself to be his disciple. Here are three steps to becoming a better disciple:

1. Emanating from God's call, the first step to discipleship is learning from Jesus's teaching. At this initial stage, discipleship is primarily an activity of the intellect. Disciples gather knowledge about what Jesus taught, who he is, and what he expects of them. This first step is very important. Knowing someone well can lead to a lasting personal relationship. The true disciples are those who get to know Jesus so well that they want to be with him and do what he asks. The challenge here is to understand how Jesus defined discipleship. The first disciples found this difficult to do. Fortunately, now we can learn from their misunderstandings.

2. It is Jesus himself who initiates the second step of discipleship—a deep and loving commitment—by inviting you to be his friend. In John's Gospel, Jesus says, "I have called you friends. . . . It was not you who chose me, but I who chose you and appointed you to go and bear fruit" (Jn 15:15–16).

3. The third step of discipleship is helping Jesus to share his message. This is the part of discipleship exhibited boldly by Mary, St. Peter, St. Paul, and countless other saints over the centuries. Reading about the lives of these saints and other disciples will help you stand firm in the face of challenges and remain committed to Jesus and the Church in a way that may be uncomfortable at times but also exhilarating and very much worth it.

The task of being a disciple of Jesus is to conform your life to his. This doesn't mean you have to give up your own identity; rather, when you conform your identity to his, you will discover your authentic self, who you were really created to be.

SECTION Assessment

Comprehension

1. What question did the rich man ask Jesus?

2. What was Jesus's answer?

3. What are three steps to becoming a better disciple of Jesus?

Reflection

4. What is the main reason young people drift away from practicing the Catholic faith?

5. List two possible remedies the Church might offer to keep teens from leaving the Church.

6. Name and explain three adjectives that describe being a disciple of Jesus today.

WHAT DID JESUS TEACH ABOUT DISCIPLESHIP?

Like the other Gospels, Mark's Gospel provides a focused study of what Jesus taught about discipleship. Much of this lesson on discipleship is connected with the unfolding of the mystery of God's Kingdom. In revealing to his disciples lessons about the Kingdom through miracles, parables, and other teachings, Jesus also taught them what it means to be his disciple.

As a twenty-first-century reader of Mark's Gospel, you have the opportunity to better understand Jesus's teaching on the meaning of discipleship. Note that the very first verse (1:1) of Mark is described as the "beginning of the gospel of Jesus Christ [the Son of God]." This means that you, the reader, have been given information that the first disciples did not know when they first traveled with Jesus—that he is the Christ and the Son of God. As the mystery of Jesus's identity is revealed in the Gospel of Mark, Jesus also teaches what he expects from his disciples.

Toward a Growing Understanding of Jesus and Discipleship

In the section of Mark's Gospel between 8:27 and 10:52, Jesus begins to reveal his divine mission to his disciples. As he does so, his followers come to a new and different understanding of what it means to be his disciple.

This important section is bracketed with two stories of blind men who come to Jesus for healing.∞ Note that in the first story (Mk 8:22–26), after Jesus rubs spittle in the blind man's eyes and lays hands on him, the man still has blurry vision. It takes a second effort for Jesus to restore the man's sight so that he can see everything clearly. When the miracle is complete, Jesus sends the man home, telling him to "not even go into the village" (Mk 8:26). In the healing of Bartimaeus, which concludes the section where Jesus's identity is

Christ Giving Sight to Bartimaeus by William Blake.

revealed (Mk 10:46–52), Jesus heals Bartimaeus on the first try, with only his words. "Immediately" the man receives his sight. Also, note that even though Jesus tells the healed Bartimaeus to go on *his* way, the man instead follows Jesus "on *the* way" (Mk 10:52).

Jesus uses these miracles to teach about his divinity and divine mission. "The way" is language that aptly describes discipleship. At the Last Supper,

∞ Note

Mark employs the bracketing or framing effect of placing important content between two related stories in other places in his Gospel; for example, the story of Jairus's daughter in Mark 5:21–24 breaks off to tell the story of a hemorrhaging woman in 5:25–34 only to bring the initial story to conclusion in 5:35–42. This technique encourages the reader to look to the middle of the frame for a lesson. In this example, the lesson concerns the great faith of the woman with the hemorrhage in believing that she will be healed if she just touches Jesus's cloak. Her faith stands in contrast to the doubt of those around Jairus who at first believe that Jesus cannot save the daughter from death. Taken together, the two stories highlight that faith is essential.

Jesus says, "I am the way and the truth and the life. No one comes to the Father except through me" (Jn 14:6). The early Christians used "the way" to describe the Church itself (see, e.g., Acts 9:2; 18:26; 19:9). "The way" is not a path to heaven and the Father that one travels half-heartedly. Rather, as Jesus said, he himself is "the way." To follow Jesus "on the way" as Bartimaeus did means forging a deep friendship and bond with Jesus. It means incorporating the pattern of Jesus's life into our own life. This is part of what it means to be a disciple.

The Meaning of Discipleship

Within the "picture frame" of the two blind-man stories in Mark 8:27–10:52, Jesus's three predictions of his Passion and Death provide the key lessons about the meaning of discipleship. Just as you would look closely at the picture that is bordered by a frame, this is the part of this section of the Gospel that Mark wishes you to look at intently.

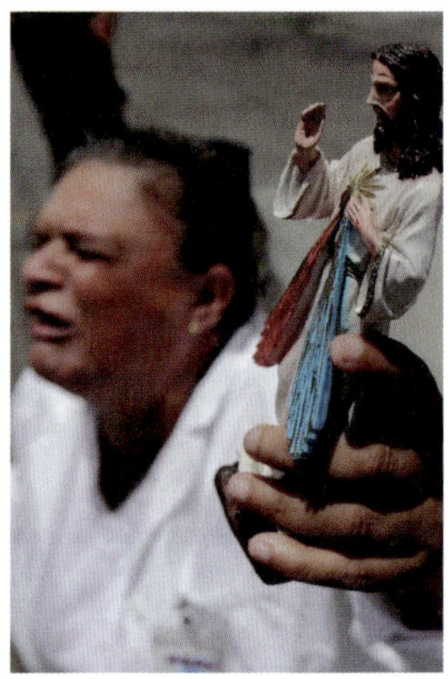

Catholics face hardships today walking the road of discipleship. In the first four years of the presidency of Daniel Ortega in Nicaragua there were 190 attacks on Catholic churches. After fourteen Catholics died at the hands of government forces in 2018, this woman knelt in prayer as a motorcade with the Catholic bishop passed by.

In the first prediction, Jesus tells the disciples "that the Son of Man must suffer greatly and be rejected" (Mk 8:31). When Peter argues with Jesus for saying this, Jesus tells Peter to "get behind me" and calls him "Satan." Jesus says that Peter is thinking not like God but like a human being. Jesus then explains the conditions of discipleship: "Whoever wishes to come after me must deny himself, take up his cross, and follow me. For whoever wishes to save his life will lose it, but whoever loses his life for my sake and that of the gospel will save it" (Mk 8:34–35).

A second prediction of his Passion and Death, in Mark 9:30–32, is followed by another lesson on discipleship. Overhearing the disciples argue about which one of them is the greatest, Jesus explains, "If anyone wishes to be first, he shall be the last of all and the servant of all" (Mk 9:35). He puts a child in their midst to emphasize that the work of a disciple is to minister to the poor and lowly. Jesus uses the child as a symbol for the *anawim*—that is, the poor in spirit he speaks of in the Beatitudes.

Finally, just before arriving at the gates of Jerusalem, Jesus tells his disciples for the third time what will happen to him: he will be handed over to Gentiles, who will treat him cruelly and put him to death. But on the third day he will rise. From reading the gospel account, it seems that at least two of the disciples still do not understand that being a follower of Jesus means giving up one's own possessions and desires and serving others, especially the poor and lowly. James and John ask Jesus if they might be the ones to sit at his right and left when he enters the Kingdom. Clearly they don't grasp his message of service and humility. But there is a positive sign: the other ten Apostles "became indignant at James and John" (Mk 10:41) for even asking this question. This portion of the Gospel ends with the Apostles beginning to know the meaning of discipleship. What Jesus says to them next is, in many ways, the climax of the Gospel because both the mystery of Jesus's identity as Messiah and the full criteria of discipleship are revealed:

> You know that those who are recognized as rulers over the Gentiles lord it over them, and their great ones make their authority over them felt. But it shall not be so among you. Rather, whoever wishes to be great among you will be your servant; whoever wishes to be first among you will be the slave of all. For the Son of Man did not come to be served but to serve and to give his life as a ransom for many. (Mk 10:42–45)

Jesus's teachings about discipleship apply to us today, especially in these ways:

We must put God's desires for our life above our own.

Maybe this means something simple, like going to a younger sibling's school open house instead of spending the evening out with friends. It could mean accepting the fact that we have to attend the local college rather than our "dream school." Or it could mean something more serious, such as accepting an illness that befalls us or someone close to us.

> *We must be the humble servant of others, especially the poor.*

In everyday life situations around high school, this can be translated to interacting with *everyone*, not just those in our peer group, class, ethnic group, with the same economic status, and so on. Taken further, this type of service means intentionally seeking out those in our family, local community, and the larger world who are in need and providing them assistance.

Finally, being a disciple of Jesus Christ means being willing to give up everything for him, even our life. This is what so many Christian martyrs have done in the Church's history.

SECTION Assessment

Comprehension

1. Give three examples of how Jesus lived out his words in Mark 10:45.

2. What were the differences in the healings of the two blind men in Mark's Gospel? What are those differences meant to represent?

3. How does the Church understand the meaning of "the way"?

Reflection

4. Name a practical way you or someone you know "takes up the cross" for Jesus in everyday life.

5. If you were going to name a symbol of *anawim* from today's world, who would it be?

COMMITMENT TO JESUS IS ASSOCIATED WITH FRIENDSHIP

In the pivotal section of Mark's Gospel (8:27–10:52) described in the previous section, Jesus both reveals his identity as Messiah (the Christ) and defines the meaning of discipleship. By the time this section of the Gospel concludes, the disciples begin to understand that discipleship involves suffering and sacrifice. The second blind man, Bartimaeus, who was healed immediately by Jesus, symbolizes the goal of all disciples: to be able to follow Jesus, "the way," into God's Kingdom.

In the first step of discipleship, followers of Jesus focus on learning about him and what discipleship entails. We gather knowledge about what Jesus taught and who he is. We do so with an open heart to God in prayer and to the witness of other Christians. This "head knowledge" of Jesus leads to "heart knowledge." Knowing Jesus leads to friendship with him. It leads to loving him.∞

It is Jesus himself who invites us to take the second step of discipleship—a deeper commitment to him in love. He takes the initiative by calling us friends (see John 15:15–16).

∞ Note

Faith is relational; God is a personal God who loves us and wants to be our friend. Jesus told his disciples, "I no longer call you slaves, because a slave does not know what his master is doing. I have called you friends, because I have told you everything I have heard from my Father" (Jn 15:15). Faith is also intellectual. It is an act of our intellect conforming to God's will. St. Thomas Aquinas wrote that our intellect must be well formed in order to affirm our faith. Finally, faith is connected with hope. The more we understand what we say we believe, the more we have hope in its outcomes.

Jesus Formed Many Deep Friendships

Among his disciples, Jesus formed many deep friendships. His Apostles were certainly counted among his closest friends. Commitment and friendship go hand in hand. Think about the friends in your life you have been loyal to and willing to follow.

Imagine the particulars of Jesus's friendship with the Apostles. With these Galilean men Jesus traveled dusty roads, encountered a variety of weather conditions, cooked and shared meals, and slept under the open sky. The Gospels tell of a close friendship Jesus had with one of the Apostles: John, son of Zebedee. This is the Apostle who is known as "beloved" or "the disciple Jesus loved." It was to John that Jesus entrusted the care of the Blessed Mother, saying to him as he hung from the Cross, "Behold, your mother" (Jn 19:27).

Jesus had other close friends, for whom he was literally willing to risk his life. We see this in the story of Lazarus, related in John 11:1–44. Jesus received word from sisters Mary and Martha that their brother, Lazarus, had died.

Christ in the household of Martha and Mary.

They wanted Jesus to come to their home in Bethany, a village just outside of Jerusalem. The problem for Jesus and those who were traveling with him was that he had just been chased from nearby Jerusalem by a stone-throwing mob (see John 10:31–32). When Jesus told his disciples they were going back to Judea, they said to him, "Rabbi, the Jews were just trying to stone you, and you want to go back there?" (Jn 11:8). When Jesus insisted that they go, the Apostle Thomas said, "Let us also go to die with him" (Jn 11:16).

Jesus's raising of Lazarus showed the depth of his friendship. When Jesus saw how upset Mary and the other friends of Lazarus were, "he became perturbed and deeply troubled" (Jn 11:33). When he reached the tomb where Lazarus was laid, Jesus displayed the deepest emotions of friendship. The Gospel reports that "Jesus wept" (Jn 11:35). Some of the Jews who were there to witness the miracle of Jesus's raising of Lazarus noted, "See how he loved him" (Jn 11:36).

Along with Mary and Martha, Jesus counted many other women among his friends. For example, Salome, the mother of the Apostles James and John, traveled openly along with other women and Jesus's disciples. This was unique because, in Jesus's time and culture, women were viewed as inferior. Jesus did not abide by that judgment. Such friendships would have certainly attracted attention. Even Jesus's own disciples were amazed that Jesus associated with women. Note their reaction to Jesus's encounter with the Samaritan woman in John 4:27.

Mary Magdalene, by all accounts, was one of Jesus's closest friends. Her name is mentioned fourteen times in the Gospels, more than many of the Apostles. Whenever the women who traveled with Jesus are listed in the Gospels, Mary Magdalene is always named first. In fact, the only time her name does not appear first is when she is identified at the foot of Jesus's Cross. On that occasion, the name of Mary, Jesus's mother, appears first. Jesus first encountered Mary Magdalene and other Galilean women while traveling from village to village. He cured them of evil spirits and Mary Magdalene, in particular, of "seven demons" (Lk 8:2).

With friendship also comes the risk of betrayal. Certainly this is a common experience in friendships today. Jesus was aware of the shortcomings of his friends. He forgave Peter, who denied knowing him, and Thomas, who doubted his Resurrection. His cruelest betrayal occurred when Judas Iscariot turned him over to be arrested by Roman soldiers in the Garden of Gethsemane. When Judas approached Jesus to identify him

St. Mary Magdalene was the first to encounter the Risen Jesus.

with the sign of a kiss, Jesus said, "Friend, do what you have come for" (Mt 26:50).

Being a disciple of Jesus involves a lasting commitment. It's pretty hard to make a commitment to someone you don't know or like as a friend. Certainly the Apostles and the women who traveled with Jesus would not have been so deeply committed to him if they did not relate to him as a friend. Our task for discipleship is similar to theirs: to grow in friendship with Jesus.

Deepening Your Friendship with Jesus

Because you have human friends, you have a concept of what friendship means. But it's important to view the subject at a deeper level when considering your friendship with Jesus, the Son of God and the Second Divine Person of the Holy Trinity. Jesus Christ is not merely *a* friend; he is *the* answer to every human longing. You are called to actually become one with Christ, primarily through reception of him in the Eucharist. Therefore, friendship with him is unlike any human friendship.

Jesus is always with you. In fact, it is precisely because Jesus is alive—risen from the dead—that you can have a personal relationship with him. He is a friend who carries you through life, shares your joys, and picks you up when you are struggling. It is by his grace alone that you are able to endure the sufferings of life. He is constantly beckoning you into relationship, but you have free will in choosing whether to respond to him in prayer and take notice of the different ways he comes to you. Jesus lives out his friendship with self-sacrificing love and generosity. In his commitment to people, Jesus both invites us to friendship and defines the true meaning of friendship. At the Last Supper, he says,

> No one has greater love than this, to lay down one's life for one's friends. You are my friends if you do what I command you. I no longer call you slaves, because a slave does not know what his master is doing. I have called you friends, because I have told you everything I have heard from my Father. It was not you who chose me, but I who chose you and appointed you to go and bear fruit. (Jn 15:13–16)

Directly before these verses on friendship, Jesus says that he is the "true vine" (Jn 15:1). He exhorts his disciples, "Remain in me, as I remain in you. Just as a branch cannot bear fruit on its own unless it remains on the vine, so neither can you unless you remain in me. I am the vine, you are the branches. Whoever remains in me and I in him will bear much fruit, because without me you can do nothing" (Jn 15:4–5). This shows the type of friendship to which he is calling his disciples. It is a friendship of *remaining* or *abiding*. Christ isn't just someone who walks next to you; rather, you are to enter into profound *communion* with him. Again, this is more intensely life-changing than any human friendship.

"I have given you a model to follow, so that as I have done for you, you should also do" (Jn 13:15).

Jesus has chosen us to be his friends, but a friendship with Christ has a profound impact on every aspect of our life. To be friends with Jesus, our life must change. Again, this is only possible by his grace. We must keep the two greatest commandments, love of God and love of neighbor (see Matthew 22:34–40). Expanding on this, Jesus's own words, recorded in the New Testament, offer several additional ways our lives should be transformed by friendship with Jesus. Also, these very words are ways to form a friendship with Jesus, acknowledging that he is unlike other friends because he is not standing before us in flesh and bone as they are. His words uncover a way for us to be friends with him in a different way, a deeper way.

1 Believe in Jesus

I am the resurrection and the life; whoever believes in me, even if he dies, will live, and everyone who lives and believes in me will never die. Do you believe this? (Jn 11:25–26)

2 Invite Jesus into Your Life

Behold, I stand at the door and knock. If anyone hears my voice and opens the door, [then] I will enter his house and dine with him, and he with me. (Rv 3:20)

3 Love God

You shall love the Lord, your God, with all your heart, with all your soul, and with all your mind. This is the greatest and the first commandment. (Mt 22:37–38)

4 Put the Son of God First

Whoever loves father or mother more than me is not worthy of me, and whoever loves son or daughter more than me is not worthy of me. (Mt 10:37)

5 Love Others

Love one another. As I have loved you, so you also should love one another. This is how all will know that you are my disciples, if you have love for one another. (Jn 13:34–35)

6 Serve Others

If I, therefore, the master and teacher, have washed your feet, you ought to wash one another's feet. I have given you a model to follow, so that as I have done for you, you should also do. (Jn 13:14–15)

7 Forgive Others

Then Peter approaching asked him, "Lord, if my brother sins against me, how often must I forgive him? As many as seven times?" Jesus answered, "I say to you, not seven times but seventy-seven times." (Mt 18:21–22)

8 **Witness to Jesus without Fear**

Do not be afraid. . . . I tell you, everyone who acknowledges me before others the Son of Man will acknowledge before the angels of God. (Lk 12:7, 8)

Because he is the Son of God, Jesus cares about every detail of our life, even those aspects that may seem mundane or unimportant. He has a true concern regarding what we are interested in, whether it's sports, music, drama, and so forth. Who, after all, put those interests and desires within us? In return, Jesus wants us to use and develop those talents. When we do, we are praising God and drawing others to him.

SECTION *Assessment*

Comprehension

1. Describe four occasions from the Gospels in which Jesus treated others as friends.

2. Tell how Jesus took risks in offering his friendship—relating to people who were usually rejected or hated by others.

Reflection

3. Which three of the eight requests Jesus made about friendship do you find the most important? Explain your response.

4. What would be some benefits for you in becoming a better friend with Jesus?

5. What are at least three ways you can work with God's grace to improve your friendship with Jesus?

DISCIPLES HELP TO SPREAD THE GOSPEL

Rising above the pressures of peers, family members, and society itself in order to live a life of committed discipleship will never be a passive exercise. Disciples must do much more than simply learn about Jesus and cultivate a personal friendship with him and commitment to him. A practical step of discipleship is putting our faith in Jesus into action. We do this by sharing the Gospel with others, an exercise called **evangelization**.

The first disciples took seriously Jesus's Great Commission to evangelize the world, described at the end of the Gospel of Matthew (28:16–20). Jesus sent his followers out to the ends of the earth to make even more disciples. As Jesus had commanded them, they went to baptize and teach everything that he had taught them:

- to forgive others
- to repent for sins
- to love God above everything and one's neighbor as oneself
- to serve
- to share Jesus's message of peace, justice, and mercy with everyone

Young pilgrims wait outside of a municipal building in Rio de Janeiro in 2013 hoping to catch a glimpse of Pope Francis, who was meeting with Brazilian leaders.

This task of evangelization is a "messy" business for a disciple. Who says so?

evangelization The bringing of the Good News of Jesus Christ to others through words and actions.

Pope Francis. At the 2013 World Youth Day in Brazil, he told thousands of young people,

> I expect a mess. There will be one. There will be a mess here in Rio. But I want a mess in dioceses! I want people to go out! I want the Church to go out to the street! I want us to defend ourselves against everything that is worldliness, that is installation, that is comfortableness, that is clericalism, that is being shut-in on ourselves. The parishes, the schools, the institutions exist to go out![2]

The need for the Church to go out in the world is also the central theme of Pope Francis's apostolic exhortation *Evangelii Gaudium* (*The Joy of the Gospel*). The title refers to the way the pope views the details of evangelization; "An evangelizer must never look like someone who has just come back from a funeral," he wrote (para. 10). In other words, the joy of the Good News must always reverberate as we live out the challenges of discipleship.∞

∞ Note

Similarly, in the closing words of the Second Vatican Council on December 8, 1965, Pope Paul VI addressed his message to the youth. Think about how his words have been enacted in the years since and how they apply to today's generation:

> It is for you, youth, especially for you that the Church now comes through her council to enkindle your light, the light which illuminates the future, your future. The Church is anxious that this society that you are going to build up should respect the dignity, the liberty and the rights of individuals. These individuals are you. The Church is particularly anxious that this society should allow free expansion to her treasure ever ancient and ever new, namely faith, and that your souls may be able to bask freely in its helpful light. She has confidence that you will find such strength and such joy that you will not be tempted, as were some of your elders, to yield to the seductions of egoistic or hedonistic philosophies or to those of despair and annihilation, and that in the face of atheism, a phenomenon of lassitude and old age, you will know how to affirm your faith in life and in what gives meaning to life, that is to say, the certitude of the existence of a just and good God.

Joyful Teen Disciples

Do you know any people your age who are truly committed disciples? You might want to pause before you answer that question. You certainly do know many committed people your own age. The high school years are chock-full of examples of dedicated commitment. Consider, for example, the commitment it takes to

complete a broad academic course of study, often including college preparatory classes

make an athletic team and compete against rival schools

memorize a part in a school play

master a musical composition, maybe while learning marching steps

work at a part-time job, maybe in a high-pressure retail situation

The list is more encompassing than these examples, of course. Add to it the commitments necessary to meet the requests of immediate family members and close friends, and you can make a case that high-school-age teens live some of the most committed lives of all.

What about a commitment to Jesus and the Catholic faith? Certainly there are teens who are among the most committed disciples. Again, you can probably look around your school and see daily examples of service, prayer, and worship. But it's important in modern society (with statistics backing up

South Korean pilgrims celebrate the announcement by Pope Francis that their nation will host the 2025 World Youth Day.

the reality that teens and young adults are straying from the faith) to reach out to Catholics your age who have left or have considered leaving the Church. This task isn't for a select few; it is for everyone.

Ten years after the World Youth Day in Rio de Janeiro, Pope Francis told those gathered at the 2023 World Youth Day in Lisbon, Portugal, that the Church is meant to be a home for "everyone, everyone, everyone!" ("*todos, todos, todos,*" in Spanish and Portuguese). "This is the Church," the pope said, "the mother of all; there is room for all." It is our task to make sure that everyone hears these welcoming words.

How do you do so? Think about strong action words that accompany the work of evangelization. You can start with the following actions:

Greet. A sincere smile, nod, or glance toward another is a friendly, simple step to acknowledge their presence and worth.

Engage. Who do you know who is in need of a friend? How can your offer of friendship be a sign of Christ's love?

Question. What is it that keeps your peers from the love of Christ and participation in the Church? Some may cite certain issues that are bothering them. Others may be at a loss for words, perhaps acknowledging that their faith has been idle because of their own lack of effort. In any case, bring them the offer of Christ's promise of fullness of life in this world and the next. As Pope Francis preached at the 2013 Brazil World Youth Day, "[Jesus] never disappoints anyone! Only in Christ crucified and risen can we find salvation and redemption. With him, evil, suffering, and death do not have the last word, because he gives us hope and life."

Invite. Certainly, an invitation to Mass or a parish-sponsored youth event would be an appropriate step here. But it's not the only step. Remember, Jesus's call to discipleship is rooted in friendship. As a disciple of Christ, you can be a friend to those you wish to reach. Jesus connected and formed friendships with people of all kinds. Do the same. This isn't an exercise in popularity. Rather, make a sincere effort to be friends to all, especially those with the most need.

We live in a world where information is ever flowing and attention spans seem to be growing ever shorter. Pope Francis admitted, "We are impatient, anxious to see the whole picture, but God lets us see things slowly, quietly." He calls for a Church that accompanies all people on their journey of faith—"a Church which realizes that the reasons why people leave also contain reasons why they can eventually return."

Heaven Is the Goal of Discipleship

At the 1994 Miss America competition, Miss Alabama, Heather Whitestone, was asked, "Would you want to live forever?" She responded in part, "I would not want to live forever. Because if we were supposed to live forever, then we would live forever." Obviously Whitestone was associating the question with living forever on earth. However, God does want us to live forever with him in

The Issue of **Wealth** and **Discipleship**

Focus Question: What does it mean to be an authentic disciple of Jesus Christ?

In the Gospels, Jesus never specifically condemns wealth in relation to being his disciple; however, he makes it clear that wealth can be an extra burden to discipleship. To illustrate this, he uses the analogy of a camel moving through the eye of a needle (see Matthew 19:24). Many Scripture scholars suggest that in this story Jesus is actually referring to one of the gates of Jerusalem, a gate called "The Needle's Eye." To help protect the city, this gate was built so low that a camel could only enter on its knees and without baggage strapped to its back. Since being on one's knees is a sign of submission, Jesus is also saying something about the attitude or disposition of a wealthy person's heart.

In describing wealth as a burden, Jesus questioned traditional Jewish teaching. To the Jews, great wealth had long been seen as a sign of God's favor. The Apostles and others who heard Jesus talking about the "burdens of wealth" were shocked. Today, the Church echoes the gospel teaching of Jesus. Although in itself wealth is not evil, excessive attachment to affluence *is* evil and violates the mandate Jesus issued in Matthew 25, in the parable of the judgment of the nations. Those who do not answer the needs of the hungry, the thirsty, the naked, and the imprisoned will be judged harshly, Jesus warns.

The obligation to share one's material wealth for the good of others is one of the **precepts of the Church**. This precept, or law, requires Catholics to help

---

precepts of the Church Basic obligations all Catholics are called to follow to help them become good and moral people. The precepts include attending Mass on Sundays and holy days of obligation, confessing one's sins at least once a year, receiving Holy Communion as a minimum requirement during the Easter season, observing days of fasting and abstinence, and providing for the needs of the Church.

provide for the needs of the Church and her outreach to the needy. Tithing of a percentage of income has long been advised as part of both Christianity and Judaism. The word *tithe* has origins in an Anglo-Saxon word that means "a tenth," with the goal of offering 10 percent of one's income to support the needs of the Church. The Church uses the income from tithing to offer divine worship, for apostolic works and works of charity, and to sustain the lives of priests. This income is also used to support the needs of the poor. Regarding tithing, a Catholic may choose to divide the total tithing amount among a variety of worthy causes within and outside of the Church, such as Catholic Relief Services, right-to-life organizations, and local food pantries. As the *Catechism of the Catholic Church* states, "Love for the poor is incompatible with immoderate love of riches or their selfish use" (2445).

Being generous with our monetary wealth is just one aspect of the generosity required of a Christian disciple. God was completely generous in his entire life, Death, Resurrection, and glorious Ascension into heaven. We can never match God's generosity through our own actions. Also, neither God nor the Church demands a set amount of money. Rather, he wants us to give not only from our monetary wealth but from the wealth of our heart, which can also translate to our actions that serve those in most need.

Comprehension

1. What do you think Jesus is saying about wealth through his analogy of a camel passing through the eye of a needle?
2. What is the warning in Matthew 25 that Jesus wants us to pay attention to?
3. How does the Church use income from tithing?
4. Besides donating monetarily to the Church, what is another charitable institution you might give to?

Reflection

How might you designate your donation of charitable gifts? Be specific.

heaven—a perfect life of supreme happiness with God and the **Communion of Saints** for all eternity. Heaven is the goal of discipleship and our faith in Jesus.∞

Jesus wants everyone in heaven, "but," in the words of Pope Benedict XVI, "with one and the same condition: that of making the effort to follow him and imitate him, taking up one's cross, as he did, and dedicating one's life to the service of our brothers and sisters." **Taking up our cross—that is, accepting and offering the challenges that come before us—is not an easy, accepted, or fashionable course of life these days.** But Jesus makes it the very criterion of how he will judge us and others.

Jesus said, "Whoever wishes to come after me must deny himself, take up his cross, and follow me" (Mt 16:24).

In the parable of the judgment of the nations (Mt 25:31–46), Jesus is very clear about how he will judge: "Amen, I say to you, whatever you did for one of these least brothers of mine, you did for me" (Mt 25:40). The basis for our own judgment as an effective disciple will be what we did or did not do for others.

∞ Note

Twentieth-century media evangelist Archbishop Fulton J. Sheen once explained that the reason we wouldn't want to live on earth for unlimited years is because we are living in time. However, in heaven, we will live apart from time, which will make it happy and blissful. Sheen explained, "Have you ever noticed that your happiest moments have come when eternity almost seemed to get inside your soul? When you are not conscious of time at all. This is a hint of what heaven must be. It must be outside of time, where you can possess all joys at one and the same full moment.

Communion of Saints The unity among members of Christ's Body, living and deceased, made possible by Baptism. The Communion of Saints is the Church on earth, in heaven, and in Purgatory.

SECTION Assessment

Comprehension

1. How did Pope Francis describe *evangelization*?

2. What are the criteria for judgment?

Vocabulary

3. What does it mean to say that evangelization is a "messy" business for a disciple?

4. Who are members of the Communion of Saints?

5. Name the precepts of the Church.

Reflection

6. Who is someone your age who is a committed disciple of Jesus? Explain why.

7. Has there been a time when you noticed that your own faith and participation in the Church were waning? What did you do about it?

8. Who is someone in your school or class who would make a good priest or consecrated religious? How can you let this person know that you think so?

JESUS TAUGHT HIS DISCIPLES HOW TO PRAY

Prayer is an indispensable component of discipleship. Prayer is essentially "conversation with God." It is the form of communication between you and your friend Jesus. In the case of your own close friends, you probably communicate with each other in some form several times a day. Imagine if you didn't. Your friendship would certainly diminish and eventually just fade away. You can probably look back to a person who was once a close friend in grade school or middle school who you aren't as close with now. It's a good chance one of the reasons is that you stopped communicating with each other.

Pope Francis suggested treating prayer like training to get in top physical shape. At the 2013 World Youth Day he told teens and young adults that "Jesus offers us the possibility of a fruitful life, a life of happiness; he also offers us a future with him, an endless future, in eternal life. . . . But he asks that we train ourselves 'to get in shape,' so that we can face every situation in

World Youth Day, Kraków, 2016, soccer game.

life undaunted, bearing witness to our faith." **The "training" Pope Francis suggested is the resolve to love, listen to, and forgive one another. It is also to participate in the sacraments, "which make [Christ's] life grow within us and conform us to Christ."** The training for discipleship demands a commitment to deepen our relationship with Jesus through personal prayer. "How do we get in shape?" Pope Francis asked the youth. "By talking with him: by prayer, which is our daily conversation with God, who always listens to us."∞

Through his own words and example, Jesus taught several important practices of prayer and even how to pray, sharing the words of the Lord's Prayer, or Our Father.

Jesus Teaches about Prayer

The Gospels—especially the Gospel of Luke—include many occasions when Jesus went off to pray by himself. For example, after his Baptism and before beginning his ministry, Jesus went into the desert to pray for forty days (see Luke 4:1–13). He also retreated to prayer before making important decisions, including the night before choosing his Apostles (see Luke 4:42). Note as well these other times Jesus prayed:

Jesus teaches his disciples to pray.

- After healing those who were ill, "he would withdraw to deserted places to pray" (Lk 5:16).

- Just prior to Peter's first confession of Jesus as Messiah, Jesus "was praying in solitude" (Lk 9:18).

- After the miraculous feeding of the five thousand, Jesus dismissed the crowds and "went up on the mountain by himself to pray" (Mt 14:23).

Of course, Jesus also prayed in solitude the night before he died. The Gospel of Luke describes this as Jesus's "custom" to seek out a place and time for prayer.

∞ Note

Pope Francis strongly encourages making prayer a habit that we do at the same time each day, preferably in the morning so that we can extend an invitation to God to walk with us through each moment of our day. "It is prayer that transforms this day into grace, or better, that transforms us: it quells anger, sustains love, multiplies joy, and instills the strength to forgive" (General Audience, February 10, 2021).

Here are seven lessons Jesus taught about prayer.

1 Pray with Sincerity

Sincerity, associated with truthfulness, is a virtue that Jesus practiced and preached about. He said (in regard to taking oaths), "Let your 'Yes' mean 'Yes,' and your 'No' mean 'No'" (Mt 5:37). With this level of sincerity, taking an oath is unnecessary as all of our words and actions will be imbued with sincerity. We take our true selves to God in prayer. He sees us as we truly are. To counteract any temptation to hypocrisy when we pray, Jesus said to "go to your inner room, close the door, and pray to your Father in secret" (Mt 6:6). In a quiet room we can spend some time in peace with God. Being alone helps us to keep our motives pure. When we are alone, we aren't there to impress anyone. We are there to talk with God.

2 Pray with Confidence

Jesus taught that we should pray with the confidence of little children, who, when they ask their parents to take care of a need (e.g., "I want dinner" or "Wipe my nose"), are 100 percent confident that their parents will respond and come to their aid. Addressing parents, Jesus said, "Which one of you would hand his son a stone when he asks for a loaf of bread, or a snake when he asks for a fish? If you then, who are wicked, know how to give good gifts to your children, how much more will your heavenly Father give good things to those who ask him" (Mt 7:9–11).

3 Pray with Persistence

Do you recall the parable Jesus told of a widow and a judge (see Luke 18:1–8)? The judge was one-sided and powerful, and he ignored the widow. The widow was powerless and defenseless. There was no way she could influence the judge to decide for her, and there were little consequences to him if he ruled against her. But he did decide for the widow because she kept badgering him and would not take no for an answer. Jesus adds, "Will not God then secure the rights of his chosen ones who call out to him day and night?" (Lk 18:7). Pope Francis said to think of persistence in prayer like a houseplant. "We need to water it consistently every day. We cannot soak it and then leave it without giving it water for a week. Even more so with prayer," the pope said.[3]

4 Pray with Faith

An increase in faith should accompany your persistence in prayer. Jesus told the Apostles, "If you have faith the size of a mustard seed, you would say to [this] mulberry tree, 'Be uprooted and planted in the sea,' and it would obey you" (Lk 17:6). St. Thérèse of Lisieux (see the Faithful Disciple profile "St. Thérèse of Lisieux" in Chapter 6) said that when we pray, "We must abandon the future into the hands of God." Praying with faith is both a sign of our faith and a request for more faith. The Apostles said to Jesus, "Increase our faith" (Lk 17:5). Jesus tells them even with faith as small as the mustard seed they will be able to do momentous things. "Whatever you ask for in prayer with faith, you will receive" (Mt 21:22), Jesus also said.

5 Pray with a Forgiving Heart

Jesus said, "When you stand to pray, forgive anyone against whom you have a grievance, so that your heavenly Father may in turn forgive you your transgressions" (Mk 11:25). The Lord's Prayer (see the subsection "Prayers" in the Appendix) states this as a requirement in one of its petitions: "And forgive us our trespasses, as we forgive those who trespass against us." According to the second part of the petition, our prayer will not be heard unless we meet the strict requirement of forgiving anyone who has sinned against us. Christian forgiveness extends to forgiveness of our enemies: "Forgiveness is a high-point of Christian prayer; only hearts attuned to God's compassion can receive the gift of prayer" (*CCC*, 2844).

6 Pray with Others

We are also to pray with others and in public, for Jesus said he is present "where two or three are gathered together in my name" (Mt 18:20). These occasions of prayer include small prayer groups, praying with your family, and praying with a friend. Of course Christ is also present when we pray with the larger church community in a sacramental liturgy. Sacramental liturgy is different from informal small group prayer in that it is a public rite. Pope Francis said, "Every time we celebrate a Baptism, or consecrate the bread and wine in Eucharist, or anoint the body of a sick person with holy oil, Christ is here! It is he who acts and is present just as when he healed the weak limbs of a sick person, or when he delivered his testament for the salvation of the world at the Last Supper."[4]

7 Pray with Him

Jesus asked his disciples in the garden the night before his Death to keep watch with him for one hour (see Matthew 26:40). Jesus also wants us to remain near. At the World Youth Day in Lisbon, hundreds of thousands of young Catholics dropped to their knees at the presence of the **monstrance** after Pope Francis's address. Prayer before the Blessed Sacrament in adoration is like hanging out with a good friend without having to say a word. You know and experience the love between you just by being close.

Jesus also used the example of prayer when teaching important religious lessons. For example, in the parable of the Pharisee and the tax collector (Lk 18:9–14), the Pharisee prays with an air of superiority ("O God, I thank you that I am not like the rest of humanity"), while the tax collector approaches God as a humble sinner. Jesus uses this example to teach that those who humble themselves will be exalted. Jesus also reminded his disciples that he is their intercessor. They can ask the Father for anything in his name, and "I will do it" (Jn 14:14).

Jesus Teaches the Our Father

Jesus taught his disciples the Our Father, the perfect Christian prayer. Church Father Tertullian called the Lord's Prayer "the summary of the whole Gospel." The Our Father appears in both Matthew's and Luke's Gospels.

monstrance A sacred vessel that holds the Blessed Sacrament when it is exposed for veneration. The word *monstrance* comes from the Latin word for "show."

The version in Matthew 6:9–13 appears in the context of the Sermon on the Mount, where Jesus instructs his followers to be authentic, to pray with trust in God, and to forgive others. The *Catechism of the Catholic Church* addresses the connection: "The Sermon on the Mount is teaching for life, the Our Father is a prayer; but in both the one and the other the Spirit of the Lord gives new form to our desires" (2764). In Luke's Gospel, Jesus is praying in a quiet place when the Apostles come and ask him to teach them to pray, "just as John [the Baptist] taught his disciples" (Lk 11:1). Jesus then teaches them the Our Father.

The uniqueness of the Our Father is that Jesus offers more than just a mechanical formula for prayer. **Jesus infuses in those who pray the Our Father the Holy Spirit, "by whom these words become in us 'spirit and life'" (*CCC*, 2766).** This means that in praying the Our Father, we are assumed into the mission of the Second and Third Persons of the Blessed Trinity. We are invited to participate by divine adoption in the unique and intimate relationship of Christ as the eternal Son of the Father.

SECTION Assessment

Comprehension

1. Name two occasions when Jesus withdrew to pray by himself.

2. What did St. Thérèse of Lisieux say about the meaning of prayer?

3. What are the two settings for Jesus's sharing the Our Father?

Reflection

4. Write your own definition of prayer.

5. How can you apply Jesus's custom to seek out a time and place for regular prayer to your own life?

Section Reviews

Focus Question

What does it mean to be an authentic disciple of Jesus Christ?

Complete one of the following:

- Read the entire story of Jesus's encounter with the rich man in Mark 10:17–31. Then create a scenario in which the rich man changes his mind and returns to Jesus. Write an introduction to the scene and some dialogue between the rich man and Jesus. *Optional*: Choose a classmate to read your script and enact the scene with you.

- The First Letter of John (2:5–6) shares a concise summary of discipleship: "This is the way we may know that we are in union with him: whoever claims to abide in him ought to live [just] as he [Jesus] lived." Write a story about a moral dilemma that teens face each day. Resolve the dilemma by telling how the main character in the story should behave like Jesus.

- Read Galatians 3:1–29. Imitate St. Paul's fiery style by writing a letter to a group of Catholics your age who have stopped going to Mass. Use persuasive language to convince them that the Church needs them.

Introduction

Becoming a Disciple (or Not)

Review

An effective disciple of Jesus cannot be lukewarm in belief or practice. Unfortunately, many Catholics—including teenagers—are drifting away from the faith. They list several reasons for this, though only a small number of people say they do not believe in God. Declining commitment to the Church is a discouraging phenomenon because the rewards of discipleship are so great: developing a friendship of communion with Jesus, the one who redeemed the world and makes a place for you in heaven.

Assignment

Interview two people you know, one who is a practicing Catholic and another who has strayed away from the practice of the faith. Ask each to name at least three reasons for his or her current choice. Write down their reasons. Write something you said to each person at the end of the interviews.

Section 1

What Did Jesus Teach about Discipleship?

Review

During the central part of the Gospel of Mark (8:27–10:52), Jesus not only reveals his identity as the Messiah but also explains what it means to be his disciple. He teaches that discipleship means denying yourself, taking up your cross, and following the Lord. This translates to putting God's desires for your life above your own and being a humble servant of others, especially the poor.

Assignment

Why did Jesus say that wealth often gets in the way of discipleship commitments? How would you describe the proper use of wealth?

Section 2

Commitment to Jesus Is Associated with Friendship

Review

Discipleship is more than just knowing *about* Jesus. Rather, knowing about Jesus leads to a second step of discipleship: forming a deep friendship and intimate communion with him. Jesus modeled friendship throughout his time on earth. He had many friends, including his Apostles and a group of women followers who traveled with him. He was also friends with sisters Mary and Martha and their brother, Lazarus. He proved the depth of his love for them when he raised Lazarus from the dead. You can participate in God's grace to develop your friendship with Christ by believing in him, inviting him into your life, loving God, putting God first, loving others, forgiving others, and witnessing about Christ to the world without fear.

Assignment

Read paragraph 1391 of the *Catechism of the Catholic Church*. What is the connection between the Eucharist and friendship with Jesus? How does the Eucharist strengthen your bond of friendship with Jesus?

Section 3
Disciples Help to Spread the Gospel

Review

Discipleship is never a passive exercise. The third step of discipleship is evangelization—that is, putting your faith in action and sharing the Gospel with others. Often evangelization involves reaching out to Catholics who have strayed from their faith as well as those who may not have ever heard the Good News of Christ. There are several things you can do to be a good evangelizer. Most of these involve being present to others and treating them with respect and kindness. Your love for Christ will shine through. At the end of the process, you can invite the person to participate in Mass or a parish-sponsored event. Because heaven is both a reward and goal of discipleship, you have something very valuable to share with others.

Assignment

Write down your responses to these questions of St. Ignatius of Loyola: What have you done for Christ? What are you doing for Christ? What will you do for Christ?

Section 4
Jesus Taught His Disciples How to Pray

Review

Because discipleship involves deepening a friendship with Jesus, prayer is an essential part. Prayer is communication between you and God. By the way he prayed, including retreating to solitude before making important decisions,

Jesus presents a model of prayer. Several of his teachings and parables also teach us about prayer. When his disciples asked Jesus to teach them to pray, he taught them the Our Father, a prayer that lets you know that God is a loving Father to you and all other people. Because of this, you can know that all people are brothers and sisters to you.

Assignment

Name at least three instructions Jesus gave his followers on how to pray. Explain how you could put these instructions into practice today.

Chapter Projects

Choose and complete at least one of the following projects to assess your understanding of the material in this chapter.

✿ 1. Respond to Questions about Mary Magdalene as the "Apostle of the Apostles"

St. Mary Magdalene is honored among the disciples of Jesus. She was faithful to Jesus through his Passion and Death, remaining with him at the foot of the Cross. She was also the first disciple to discover the empty tomb and to encounter the Risen Lord. In 2016, Pope Francis raised the liturgical celebration of the memorial of St. Mary Magdalene to the dignity of a feast, the same level of liturgical celebration given to the Apostles. In doing so, the pope called Mary Magdalene the "Apostle of the Apostles." Research and write your answers to *all* of the following:

- Who are the "three Marys" described in John 20:11–18, Luke 7:36–50, and Luke 10:38–42?

- Why did Pope Gregory the Great fuse these women together?

- What are three honors given to St. Mary Magdalene according to St. Thomas Aquinas?

- What is the date of St. Mary Magdalene's feast?

- What is the difference between a solemnity, feast, and memorial on the liturgical calendar?

- Print the words of the preface of the Eucharistic prayer on St. Mary Magdalene's feast day.

- How was St. Mary Magdalene a true evangelizer for the faith? Cite at least three specific examples to back up your answer.

✿ 2. Survey Agencies That Practice the Corporal Works of Mercy

Corporal (or bodily) works of mercy are practical instructions the Church gives Catholics to help meet the basic physical needs of others. The corporal works of mercy are to (1) feed the hungry; (2) give drink to the thirsty;

(3) clothe the naked; (4) visit the imprisoned; (5) shelter the homeless; (6) visit the sick; and (7) bury the dead. For each of these works of mercy, research an agency in your local community or diocese that focuses on that particular need. Write the following:

- the name of the agency
- how it supports the particular corporal work of mercy (who it serves, how it serves, where it serves)
- ways someone your age can support this agency in its work

⚙ *3. Write Your Impressions of The Imitation of Christ*

The Imitation of Christ is a classic spiritual text discovered in the Netherlands in the fifteenth century. Among all spiritual texts, it is second to the Bible in all-time popularity. Although officially labeled an anonymous work, *The Imitation of Christ* is usually credited to Thomas à Kempis, a German canon regular (a member of the clergy who lived in community). The text presents a dialogue between a disciple and Jesus. It is divided into four parts:

- Book One: Useful Reminders for the Spiritual Life
- Book Two: Suggestions Drawing One Toward the Inner Life
- Book Three: Of Inner Comfort
- Book Four: The Book on the Sacrament

Locate a copy of *The Imitation of Christ*. Then complete each of the following parts of this assignment:

1. Write a paragraph detailing the origins of *The Imitation of Christ*.
2. Write one page explaining the purpose of each of the books (listed above) of *The Imitation of Christ*.
3. Read several of the dialogues between the disciple and Jesus in Book Three, "Of Inner Comfort." Summarize three particular instructions of Jesus that you find helpful from this material. Explain why the instructions you chose are meaningful to you.

⚙ *4. Illustrate the Gospel Passage "I Am the Vine, You Are the Branches"*

As you read in Section 2, Jesus describes the close relationship he desires with you in John 15:1–7. Read the passage from Scripture. Illustrate its meaning in one of the following ways:

- creatively designed words
- a drawing to accompany the passage
- a bookmark
- your own song (You may wish to listen to a recording of John Michael Talbot's "I Am the Vine.")

Use one of these ways to represent the communion between you and Jesus, and you and others in Jesus's name.

⚙ *5. Define Types of Prayer and Psalms*

Read about the types of prayer described in the *Catechism of the Catholic Church*, paragraphs 2629–2643. Write a definition for these types of prayer:

- Petition
- Intercession
- Thanksgiving
- Praise

Next, read the following psalms. Indicate which type of prayer each psalm is most closely identified with. (There are two examples for each type.) Besides naming the type of prayer, list at least one verse that exemplifies the type of prayer that you named.

- Psalm 118
- Psalm 148
- Psalm 20
- Psalm 38
- Psalm 104
- Psalm 30
- Psalm 88
- Psalm 86

Faithful Disciple
St. Josephine Bakhita

Born in Sudan in 1869, St. Josephine Bakhita was kidnapped from her family by Arab slave traders before she was ten years old. Before gaining her freedom, Bakhita was sold several times to abusive masters and endured the humiliation and suffering of slavery. When an Italian consul, Callisto Legnani, bought Bakhita and allowed her to live with his family, it was the first time since childhood she had been with people who treated her lovingly. When Legnani needed to return to Italy, Bakhita asked if she could accompany him. She was brought to Italy and given to another Italian family, the Michielis. Bakhita became the primary caretaker and friend of the Michielis' only daughter.

Eventually, when both Michieli parents needed to return to Africa, they entrusted Bakhita and their daughter to the care of the Canossian Sisters of the Institute of Catechumens in Venice. Members of this religious order taught Bakhita about God, Jesus, and the Gospel. She recalled that before she had been taken a slave, she had looked lovingly at the sun, moon, and

St. Josephine Bakhita

stars and wondered, "Who is the Master of these beautiful things?" and had "a great desire to see him, and know him, and worship him." Bakhita entered the Catholic Church and was baptized with the name Josephine. Though the Michielis later wanted to bring Bakhita to Africa to live with them, she asserted herself and said that she wanted to stay with the sisters. This was her right under Italian law. After staying with the sisters for a time, she realized that God was calling her to join their community. On December 8, 1896, she was consecrated to God, whom she continued to refer to as "Master."

Sr. Josephine spent fifty years living in the Canossian community doing simple tasks such as answering the door, sewing, and cooking. She encouraged children and people who were poor and suffering who came to the door. Sr. Josephine was loved and admired by the other sisters as well as by the people outside of the community. She was humble, simple, and constantly smiling. She had a great desire to make God known to all, saying, "Be good, love the Lord, pray for those who do not know him. What a great grace it is to know God." She died in Italy in 1947 after a difficult illness.

To St. Josephine, God was always "my Master." Having known cruel masters, she appreciated God's goodness all the more. St. Josephine Bakhita was beatified in 1992 and canonized on October 1, 2000.

Comprehension

1. Where was St. Josephine Bakhita born and enslaved?
2. Whom did St. Josephine care for when she moved to Italy?
3. How did St. Josephine learn about God?
4. What was St. Josephine's role in her community of sisters?

Application

Describe St. Josephine's understanding of God as "Master." Compare her understanding of God under this title with your own experience of God.

Prayer

St. Augustine of Hippo (354–430), who took a long course to Baptism and becoming a disciple of Jesus Christ, dedicated himself wholly to the task of discipleship after his conversion. He became a bishop and theologian and is a Doctor of the Church. This prayer of reflection on the meaning and challenges of discipleship is credited to him.

Prayer of St. Augustine

Lord Jesus, let me know myself and know you,
And desire nothing, save only you.
Let me hate myself and love you.
Let me do everything for the sake of you.
Let me humble myself and exalt you.
Let me think of nothing except you.
Let me die to myself and live in you.
Let me accept whatever happens as from you.
Let me banish self and follow you,
And ever desire to follow you.
Let me fly from myself and take refuge in you,
That I may deserve to be defended by you.
Let me fear for myself, let me fear you,
And let me be among those who are chosen by you.
Let me distrust myself and put my trust in you.
Let me be willing to obey for the sake of you.
Let me cling to nothing, save only to you,
And let me be poor because of you.
Look upon me, that I may love you.
Call me, that I may see you,
And for ever enjoy you.
Amen.

Jesus Calls You

Jesus Is Our Bridge to Heaven

➤Elizabeth Wang

After her conversion to Catholicism in 1968, English artist Elizabeth Wang (1942–2016) became active in her parish in her hometown of Harpenden, England. As with many converts, she found her entrance into the Church somewhat difficult because of the various reactions of her family and friends. But these reactions were outweighed by the great peace she found. "I can't describe how fulfilling I found it to be able to receive the sacraments, and to discover the plain truth about what is right and wrong. I found the sole Church which had been founded by Christ," she explained.

While her entrance into the Church came in her twenties, Elizabeth began painting "as soon as I could hold a paintbrush, and found paints available. In childhood, I enjoyed making colored marks." This attraction to bright color never dissipated, as evidenced in the painting reproduced above, *Jesus Is Our Bridge to Heaven*. Inspired by Impressionist and Expressionist artists, Elizabeth said that using color gave her "the exact sort of pleasure and experience as to when she hears a great choral work with interweaving harmonies." Light is also a main theme of her work. In this painting, note the lightness and brightness that emanate from those who have crossed over the chasm from this world to heaven.[1]

The theme of Christ as a bridge has been popular among the saints. For example, St. Catherine of Siena recorded a conversation she had with God while in ecstasy in which she saw that Jesus, through obedience to the Father, made himself a bridge between heaven and earth. She wrote that it was necessary for Jesus to become a bridge "so that you might pass over the bitterness of the world and reach life." God also told St. Catherine, "My Son's having made himself of a bridge for you could not bring you to life unless you make your way along that bridge."[2]

If you would like to draw your own representation of the bridge between earth and heaven, see Chapter 8 Review, Chapter Project 1.

How does the light of Christ shine through me?

Chapter Overview

Introduction

Jesus Christ at the Center of Your Life

Section 1

What It Means to Be Human

Section 2

What It Means to Gain Salvation

Section 3

What It Means to Be Happy

Conclusion

What It Means to Live for Jesus

JESUS CHRIST AT THE CENTER OF YOUR LIFE

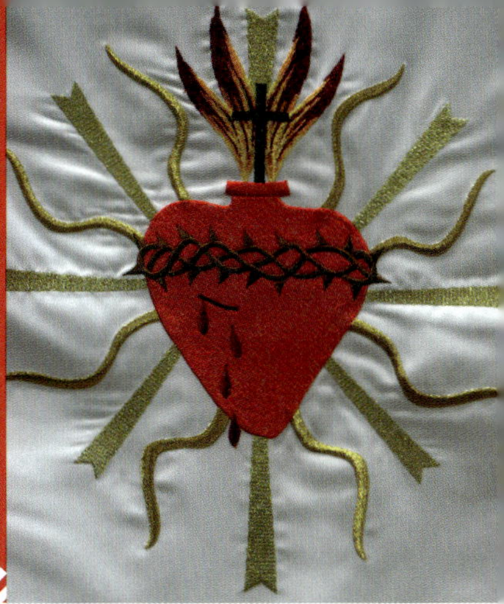

While Apostles, martyrs, and saints (including Mary, the Mother of God) are important, without Jesus none of them would exist. **In a homily after a Monday morning Mass, Pope Francis said that we must ask ourselves these questions: "Is Jesus Christ at the center of my life? And what is my relationship with Jesus Christ?"∞**

Our lives only make sense with Jesus at the center. On an earlier occasion, in his opening remarks on World Youth Day to one million young Catholics on Copacabana Beach at Rio de Janeiro, Brazil, in 2013, the pope also said, "With Christ at the center of your life, you will never be disappointed. Put on Christ and you will find a friend in whom you can always trust and your life will be full of his love. Your journey will be joyful because you will find many friends to journey with. Your horizon will never be dark."[3]

Getting to know Jesus, forming a friendship with him, and sharing the Good News of his promise of salvation have been the focus of this text. But remember: if this has only been an academic study of the life of Christ, in the same way you would study the life of Louis Pasteur in chemistry class or Mark Twain in American literature, you have missed its essential message. **A study of the life of Christ invites, persuades, and demands that you incorporate all of Jesus into your life and make him its center.** In another one of his daily

∞ Note

In his homily on January 9, 2017, Pope Francis said that to put Jesus at the center, we must make sure we know him and are able to recognize him. To get to know him, there is "prayer, the Holy Spirit, and also the Gospel, which we should carry with us and read a passage every day. It is the only way to get to know him."

homilies at the Vatican, Pope Francis put it this way: "Jesus didn't say to Peter and to his Apostles, 'Know me!' He said, 'Follow me!' And this following of Jesus makes us know him."

You follow Jesus because, in doing so, you know what God is really like. Jesus is completely divine. He is the Second Divine Person of the Blessed Trinity. You also follow Jesus because he is completely human and lived as the perfect model of God's creation. His words and actions teach about how to live your life on earth in order to guarantee everlasting happiness in heaven. St. Paul wrote about Jesus,

> He is the image of the invisible God,
> the firstborn of all creation.
> For in him were created all things in heaven and on earth,
> the visible and the invisible . . .
> all things were created through him and for him.
> He is before all things,
> and in him all things hold together. (Col 1:15–17)

Jesus Asks You to See Yourself through the Eyes of God

St. Paul called Jesus the "last Adam" (1 Cor 15:45). What this means is that at the Incarnation, Jesus appeared as a New Adam in history to give the human race a brand-new start: "Jesus is conceived by the Holy Spirit in the Virgin Mary's womb because he is the New Adam, who inaugurates the new creation: 'The first man was from the earth, a man of dust; the second man is from heaven'" (*CCC*, 504, quoting 1 Cor 15:45, 47). As the last or New Adam, Jesus intends for humanity to look back at creation prior to Original Sin and to consider how God first intended people to live. In fact, Christ's victory over sin has given the world even greater blessings than before sin entered the world.

For example, if you look closely at the teaching of Jesus about marriage and divorce in Mark 10:2–12, you can get a sense of how our lives would have been different if we had not been born into sin. Some Pharisees who wished to challenge Jesus and his teaching authority ask him, "Is it lawful for a husband to divorce his wife?" (v. 2). It is likely that, like other religious leaders of their day, the Pharisees were permitting men to divorce their wives under certain circumstances. Referring to two passages in the Book of Genesis (1:27 and 2:24), Jesus responds by teaching about what God originally intended for

Colette and Ken Santucci on their wedding day and at their fiftieth-anniversary Mass at St. Bartholomew Catholic Church in Long Beach, California.

marriage. Jesus says that God does not want people to separate what he has joined together. He explains that only due to the "hardness of your hearts" did Moses permit divorce.

In answering the Pharisees this way, Jesus indicates that he would like his listeners to go back and study what God revealed before Original Sin spread sinfulness in the world. In the case of marriage, spouses are given the grace to deny themselves, take up their crosses, and remain faithful to each other out of their love for Christ and accompanied by his grace. For others, God invites them to a life of consecrated virginity for the sake of the Kingdom. These are two ways disciples of Jesus make him the center of their lives.

You may wonder why it had to be this way. Why didn't God prevent the first humans from sinning? The human race could then have lived as God first intended. St. Leo the Great responds this way: "Christ's inexpressible grace gave us blessings *better* than those the demon's envy had taken away."[4] Do you see that it was only because of the sin of Adam that we have been able to know

Jesus? The **Exsultet**, an ancient proclamation sung at the Easter Vigil, speaks of the grace that it is only through the "happy fault" of Adam that we have gotten to know so great a Savior as Jesus:

> O truly necessary sin of Adam,
> destroyed completely by the Death of Christ!
> O happy fault
> that earned for us so great, so glorious a Redeemer!

Only with Jesus do we know the full meaning of friendship, love, and what it means to be a human. Pope John Paul II echoed these words and what they mean for us today: "When you wonder about the mystery of yourself, look to Christ who gives you the meaning of life. When you wonder about what it means to be a mature person, look to Christ who is the fullness of humanity."∞

∞ Note

Pope John Paul II spoke these words in a gathering with teenagers at Madison Square Garden in New York City in 1979, just months after the release of his encyclical *Redemptor Hominis* (*The Redeemer of Man*), in which the very first line states, "Christ is the center of the universe and human history."

Exsultet The first words in Latin of the proclamation sung at the Easter Vigil. The opening words in English are, "Now let the angelic host of heaven exult, exult the mysteries divine; and for the victory of so great a King, sound the trumpet of salvation." The Exsultet was originally credited to St. Augustine in the fifth century, but it was probably composed later.

SECTION Assessment

Comprehension

1. What is the difference between studying a historical figure like Louis Pasteur or Mark Twain and studying Jesus?

2. How did Pope Francis explain a way to follow Jesus or make him the center of your life?

3. What does it mean to say that Jesus is the last or New Adam?

4. Besides offering a teaching about marriage and divorce, what else was the purpose of Jesus's lesson in Mark 10:2–12?

Reflection

5. Write a sentence describing what God intended for people prior to Original Sin.

6. On a scale of 1 to 10, rate yourself on how well you make Jesus the center of your life. Explain your rating.

WHAT IT MEANS TO BE HUMAN

The first creation account in the Book of Genesis ends with a description of the creation of humans and the responsibilities God gives them (1:26–31). These verses reveal a great deal about how we are expected to live and also tell us a great deal about God, the Creator.

Sometimes people forget that God did not have to create anything, much less humans. The *Catechism of the Catholic Church* teaches that "God created the world according to his wisdom. It is not the product of any necessity whatever, nor blind fate or chance" (295). **God created the world for his own glory—according to St. Bonaventure, "not to increase his glory but to show it forth and to communicate it."** God had no reason to create other than to share his love and goodness.

It is important for us to keep in mind that we are creatures, not the Creator. God remains our Creator whether we think about him or not and whether we believe in him or not. However, life is most complete when we acknowledge God. St. Irenaeus asked, "How much more will the Word's manifestation of the Father obtain life for those who see God?"

History shows that when humans forget about God or, worse, make themselves into gods, sinfulness abounds. They wreak havoc on themselves and the rest of creation. When we remember our place in God's creation and name him as our Creator, we give God glory. St. Irenaeus famously pointed out that "the glory of God is a person fully alive; moreover, a person's life is the vision of God."

Jesus had good reason for wanting us to understand what God intended for humans before Original Sin. Several lessons from the creation accounts in Scripture relevant for our life today follow in the next sections.

Humans Have a Privileged Place in Creation

Genesis 1:26 tells us what sets human beings apart from the rest of the created world: "Then God said: Let us make human beings in our image, after our likeness." We are created in the likeness of God. Because of this, each of us possesses "the dignity of a person, who is not just something, but someone" (*CCC*, 357). As someone created in the image of God, you are capable of knowing yourself, of being in control of your own life, of giving yourself to others, and of responding to God, your Creator, with faith. People are the only visible creatures who can know and love God. Consider what else you can do because you are human:

"I can think!"

"My intellect allows me to learn things and pass on this knowledge to future generations. Most importantly, I can discover truth. I can discover the meaning of life and death. I can recognize God's voice.

"I use my mind to discover objective and eternal laws that God has implanted in creation. I hear his call to me to do good and avoid evil."

"I can choose!"

"Because God gave me **free will**, I have the ability to make choices. This gift of freedom is so important to God that he allows the possibility that I may even choose not to acknowledge or follow his will.

free will The capacity to choose among alternatives. Free will is "the power, rooted in reason and will . . . to perform deliberate actions on one's own responsibility" (*CCC*, 1731).

This makes me accountable for my choices—whether they are good or evil.

"My freedom to choose means that I can always change to be better. I don't have to remain intolerant or uncaring. I don't have to remain judgmental or prejudiced. I can become better."

"I can love!"

"I am most human when I love. This only makes sense. I am made in God's image and God is love. I know this because Jesus told me so.

"I learn most about love directly from Jesus. He teaches me to care for others with respect, equality, and mutual self-giving. He has told me that I am a child of his Father in heaven as are all other people. For that reason, I love others as sisters and brothers."

"I can relate!"

"I belong to this world. This means I belong to other people. I have relationships. They can't go it alone, and neither can I. We all need help. For this reason I work to build up my family, my community, my Church, my nation, and the entire world by working for justice and solidarity for all."

Your ability to do each of these things in your own unique way comes from being made in God's image. This fact enables you to share in God's own life.

God does not have physical or material qualities. He is pure spirit. **By making you in the divine image, God endowed you with the spiritual qualities that he possesses: the ability to think, to choose, to love, and to relate to others in community.** (Remember that God is a community of Divine Persons: Father, Son, and Holy Spirit.) These traits enable you to share, through knowledge and love, in God's own life. These capacities also separate humans from any other earthly creatures.

Another special distinction of being human that can be gleaned from the second creation account in Genesis 2:4–25 is that people are created in friendship with God. The first people—named Adam and Eve—were in complete harmony with God, with each other, and with the rest of creation.[∞] In this way, they shared in God's life. He placed them in the Garden of Eden "to cultivate and care for it" (Gn 2:15). This shows their familiarity and closeness with God. Their work was not hard labor but rather a collaborative effort with God, their Creator. Together they worked to perfect God's creation. This was the state of life God intended for all of us to live—and intends for us to achieve in the fullness of time.

Though friendship with God was the intended lot for humans at the time of creation, because of the Original Sin of Adam and Eve, this harmony was lost. Human beings became subject to suffering and death. But the fundamental goodness of human beings and all of God's creation was never lost. The proof of this is that God loves the world so much that "he gave his only Son, so that everyone who believes in him might not perish but might have eternal life" (Jn 3:16).

Humans Are Made Male and Female

As the Incarnate Son of God, Jesus was fully human. His gender was male. Although this is obvious, it is an important point for reflection in light of the second creation account, which teaches that God created humans as complementary beings, male and female. Complementary means "making up for what is lacking in another." Humans need one another in many ways. God

---

∞ Note

This was the state of original holiness and original justice introduced in Chapter 2, Section 3.

builds interdependence into human nature, creating males and females to be helpmates, a communion of persons. Together, man and woman as married spouses and parents "cooperate in a unique way in the Creator's work" (*CCC*, 372).

The cooperation between man and woman is truly an equal one. Neither male nor female is superior or inferior to the other. **God created man and woman equal in dignity and worthy of the same esteem and respect.** The *Catechism of the Catholic Church* teaches that "man and woman are both with one and the same dignity 'in the image of God.' In their 'being-man' and 'being-woman,' they reflect the Creator's wisdom and goodness" (369).∞

The fact that God's Son had a human body and was part of the material universe means that both are very good. Your human body, especially, shares in the dignity of the image of God for two reasons:

- Your body is a temple of the Holy Spirit (*CCC*, 2519).

- Your body will rise again on the last day (*CCC*, 1003).

Your whole human person—body and soul—gains knowledge through your five senses in collaboration with your intellect and will. You express your humanity and experience reality through your emotions and feelings, passions and drives, preferences and dislikes. What's more, each individual has a unique, one-of-a-kind genetic makeup. There's only one of you. You are an unrepeatable creation of God.

∞ Note

The Church opposes what is sometimes known as "gender ideology," which holds that humans can choose their own sex. "Gender ideology is one of the most dangerous ideological colonizations," Pope Francis said in a 2023 interview. "Why is it dangerous? Because it blurs the differences and value between men and women." At the same time, Pope Francis showed great pastoral care for those who call themselves "transgender." On numerous occasions—and usually out of the public eye—the pope met with transgender people in Rome. "Pope Francis didn't judge us— he listened," said Minerva Motta, a Peruvian. "He told me: 'Remember that we are all equal before the eyes of God.'" After that visit, the pope continued to send cards and prayers to those whom he met.

SECTION Assessment

Comprehension

1. What book of the Bible confirms that God has a plan for every creature but especially for human beings?

2. What words in Genesis 1 verify that God gave human beings a special place among all the creatures on earth?

3. Name four spiritual qualities God gave to human beings.

Vocabulary

4. Define *free will*. Give one example of how a person might use free will.

Reflection

5. Write about the God-given dignity you observed in another person today. Be specific.

WHAT IT MEANS TO GAIN SALVATION

Just as learning about and reflecting on God's gift of creation can teach us more about ourselves and what it means to be human, so too keeping in mind the basic facts about God's Incarnation in the Person of Jesus Christ can be constructive for our life.

The first lesson of the Incarnation is easy to comprehend and is much like one gleaned from the creation accounts in Genesis: we have been created fundamentally good. If not, why would God have bothered to send Jesus, his own Son, to be one with humanity? The second lesson is a bit more difficult to grasp: What does it mean to be saved? Why is it necessary to be saved? The Incarnation answers these questions as well. Jesus would not have come to live, suffer, and die for humanity unless there was no other solution to rid the world of sin and death. Jesus Christ rescued the world from sin and death so that you and others can have a life of eternal joy with the Blessed Trinity. For this, he is the Savior of the World.

Why We Need a Savior

At the beginning of time, human beings were wounded by sin and inclined toward evil and selfishness. Genesis 2:15–3:24 reports that Adam and Eve chose to follow their own desires and ignore God's plan for

Pilgrims holding candles pray during the candle procession at the Sanctuary of Fatima.

them. The sin of pride led to their downfall and expulsion from the Garden of Eden. There were many consequences:

> **They were alienated from God.**

> **They were subject to suffering and death.**

> **Their ancestors—the whole human race—became prone to sin.**

All of this translates to our life in the form of concupiscence. Recall that concupiscence means that even though we often have good intentions, we have trouble resisting temptation and thus sometimes commit personal sins. This inclination can lead to many types of sin (e.g., cowardice, selfishness, deceit, anger, violence, jealousy).

Although humans were created in goodness, we are weak-willed and inclined to sin. Salvation history provides example after example of the moral battle that takes place within every person. You may have experienced this as

Vices can be linked to both the virtues they oppose and to "capital" or "deadly" sins, which are pride, avarice, envy, wrath, lust, gluttony, and sloth or acedia. "They are called 'capital' because they engender other sins and vices" (CCC, 1866).

a struggle or even a battle within yourself. St. Paul described this battle in the Letter to the Romans: "What I do, I do not understand. For I do not do what I want, but I do what I hate. . . . For I do not do the good I want, but I do the evil I do not want. Now if [I] do what I do not want, it is no longer I who do it, but sin that dwells in me" (Rom 7:15, 19–20). St. Paul's insight helps explain the need for a Savior. No one is strong enough to save themselves from the inclination to sin. This is the reason that God sent his Son into the world in the form of human flesh.

Our Life as Saved Sinners

Through the Paschal Mystery—the Passion, Death, Resurrection, and Ascension of Jesus Christ—we have been saved from sin. In short, God the Son gave up his life so that we might live. God the Father rewarded this effort and rescued Jesus from death. Together, the Father and the Son send the Holy Spirit to provide us the grace to live as saved disciples. Other tangible graces abound: Christ continues his work of salvation in his Body, the Church. The Seven Sacraments provide particular graces and are fountains of his saving work. The first task of a saved sinner is to follow the instruction of St. Paul:

> Throw off the works of darkness [and] put on the armor of light; let us conduct ourselves properly as in the day, not in orgies and drunkenness, not in promiscuity and licentiousness, not in rivalry and jealousy. But put on the Lord Jesus Christ, and make no provision for the desires of the flesh. (Rom 13:12–14)

This reforming of our life is known as *repentance*. It means turning from sin and avoiding anything that might lead to sin. Another name for repentance is the Greek word **metanoia**. Repentance was Jesus's very first instruction recorded in the first chapter of the Gospel of Mark: "This is the time of fulfillment. The kingdom of God is at hand. Repent, and believe in the gospel" (Mk 1:15).

---

metanoia A change of heart from sin to the practice of virtue. Literally, "repentance" or "penance."

Of the Seven Sacraments, two figure prominently in the reforming of our life from sin to discipleship. The first is the Sacrament of Baptism. At Baptism, we are showered with graces, including:

- *The forgiveness of sin.* Baptism forgives Original Sin and personal sin—as well as the punishment due to sin. However, some consequences of sin remain, such as suffering, weakness of will, the inclination to sin, and ultimately death.

- *Sanctifying grace.* This type of grace heals fallen human nature and gives us a share in the divine life of the Blessed Trinity. Sanctifying grace is a habitual, supernatural gift that makes us perfect, holy, and Christlike.

- *Initiation and incorporation.* Baptism, along with Confirmation and Eucharist, is one of the Sacraments of Christian Initiation.

- *Sealing.* The sacrament provides an indelible spiritual character that marks us as belonging to Christ.

- *Birth into a new life in Christ.* Through Baptism we become a child of God and a temple of the Holy Spirit. Baptism is necessary for our salvation, as is membership in the Church herself.

Enjoying the graces of a "saved sinner" does not end at Baptism. Repentance is not a one-time event, nor even an every-so-often action. **Rather, God the Father's pinnacle offering of his own Son as payment for the world's sins demands a constant and lifelong commitment to reordering our life**

to follow Christ as his disciple. It is an endless process of repenting for our sins and failings, and turning more and more to God. One support is the Sacrament of Penance—sometimes called a "second Baptism"—in which we can confess our sins, receive God's forgiveness, and be reconciled with the Church. The grace of this sacrament also helps us to live more faithfully as Jesus's disciples.

SECTION Assessment

Comprehension

1. What is the first lesson of the Incarnation?

2. What were the consequences of Original Sin?

3. What are two sacraments that figure prominently in repentance?

4. Name the graces of the Sacrament of Baptism.

Vocabulary

5. Define *metanoia*.

Reflection

6. How do St. Paul's words "put on the Lord Jesus Christ" translate to your own human behavior?

7. Why do you need to be saved?

WHAT IT MEANS TO BE HAPPY

If Christ "won" salvation for humankind, what exactly is the prize? Don't ever forget the heart of the Good News: God raised his Son from the dead, "the firstfruits of those who have fallen asleep" (1 Cor 15:20). St. Paul wrote about the importance of remembering this message. He called a Christian's preaching and faith "empty" unless we hold fast to the belief in the Resurrection, first for Christ and then "each one in proper order" (1 Cor 15:23). "If the dead are not raised," Paul pondered, then "why are we endangering ourselves all the time?" (1 Cor 15:29, 30).

In fact, God wants us to focus on the rewards of Christ's victory. **Our goal of knowing, loving, and serving God through his Son, Jesus, is eternal happiness in heaven. In a sense, God programmed us with a desire for eternal happiness.** Nothing in this world can fully satisfy this quest to be happy. Not wealth, not straight As, not getting into the best college, not fame, not power, not a huge bank account, not awesome looks for you or a spouse. None of these things are bad, but they can't really quench the desire for happiness. Only God's goodness and love can satisfy our deepest hunger for true and lasting happiness.

This doesn't mean we can't be happy on earth. In fact, we can be deeply happy, but not in the way the world defines happiness. The blueprint Jesus left for happiness is the Beatitudes. Recall that the word *beatitude* means "supreme happiness." The Beatitudes direct our lives away from an overconsumption of worldly possessions and toward a participation in God's nature and the Kingdom of God. They condition us to love.

Living the Beatitudes

The eight Beatitudes appear at the beginning of the Sermon on the Mount (Mt 5:3–10). They are also found in the Sermon on the Plain in Luke 6:20–26. The Beatitudes complete the promises that God made to Abraham, the father of the Jewish faith. They show how we are to fulfill our desire for happiness and teach us how to live in order to reach our eternal destiny of union with God. The Beatitudes also explain how we should love God and neighbor in a Christlike way.

If you are already familiar with the Beatitudes, you know that they do not prescribe happiness in the way that we are used to or in a way that much of secular society does. The Beatitudes offer a very untraditional and unpracticed path to happiness, a path characterized by poverty, meekness, and purity of heart. **The Beatitudes call us to separate ourselves from our culture and to become poor in several ways. We are called to identify with the hungry, homeless, impoverished, abused, refugees, addicts, the elderly, and victims of war.** Ironically, these groups make up the majority of the world's population. By identifying with those who are vulnerable and in need, we acknowledge the reality of the world we live in. Yet to live the Beatitudes means we

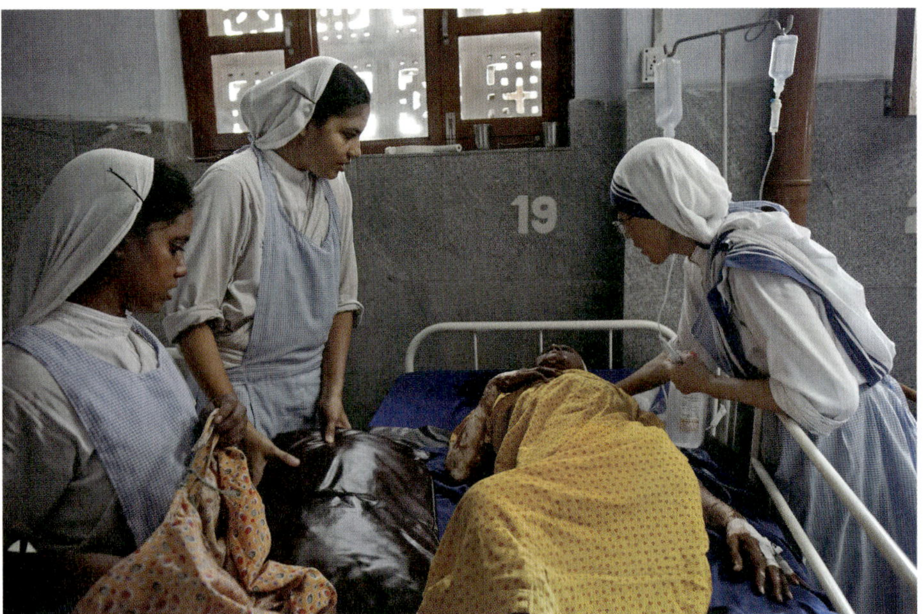

Missionaries of Charity sisters care for the sick and dying at their hospital in Calcutta, India.

must marginalize and separate ourselves from our materialistic, success-driven culture.

What happens when we follow the Beatitudes? Simply, we will be happy. This happiness is not something reserved for the future in heaven. In preaching the Beatitudes, Jesus used a present-tense verb: "Blessed *are*," not "Blessed *will be*." You might wonder how we can really be happy in practicing what seems like great suffering as described in the Beatitudes. Yet, you might have also witnessed people who are happy in this way without realizing the connection with the Beatitudes. For example, have you been in the presence of someone—maybe a religious sister or a faithful layperson—who ministers to the homeless, provides support for single mothers, or advocates for migrants? If so, you may have recognized the deep joy they possess in aligning themselves with those in such need. Closer to home, you may have witnessed family members who are sick or even dying who are more concerned about the welfare of those who are caring for them than with their own needs. These are people who find deep happiness in living the Beatitudes.

The Beatitudes Are a Blueprint for God's Kingdom

The Beatitudes ask more of what our human nature might deem reasonable. They offer the blueprint for not only our own happiness but also establishing the Kingdom of God on earth. Understood properly, the Beatitudes are a glimpse into the heart of Jesus.

> **Blessed are the poor in spirit,**
> **for theirs is the kingdom of heaven.**

Jesus associated with poor, weak, and vulnerable people and expects his followers to do the same. This Beatitude is not intended to condone the condition of material poverty, which is an evil that should be eradicated. Rather, Jesus wants us to recognize our spiritual poverty—that everything we are and everything we have are gifts from God. We show our gratitude for what we have been given by sharing what we have and what we are with others.

Blessed are they who mourn, for they will be comforted.

Jesus blesses those who mourn over injustices and evils committed against God, often resulting in the suffering of needy and innocent people. The hearts of those close to God ache for the sins of the world and for their own sins too. The Lord tells us not to lose heart, though, because he promises that he will eventually console us. Through deep mourning, we receive comfort that only God can provide.

Blessed are the meek, for they will inherit the land.

Meek people are humble and patient with others. Jesus exemplified meekness when he treated others with gentleness and compassion. He also forgave others when they hurt and taunted him. His heavenly Father treats each of us with patience, forgiveness, and gentleness when we sin. Those who live this Beatitude are patient with the shortcomings of others, working to solve disagreements with goodwill without ever giving in to hate or violence.

Blessed are they who hunger and thirst for righteousness, for they will be satisfied.

Our restless hearts cannot find true happiness until they find God. Jesus blesses those who know that only God's righteousness can fulfill us. God made us so that our hearts seek divine justice from God the Father and the loving, forgiving friendship of God the Son, who guides us in what is just and true.

Blessed are the merciful, for they will be shown mercy.

This Beatitude urges empathy. We are to think, feel, and act from another's perspective rather than our own. When we show mercy, we live this petition of the Our Father: "Forgive us our trespasses as we forgive those who trespass against us."

Blessed are the clean of heart, for they will see God.

A person with a clean heart has a single-hearted commitment to God. School, money, possessions, family, sports, friends, and everything else should come after a total commitment to accomplish God's will. The clean of heart are the opposite of people who say one thing and do another. The clean of heart are honest, sincere, and unselfish.

Blessed are the peacemakers, for they will be called children of God.

The Hebrew word for peace—*shalom*—helps us to understand the meaning of this Beatitude. In this sense, peace is not only an absence of war or trouble. Peace means helping others enjoy all that this life has to offer. This is an active, not passive action. A peacemaker does not just voice opposition to war but also looks for ways to make the local and large community a better place to live.

Blessed are they who are persecuted for the sake of righteousness, for theirs is the kingdom of heaven.

We are reminded that the life of a Christian on earth is not easy. We must live prepared to experience the same pain, suffering, and death that Jesus did. When we do experience trials, we must remember that we are living out the same pattern of life that Jesus did. Suffering for faith in Jesus is a great sign of love for him. He himself suffered misunderstanding and abuse when he preached the truth. Our Christlike words and actions will at times bring us the same ridicule and rejection. We might even suffer martyrdom or at least be willing to do so in his name.

Are You a Beatitude Person?

Focus Question: How does the light of Christ shine through me?

From the Beatitudes (see Matthew 5:3–10), we know of Jesus's love and the kind of love to which we are called. But is it really possible to live the Beatitudes as Jesus asks us to do?

At first glance, the eight Beatitudes announced by Jesus seem impossible to take seriously. How can it be a blessing to mourn, to be meek, or to be persecuted for the sake of righteousness? In asking us to live according to the Beatitudes, is Jesus asking something that human beings can't honestly accept or believe in? The answer is no.

Because Jesus began his public life by teaching the Beatitudes to a crowd, he must want his followers to take them to heart. In many ways, all of the Beatitudes say, "Now that I have come, everything is different." The logic of life is turned upside down. Jesus is ushering in the Kingdom of God, so the heartaches and tragedies that used to grieve and burden us are no longer painful or draining. In the Beatitudes, Jesus calls for a new mindset. Happiness is found in living in a new way that much of the world does not recognize. Although it may not seem possible to fully abide by the Beatitudes, we can surely learn to trust that God's ways, not the world's ways, will lead to happiness.

Reflect on the questions associated with each of the Beatitudes and write short answers for each to explain how you are currently doing and how you might further develop that Beatitude in your own life.

Reflection

The Poor in Spirit

- How do I recognize God as the source of everything in my life?
- How do I share my gifts with others?

Those Who Mourn

- How do I empathize with others?
- How do I help those less fortunate than I am?

The Gentle

- How am I a gentle and kind person?
- How do I respect others?

The Righteous

- How do I show that I am Christlike?
- How do I grow in holiness?

The Merciful

- How do I forgive others when they hurt me?
- How do I show compassion?

The Clean of Heart

- How do I live an honest life?
- How am I counted on and trusted?

Peacemakers

- How do I go out of my way to resolve conflicts?
- How do I often "turn the other cheek"?

The Persecuted

- How do I unite my suffering with Jesus's Cross?
- How do I think of difficulties and challenges as gifts from God?

Never forget that God really wants you to be happy. From the beginning, God created people to be happy both in this world and in the next, and has shown us ways to be truly happy. Unhappiness occurs when we separate ourselves from God. With the hope of salvation through Jesus, we can be happy even in a world filled with suffering. Everything Jesus shared with his disciples, and by extension the Church, was part of the offer of happiness. He said, "I have told you this so that my joy may be in you and your joy may be complete" (Jn 15:11). Jesus wants us to share in his joy. The Beatitudes teach us how.

SECTION Assessment

Comprehension

1. What did St. Paul say would make preaching about Christ "empty"?

2. Where and how did Jesus teach the Beatitudes?

3. What is an essential lesson about Jesus using the present-tense verb (Blessed *are*) rather than a future-tense verb in preaching the Beatitudes?

Reflection

4. Finish a necessary and new Beatitude for the world today: "Blessed are . . ."

5. What do you find most challenging about finding happiness in this world through living the Beatitudes?

WHAT IT MEANS TO LIVE FOR JESUS

As you conclude this course, you do so with your eyes wide open. The Gospel of Jesus Christ brings with it a message of hope for your life, both now and into eternity. You also know that there remains much pain and hurt in the world. The world needs Jesus. In that vein, the Catholic bishops of the United States recently introduced a National Eucharistic Revival to bring us to the very source of our strength—Jesus Christ, particularly in the gift of his Body and Blood in the Eucharist.

The National Eucharistic Revival launched on the Feast of Corpus Christi in 2022. Among the events of the three-year initiative are a pilgrimage and congress where Catholics and non-Catholics can draw on the presence of Jesus in the Eucharist to accomplish healing in our broken world. Pope Francis commented on the connection between celebrating Mass and our mission of evangelization as Christian disciples:

> In the Eucharist, we encounter the one who gave everything for us, who sacrificed himself in order to give us life, who loved us to the end. We become credible witnesses to the joy and transforming beauty of the Gospel only when we recognize that the love we celebrate in this sacrament cannot be kept to ourselves but demands to be shared with all.
>
> This is the sense of mission: You go, you celebrate Mass, you take Communion, you go to adoration—and afterward? Afterward you go out, you go out and evangelize; Jesus makes us this way.
>
> The Eucharist impels us to a strong and committed love of neighbor. For we cannot truly understand or live the meaning of the Eucharist if our hearts are closed to our brothers and sisters, especially those who are poor, suffering, weary or may have gone astray in life.[5]

Pope Francis also taught that in the Eucharist we partake in the Paschal Mystery and "thus, the Eucharist configures us in a unique and profound way with Jesus." **In fact, we can say that our friendship with Jesus and our desire to be his disciples is born in the gift of his Passion, Death, and Resurrection. It is his Paschal Mystery that brings us salvation and the opportunity to live an eternal life of joy in heaven.** The most practical and rewarding way to remain in union with Christ is through participating in the Sacrament of the Holy Eucharist.

Fruits of the Eucharist

In the Eucharist we receive Jesus himself. Holy Communion is a spiritual food that "preserves, increases, and renews the life of grace received at Baptism" (*CCC*, 1392). The Eucharist also separates us from sin. It strengthens love within us and unites us more closely to other members of Christ's Body. The *Catechism of the Catholic Church* puts it this way:

> *Holy Communion augments our union with Christ.* The principal fruit of receiving the Eucharist in Holy Communion is an intimate union with Christ Jesus. Indeed, the Lord said: "He who eats my flesh and drinks my blood abides in me, and I in him." Life in Christ has its foundation in the Eucharistic banquet: "As the living Father sent me, and I live because of the Father, so he who eats me will live because of me." (1391, quoting John 6:56, 57)

St. Pius X

When you receive Jesus in Holy Communion, you become more like him and are better equipped to share his presence and message with the world. In particular, the Eucharist unites you with outreach to the poor and suffering.

Living the Mission

St. Teresa of Avila once overheard a part of someone's conversation that included phrases like these: "If only I had lived in the time of Jesus. . . . If only I had seen Jesus. . . . If only I had talked with Jesus. . . ." St. Teresa interrupted and said to the person, "But do we not have in the Eucharist a living, true, and real Jesus present before us? Why look for more?"

When you celebrate the Eucharist, you receive Christ, you renew the memory of his Passion, and "your soul is filled with grace and a pledge of the life to come" (*CCC*, 1402). Jesus could have offered no greater gift of himself than the gift of the Eucharist.

As you complete this semester study of Jesus Christ and his mission, you are called to expand your knowledge of him and your commitment to him by sharing the Gospel with others. This is the command you are given in the Concluding Rite of Mass: "Go in peace to love and serve the Lord." You do this in particular by the way you speak and act. In just a few years, you will live apart from your parents and have the opportunity to explore and choose your own life's work and vocation. As you do so, continue to make Jesus the focus of your life. It is Jesus who loves and embraces you for who you are. Come to share his mission and ministry.

SECTION Assessment

Comprehension

1. What was an intention of the National Eucharistic Revival?

2. What did Pope Francis say we should do after receiving the Eucharist at Mass?

3. Name two fruits of receiving the Eucharist.

Reflection

4. How can the Eucharist deepen your relationship with Jesus and with other people?

5. What would you say to someone who told you that he or she couldn't have a relationship with Jesus because he "is not here with me in the flesh"?

Section Reviews

Focus Question

How does the light of Christ shine through me?
Complete one of the following:

- Read John 1:1–5. What do these opening verses of John's Gospel tell about Jesus's origins? What do they tell about his mission? Write your answers. Be specific.

- Peruse the epistles of St. Paul. Choose one passage that encourages you to be a better disciple of Christ. Creatively print the passage. Below it write an explanation of why it is meaningful to you.

- Pope Francis said, "Christ manifested his love by being with people and by sharing their desires and their problems. So, too, the Eucharist brings us together with others—young and old, poor and affluent, neighbors and visitors." How does the Eucharist allow you to see all people as your brothers and sisters and to see in them the face of Christ? Write your answer. Be specific.

Introduction
Jesus Christ at the Center of Your Life

Review

It is Christ who gives meaning to our life. A study of Christ is not complete as only an academic exercise. Rather, you are called to incorporate all of Jesus into your life and make him your center. There are two worthwhile reasons for making Jesus the center of your life. First, he is divine. He is the Second Divine Person of the Blessed Trinity. Second, he is completely human and models perfectly how to live. Part of understanding who you are as a child of God is envisioning the life God intended for you prior to Original Sin. In his teaching on marriage and divorce, Jesus noted the need to study how life was before sin entered the world.

Assignment

Read another version of Jesus's teaching on marriage and divorce in Matthew 19:1–12. What is the reason Jesus gave for Moses permitting divorce? How does this reason connect with Original Sin?

Section 1

What It Means to Be Human

Review

Jesus's invitation to look back to a time before Original Sin entered the world for insight on what it means to be human provides several lessons—that God created us to share his love and goodness; that God remains Creator while we will always be his creatures; that we as humans are the pinnacle of God's visible creation; and that we were made in God's image. A person most fully alive is one who acknowledges God and all that he has done. God has given us several abilities that distinguish us from the rest of creation, including being able to think, choose, love, and relate with others.

Assignment

Muhammad, the founder of Islam, is reported to have said, "One hour's concentration on the work of the Creator is better than seventy years of prayer." What do you think his statement means? What can you learn about yourself by meditating on the beauty and complexity of God, the Creator?

Section 2

What It Means to Gain Salvation

Review

Asking questions about the necessity of being saved reveals more about God's choice to send his Son to the world. The first lesson is: God loves us or he would not have sent his own Son to be one with humanity. Another lesson involves humanity's need for a Savior and what it means to be a saved human being. Because of Original Sin and the proliferation of sinfulness in the time since, people need a Savior. Through the events of the Paschal Mystery, Jesus saves us from sin. We participate in the work of salvation through Baptism, repentance, participation in the Church, and ongoing conversion.

Assignment

Read paragraph 457 of the *Catechism of the Catholic Church*. How did St. Gregory of Nyssa describe humanity's need for a Savior?

Section 3
What It Means to Be Happy

Review

God wants us to be happy. He desires our eternal happiness in heaven. For that reason, we should focus on the victory of God raising his Son, Jesus, from the dead. The Resurrection should never be far from our thoughts. Nothing on earth can ever quench our desire for happiness in the way that Christ's Resurrection and the promise of our own resurrection can. Jesus left a blueprint for happiness: the Beatitudes. These guide us to seek the Kingdom of God and to participate in God's nature.

Assignment

Write your answers: What is the main challenge to you for living out the Beatitudes? How can you overcome this challenge?

Conclusion
What It Means to Live for Jesus

Review

The best and most practical way to remain in friendship with Jesus while on earth is through participating in the Sacrament of the Eucharist. "Holy Communion augments our union with Christ" (*CCC*, 1391). The Eucharist separates us from sin. It strengthens us for love and unites us more closely with others who are part of Christ's Body on earth. When we receive the Eucharist, we are filled with grace and prepare ourselves for eternal life to come. The Eucharist helps to make Christ the focus of our life and strengthens us to share in his mission and ministry.

Assignment

Pope Francis said of the Eucharist, "When we go to Mass, we find ourselves with all sorts of people. . . . Does the Eucharist we celebrate lead me to consider all of them as brothers and sisters? Does it increase my ability to rejoice when they do and to weep with those who weep?" Answer the questions Pope Francis posed.

Chapter Projects

Choose and complete at least one of the following projects to assess your understanding of the material in this chapter.

⚙ 1. Draw a Bridge between Earth and Heaven

In a vision, God said to St. Catherine of Siena, "I want you to look at the bridge of my only-begotten Son, and notice its greatness. Look! It stretched from heaven to earth, joining the earth of your humanity with the greatness of the Godhead." Use colorful watercolors, pastel chalk, or colored pencils to draw your own representation of a bridge between earth and heaven. Include in your drawing human pilgrims, Jesus, a bridge, and two sides of the bridge: earth and heaven. A bridge can be drawn in different ways. Generally:

- Sketch out the basic structure and shape of the bridge by drawing two towers on either side of an open space.
- Connect the towers with horizonal lines.
- Add the actual roadway or path that runs across the bridge.
- Finally, add railings on either side of the roadway or path.
- *Optional*: Add suspension cables that connect the tops of the towers to the underside of the roadway or path.

⚙ 2. Develop a Plan to Build Your Self-Confidence

God expects you to be the person he created. This means being confident to live out his desires for you. One way to begin this quest is to develop a plan for improving your self-confidence. Write up a personal four-week plan for improving your self-confidence. Each week should be labeled with a primary theme. Under each week, list seven daily tasks you will do to reach your goals. Four examples of primary themes are:

- Draw on support from people who recognize your goodness.
- Replace negative thoughts with positive ones.

- Concentrate on what's really important.
- Pray.

Regarding prayer, never forget that in God you have your number one supporter. God cuts away all the excess of what you can or can't do and loves you just the way you are. In order to achieve your full potential, you must do as well as you can using all of your gifts. But as a child of God, you have been given the common need to love and to be loved. As St. Paul wrote, "Your every act should be done with love" (1 Cor 16:14).

⚙ 3. Report on the Benefits of Going to Confession

As Jesus preached at the start of his public ministry, repentance is one of the very first steps of Christian discipleship. In the Sacrament of Penance, Catholics have a "new possibility to convert and to recover the grace of justification" (*CCC*, 1446) given at Baptism. Arrange to celebrate the Sacrament of Penance in the next few days. (If the sacrament is not offered through your campus ministry program at school, use your parish's or diocesan website to locate Confession times in your area. Many parishes offer weekday opportunities.) Use the opportunity as a springboard for a renewed participation in the life of Christ and his Church. Review "Steps for Celebrating the Sacrament of Penance" in the subsection "Moral Teaching" in the Appendix.

After you go to Confession, write a report listing six benefits of receiving the Sacrament of Penance. First review the list developed by Sr. Mary Ann Walsh, writing on the United States Conference of Catholic Bishops blog. Her list appears in an article titled "Confession: It Puts You Straight with Everyone." One of the benefits Sr. Mary Ann lists is that Confession is "low-cost therapy." She also points out an outward benefit—that Confession contributes to world peace. She explains that peace of the inner heart brings a willingness to share peace outwardly with others. Make your own list, naming six new benefits in your own words. Write at least three sentences to explain each benefit.

⚙ *4. Sing the Virtues*

In addition to the theological or God-given virtues of faith, hope, and love (see Chapter 6, Section 1) are human virtues—that is, "firm attitudes, stable dispositions, habitual perfections of intellect" that are acquired by our own human effort and elevated by God's grace. These are called cardinal virtues and are pivotal or essential for Christian living. They are prudence, justice, fortitude, and temperance. Many other human virtues are grouped around the cardinal virtues, including seven capital virtues first defined by St. Gregory the Great to combat the seven capital sins (pride, greed, gluttony, lust, sloth, envy, and anger).

- Read the brief descriptions of the seven capital virtues below. Research more about their meanings.

- Choose a contemporary song currently popular with your peers. Work individually or with a group of classmates to write new lyrics that expound the positive elements of the capital virtue you have chosen and can be lip-synced to the song. Rehearse the performance. When you are ready, have your performance videotaped by a friend and downloaded to a website that can be viewed at your school. Play the performance for your classmates and teacher.

Seven Capital Virtues

1. *Humility.* This virtue involves modest and selfless behavior. It counters the capital sin of pride.
2. *Generosity.* A generous person is one who is willing to give freely of himself or herself without the need to be repaid. It counters greed.
3. *Chastity.* A counter to the sin of lust, chastity enhances wholesomeness and purity.
4. *Meekness.* Also known as patience, this virtue encourages a patient response to a conflict. This virtue counters anger.
5. *Temperance.* Centered on self-control over desires like food, alcohol, and sex, temperance opposes the sin of gluttony.
6. *Kindness.* This pure form of compassionate love for others is opposed to the sin of envy. It shows itself with a deep, genuine concern for others.
7. *Persistence.* Persistence brings about a willingness to be more zealous in practicing the Catholic faith. This virtue counters sloth or laziness, a

common sin that discourages a person from practicing his or her faith, such as by not attending Sunday Mass.

⚙ *5. Write Three Profiles in Faith*

Write profiles (minimum of three hundred words each) of three people you know (or know of) who best represent what it means to be a disciple of Jesus Christ. *Optional*: Include one or more photos of each person profiled in a notebook or online presentation. The people you choose should exhibit the following qualities of discipleship:

1. Puts personal desires aside to follow the Father's will.
2. Accepts suffering, even to the point of death.
3. Passionately serves others.

Faithful Disciple
Bl. Frédéric Ozanam

When Frédéric Ozanam was a college student at the University of Sorbonne in Paris in the 1830s, he was offended when some of his teachers made fun of the Catholic Church. Ozanam, who had once had his own doubts about the faith, politely but brilliantly defended Church teaching. His fellow students and even the professors took notice. They were especially impressed with his eloquence.

During those years, France was still settling and healing after the collapse of Napoleon's French Empire. Years of war and destruction had left the people poor and cynical. To help defend Catholicism further, Frédéric soon founded a discussion club at the university. One night, after he finished a talk about the contributions of Christianity, one student raised his hand and criticized Frédéric. "All you do is talk about faith," the man said. "Is your faith good for anything besides talk?" That comment stung Frédéric deeply because he believed it to be accurate.

Not long after hearing that remark, Frédéric and a friend began to visit and bring food to the poor in apartment houses all over Paris. They founded a small group under the patronage of St. Vincent de Paul, a sixteenth-century priest who had served the poor, calling it the St. Vincent de Paul Society. Membership in the society grew, and soon communities were established throughout Paris and eventually throughout Europe. Those who joined the groups lived and worked in the spirit of the Beatitudes, especially the

Frédéric Ozanam

fourth Beatitude: "Blessed are they who hunger and thirst for righteousness, for they will be satisfied."

Frédéric Ozanam and his friends knew they were simply doing what Jesus would do—serving and comforting the poor and needy. Frédéric continued his studies and received doctorates in law and literature. In 1841, he married Amélie Soulacroix. They became parents of a daughter, Marie.

Frédéric taught at the Sorbonne, where the students flocked to his classes. But his health began to decline. In 1858, at the age of forty, he died on a journey back to France from Italy. Frédéric's young family was shattered by the loss. But Amélie knew that her husband's work and ministry would live on. Today, the St. Vincent de Paul Society includes hundreds of thousands of members and serves the poor in about 140 countries around the world. In the United States, approximately one-fourth of all parishes have a St. Vincent de Paul chapter (4,428 chapters according to recent statistics).

Frédéric Ozanam was beatified by Pope John Paul II in 1997. Bl. Frédéric Ozanam's feast is celebrated on September 7.

Comprehension

1. How did Frédéric Ozanam first attract notice as a Catholic at the University of Sorbonne?
2. What incident inspired Frédéric to found groups with the intention of serving the poor and needy?
3. Which Beatitude inspired Frédéric's mission?
4. What is the name of the organization that Bl. Frédéric is credited with founding?

Application

The questions that stirred Frédéric to put his faith into action went something like this: "So, you boast about being Catholic, what are you doing? Where are the works that demonstrate your faith?" How would you answer this student's questions for yourself?

Prayer

The Divine Praises were written by Fr. Luigi Felici, SJ, in 1797 as a way to combat blasphemies that were prevalent against God's holy Name. Each of the Divine Praises begins with the words "Blessed be" followed by praises for God, Jesus, Mary, the angels, and the saints. Originally there were eight praises; over the years various popes added six more praises. The Divine Praises are typically recited after the blessing with the Blessed Sacrament at **Benediction**. In 1801, Pope Pius VII granted an indulgence—that is, a remission of sins—for recitation of the Divine Praises.

Divine Praises

> Blessed be God.
> Blessed be his holy Name.
> Blessed be Jesus Christ, true God and true Man.
> Blessed be the name of Jesus.
> Blessed be his most Sacred Heart.
> Blessed be his most Precious Blood.
> Blessed be Jesus in the most holy Sacrament of the altar.
> Blessed be the Holy Spirit, the Paraclete.
> Blessed be the great Mother of God, Mary most holy.
> Blessed be her holy and Immaculate Conception.
> Blessed be her glorious Assumption.
> Blessed be the name of Mary, Virgin and Mother.
> Blessed be Saint Joseph, her most chaste spouse.
> Blessed be God in his angels and in his saints.

Benediction A service in which Christ is adored in the Sacred Host exposed on the altar and in which the priest blesses the faithful with the Sacred Host. The liturgy may include the singing of Latin hymns written by St. Thomas Aquinas, and it concludes with recitation of the Divine Praises.

Appendix

BELIEFS

From the beginning, the Church expressed and handed on her faith in brief formulas accessible to all. There are early formulas of belief in the New Testament, especially in 1 Corinthians 15. Early Christians continued to develop their understanding of the God who saves in Jesus Christ and in the Church, and they formed professions of faith to pass on for generations. These professions of faith are called creeds *because their first word in Latin,* credo, *means "I believe." The following three creeds have special importance in the Church. The Apostles' Creed is an early summary of the Apostles' faith. The Nicene Creed expresses the Church's faith in the Trinitarian God who saves in Jesus Christ. It was developed from the Councils of Nicaea (325) and Constantinople (381) and remains the common profession of faith in the Churches of the East and West; it is typically recited at Mass on Sundays. The Chalcedonian Creed (also known as the Symbol of Chalecedon or the Chalcedonian Definition) was issued by the Council of Chalcedon (451). This creed summarizes the Church's understanding of the Person of Jesus Christ, rejecting the view that we can no longer distinguish Jesus's divinity from his humanity because they became commingled into one (the notion of a single nature in Christ).*

Apostles' Creed

I believe in God,
the Father almighty,
Creator of heaven and earth,
and in Jesus Christ, his only Son, our Lord,
who was conceived by the Holy Spirit,
born of the Virgin Mary,
suffered under Pontius Pilate,
was crucified, died, and was buried;
he descended into hell;
on the third day he rose again from the dead;
he ascended into heaven,
and is seated at the right hand of God the Father Almighty;
from there he will come to judge the living and the dead.

I believe in the Holy Spirit,
the holy catholic Church,
the communion of saints,

the forgiveness of sins,
the resurrection of the body,
and life everlasting. Amen.

Nicene Creed

I believe in one God,
the Father almighty,
maker of heaven and earth,
of all things visible and invisible.

I believe in one Lord Jesus Christ,
the Only Begotten Son of God,
born of the Father before all ages.
God from God, Light from Light,
true God from true God,
begotten, not made, consubstantial with the Father;
through him all things were made.
For us men and for our salvation
he came down from heaven,
and by the Holy Spirit was incarnate of the Virgin Mary,
and became man.

For our sake he was crucified under Pontius Pilate,
he suffered death and was buried,
and rose again on the third day
in accordance with the Scriptures.
He ascended into heaven
and is seated at the right hand of the Father.
He will come again in glory
to judge the living and the dead
and his kingdom will have no end.

I believe in the Holy Spirit, the Lord, the giver of life,
who proceeds from the Father and the Son,
who with the Father and the Son is adored and glorified,
who has spoken through the prophets.

I believe in one, holy, catholic and apostolic Church.
I confess one Baptism for the forgiveness of sins

and I look forward to the resurrection of the dead
and the life of the world to come. Amen.

Chalcedonian Creed

Following therefore the holy Fathers, we unanimously teach to confess one and the same Son, our Lord Jesus Christ, the same perfect in divinity and perfect in humanity, the same truly God and truly man composed of rational soul and body, the same one in being (*homoousios*) with the Father as to the divinity and one in being with us as to the humanity, like unto us in all things but sin (cf. Heb 4:15). The same was begotten from the Father before the ages as to the divinity and in the later days for us and our salvation was born as to his humanity from Mary the Virgin Mother of God.

We confess that one and the same Lord Jesus Christ, the only-begotten Son, must be acknowledged in two natures, without confusion or change, without division or separation. The distinction between the natures was never abolished by their union but rather the character proper to each of the two natures was preserved as they came together in one person (*prosopon*) and one hypostasis. He is not split or divided into two persons, but he is one and the same only-begotten, God the Word, the Lord Jesus Christ, as formerly the prophets and later Jesus Christ himself have taught us about him and has been handed down to us by the Symbol of the Fathers.

DEPOSIT OF FAITH

Deposit of Faith *refers to both Sacred Scripture and Sacred Tradition handed on from the time of the Apostles, from which the Church draws all that she proposes is revealed by God.*

Relationship between Sacred Scripture and Sacred Tradition

The Church does not derive the revealed truths of God from the Holy Scriptures alone. Sacred Tradition hands on God's Word, first given to the Apostles by the Lord and the Holy Spirit, to the successors of the Apostles (the bishops and the pope). Enlightened by the Holy Spirit, these successors faithfully preserve, explain, and spread it to the ends of the earth. The Second Vatican Council Fathers explained the relationship between Sacred Scripture and Sacred Tradition:

> It is clear therefore that, in the supremely wise arrangement of God, Sacred Tradition, Sacred Scripture, and the Magisterium of the Church are so connected and associated that one of them cannot stand without the others. Working together, each in its own way, under the action of the one Holy Spirit, they all contribute effectively to the salvation of souls. (*Dei Verbum*, 10)

THE OLD TESTAMENT

THE PENTATEUCH

Genesis	Gn
Exodus	Ex
Leviticus	Lv
Numbers	Nm
Deuteronomy	Dt

THE HISTORICAL BOOKS

Joshua	Jos
Judges	Jgs
Ruth	Ru
1 Samuel	1 Sm
2 Samuel	2 Sm
1 Kings	1 Kgs
2 Kings	2 Kgs
1 Chronicles	1 Chr
2 Chronicles	2 Chr
Ezra	Ezr
Nehemiah	Neh
Tobit	Tb
Judith	Jdt
Esther	Est
1 Maccabees	1 Mc
2 Maccabees	2 Mc

THE WISDOM BOOKS

Job	Jb
Psalms	Ps(s)
Proverbs	Prv
Ecclesiastes	Eccl
Song of Songs	Sg
Wisdom	Ws
Sirach	Sir

THE PROPHETIC BOOKS

Isaiah	Is
Jeremiah	Jer
Lamentations	Lam
Baruch	Bar
Ezekiel	Ez
Daniel	Dn
Hosea	Hos
Joel	Jl
Amos	Am
Obadiah	Ob
Jonah	Jon
Micah	Mi
Nahum	Na
Habakkuk	Hb
Zephaniah	Zep
Haggai	Hg
Zechariah	Zec
Malachi	Mal

Canon of the Bible

There are seventy-three books in the canon of the Bible—that is, the official list of books the Church accepts as divinely inspired. The canon contains forty-six Old Testament books and twenty-seven New Testament books.

THE NEW TESTAMENT

THE GOSPELS

Matthew	Mt
Mark	Mk
Luke	Lk
John	Jn
Acts of the Apostles	Acts

THE NEW TESTAMENT LETTERS

Romans	Rom
1 Corinthians	1 Cor
2 Corinthians	2 Cor
Galatians	Gal
Ephesians	Eph
Philippians	Phil
Colossians	Col
1 Thessalonians	1 Thes
2 Thessalonians	2 Thes
1 Timothy	1 Tm
2 Timothy	2 Tm
Titus	Ti
Philemon	Phlm
Hebrews	Heb

THE CATHOLIC LETTERS

James	Jas
1 Peter	1 Pt
2 Peter	2 Pt
1 John	1 Jn
2 John	2 Jn
3 John	3 Jn
Jude	Jude
Revelation	Rv

MORAL TEACHING

Morality refers to the goodness or evil of human actions. Listed below are several helps the Church offers for making good and moral decisions.

The Ten Commandments

The Ten Commandments are a main source for Christian morality. God revealed the Ten Commandments to Moses. Jesus himself acknowledged them; he told the rich young man, "If you wish to enter into life, keep the commandments" (Mt 19:17). Since the time of St. Augustine (fourth century), the Ten Commandments have been used as a source for teaching baptismal candidates.

I. I am the Lord, your God: you shall not have strange gods before me.

II. You shall not take the name of the Lord your God in vain.

III. Remember to keep holy the Lord's Day.

IV. Honor your father and your mother.

V. You shall not kill.

VI. You shall not commit adultery.

VII. You shall not steal.

VIII. You shall not bear false witness against your neighbor.

IX. You shall not covet your neighbor's wife.

X. You shall not covet your neighbor's goods.

The Beatitudes

The word *beatitude* means "supreme happiness." Jesus preached the Beatitudes in his Sermon on the Mount (see Matthew 5–7). They are:

Blessed are the poor in spirit, for theirs is the kingdom of heaven.

Blessed are they who mourn, for they will be comforted.

Blessed are the meek, for they will inherit the land.

Blessed are they who hunger and thirst for righteousness, for they will be satisfied.

Blessed are the merciful, for they will be shown mercy.

Blessed are the clean of heart, for they will see God.

Blessed are the peacemakers, for they will be called children of God.

Blessed are they who are persecuted for the sake of righteousness, for theirs is the kingdom of heaven. (Mt 5:3–10)

Theological Virtues

The theological virtues are the foundation for moral life. They are gifts infused into our souls by God:

- faith

- hope

- charity (love)

Cardinal Virtues

Virtues that are acquired by human effort are known as moral or human virtues. Four of these are known as the cardinal virtues, as they form the hinge (*cardinal* comes from the Latin word for "hinge") that connects all the others:

- prudence

- justice

- fortitude

- temperance

Works of Mercy

The works of mercy are charitable actions by which we come to the aid of our neighbor and fulfill his or her bodily and spiritual needs.

Corporal Works of Mercy

1. Feed the hungry.

2. Give drink to the thirsty.

3. Clothe the naked.

4. Visit the imprisoned.

5. Shelter the homeless.

6. Visit the sick.

7. Bury the dead.

Spiritual Works of Mercy

1.   Counsel the doubtful.

2.   Instruct the ignorant.

3.   Admonish sinners.

4.   Comfort the afflicted.

5.   Forgive offenses.

6.   Bear wrongs patiently.

7.   Pray for the living and the dead.

Precepts of the Church

The precepts of the Church are basic obligations for all Catholics decreed by laws of the Church. They are intended to guarantee to Catholics the minimum in prayer and moral effort to facilitate their growth in love for God and neighbor.

1.   You shall attend Mass on Sundays and on holy days of obligation and rest from servile labor.

2.   You shall confess your sins at least once a year.

3.   You shall receive the Sacrament of the Eucharist at least during the Easter season.

4.   You shall observe the days of fasting and abstinence established by the Church.

5.   You shall help to provide for the needs of the Church.

Understanding Sin

Being a moral person entails avoiding sin. Sin is an offense against God.

   Mortal sin is the most serious kind of sin. Mortal sin kills a person's relationship with God. For a sin to be mortal, three conditions must exist:

1.   The moral object must be of grave or serious matter. Grave matter is specified in the Ten Commandments (e.g., do not kill, do not commit adultery, do not steal).

2. The person must have full knowledge of the gravity of the sinful action.

3. The person must deliberately consent to the action. It must be a personal choice.

Venial sin is less serious sin. Examples of venial sins are petty jealousy, disobedience, or "borrowing" a small amount of money without the intention of repaying it. Venial sins, when not repented, can lead a person to commit mortal sins.

Vices are bad habits linked to sins. Vices come from particular sins, especially the seven *capital sins*: pride, avarice, envy, wrath, lust, gluttony, and sloth.

Steps for Celebrating the Sacrament of Penance

- Spend some time examining your conscience. Consider your actions and attitudes in each area of your life (faith, family, school, work, social relationships). Ask yourself: "Is this area of my life pleasing to God? What needs to be reconciled with God? With others? With myself?"

- Sincerely tell God that you are sorry for your sins. Ask God for forgiveness and for the grace you will need to change what needs changing in your life. Promise God that you will try to live according to his will for you.

- Approach the area for Confession. Wait at an appropriate distance until it is your turn.

- Make the Sign of the Cross with the priest. He may say, "May God, who has enlightened every heart, help you to know your sins and trust in his mercy." You reply, "Amen."

- Confess your sins to the priest. Simply and directly talk to him about the areas of sin in your life that need God's healing touch.

- The priest may talk to you about your life and encourage you to be more faithful to God in the future, and he will impose on you a penance for your sin. The penance corresponds as far as possible with the gravity and nature of the sins committed. It can consist of prayer, offerings, works of mercy, service to neighbor, voluntary self-denial, sacrifices, and patient acceptance of the crosses you must bear. You should continue in acts of penance, prayer, charity, and bearing sufferings of all kinds for the removal of the remaining temporal punishment for sin.

- The priest will ask you to express your contrition or sorrow and to pray an Act of Contrition. Pray an Act of Contrition that you have committed to memory. See the subsection "Prayers" in the Appendix for an example.

- The priest will then extend his hands over your head and pray a prayer of absolution for your sins. You respond, "Amen."

- The priest will wish you peace. Thank him and leave.

- Go to a quiet place in the church and pray your prayer of penance. Then spend some time quietly thanking God for the gift of forgiveness.

PRAYERS

Some common Catholic prayers are listed below. The Latin translation for four of the prayers is included. Latin is the official language of the Church. There are occasions when you may pray in Latin (for example, at a World Youth Day when you are with young people who speak many different languages).

Sign of the Cross

In the name of the Father,
and of the Son,
and of the Holy Spirit. Amen.

*In nómine Patris,
et Filii,
et Spíritus Sancti.
Amen.*

Our Father

Our Father
who art in heaven,
hallowed be thy name.
Thy kingdom come;
thy will be done on earth as it is in heaven.
Give us this day our daily bread
and forgive us our trespasses
as we forgive those who trespass against us.
And lead us not into temptation,
but deliver us from evil. Amen.

*Pater noster, qui es in caelis:
sanctificétur nomen tuum;
advéniat regnum tuum;
fiat volúntas tua, sicut in caelo, et in terra.
Panem nostrum quotidiánum da nobis hódie;
et dimítte nobis débita nostra,
sicut et nos dimíttimus debitóribus nostris;
et ne nos inducas in tentatiónem,
sed libera nos a malo.
Amen.*

Glory Be

Glory be to the Father
and to the Son
and to the Holy Spirit,
as it was in the beginning,
is now, and ever shall be,
world without end.
Amen.

Glória Patri
et Fílio
et Spirítui Sancto,
sicut érat in princípio,
et nunc et semper,
et in saécula saeculórum.
Amen.

Hail Mary

Hail Mary, full of grace,
the Lord is with thee.
Blessed art thou among women
and blessed is the fruit of thy womb, Jesus.
Holy Mary, Mother of God,
pray for us sinners
now and at the hour of our death.
Amen.

Ave María, grátia plena,
Dóminus tecum.
Benedícta tu in muliéribus,
et benedíctus fructus ventristui, Iesus.
Sancta María, Mater Dei,
ora pro nobis peccatóribus
nunc et in hora mortis nostræ.
Amen.

Memorare

Remember, O most gracious Virgin Mary,
that never was it known
that anyone who fled to thy protection,
implored thy help,
or sought thy intercession was left unaided.
Inspired by this confidence I fly unto thee,
O virgin of virgins, my Mother,
To thee do I come, before thee I stand,
sinful and sorrowful.
O Mother of the Word Incarnate,
despise not my petitions,
but in thy mercy hear and answer me. Amen.

Fatima Prayer

O my Jesus, forgive us our sins, save us from the fires of hell; lead all
souls to heaven, especially those who have most need of your mercy.

Grace at Meals

Before Meals

Bless us, O Lord,
and these thy gifts,
which we are about to receive from thy bounty,
through Christ our Lord. Amen.

After Meals

We give you thanks, almighty God,
for these and all the gifts
which we have received
from your goodness,
through Christ our Lord. Amen.

Guardian Angel Prayer

Angel of God, my guardian dear,
to whom God's love commits me here,
ever this day be at my side,
to light and guard, to rule and guide. Amen.

Prayer to St. Michael the Archangel

St. Michael the Archangel,
defend us in battle,
Be our defense against the wickedness and snares of the devil.
May God rebuke him, we humbly pray,
and do thou,
O Prince of the heavenly hosts,
by the power of God,
thrust into hell Satan,
and all the evil spirits,
who prowl about the world
seeking the ruin of souls.
Amen.

Prayer for the Faithful Departed

Eternal rest grant unto them, O Lord,
and let perpetual light shine upon them.
May they rest in peace. Amen.

Morning Offering

O Jesus, through the Immaculate Heart of Mary, I offer you my prayers, works, joys, and sufferings of this day in union with the holy sacrifice of the Mass throughout the world. I offer them for all the intentions of your Sacred Heart: the salvation of souls, reparation for sin, and the reunion of all Christians. I offer them for the intentions of our bishops and all Apostles of Prayer and in particular for those recommended by our Holy Father this month. Amen.

Act of Faith

O my God, I firmly believe that you are one God in three divine Persons, Father, Son, and Holy Spirit. I believe that your divine Son became man and died for our sins and that he will come to judge the living and the dead. I believe these and all the truths which the Holy Catholic Church teaches because you have revealed them who are eternal truth and wisdom, who can neither deceive nor be deceived. In this faith I intend to live and die. Amen.

Act of Hope

O Lord God, I hope by your grace for the pardon of all my sins and after life here to gain eternal happiness because you have promised it who are infinitely powerful, faithful, kind, and merciful. In this hope I intend to live and die. Amen.

Act of Love

O Lord God, I love you above all things and I love my neighbor for your sake because you are the highest, infinite and perfect good, worthy of all my love. In this love I intend to live and die. Amen.

Act of Contrition

O my God, I am heartily sorry for having offended thee, and I detest all my sins because of thy just punishment, but most of all because they offend thee, my God, who art all good and deserving of all my love. I firmly resolve with the help of thy grace to sin no more and to avoid the near occasion of sin. Amen.

DEVOTIONS

Devotions are external acts of holiness that are not part of the Church's official liturgy but are popular spiritual practices of Catholics. Catholics have expressed their piety through practices such as the veneration of relics, visits to churches, pilgrimages, processions, the Stations of the Cross, religious dances, the Rosary, the Chaplet of Divine Mercy, and wearing religious medals. Some popular Catholic devotions are included in this subsection.

The Mysteries of the Rosary

The Joyful Mysteries

1. The Annunciation

2. The Visitation

3. The Nativity

4. The Presentation

5. The Finding in the Temple

The Mysteries of Light

1. The Baptism of Jesus

2. The Wedding Feast of Cana

3. The Proclamation of the Kingdom, with the Call to Conversion

4. The Transfiguration

5. The Institution of the Eucharist

The Sorrowful Mysteries

1. The Agony in the Garden

2. The Scourging at the Pillar

3. The Crowning with Thorns

4. The Carrying of the Cross

5. The Crucifixion

The Glorious Mysteries

1.   The Resurrection

2.   The Ascension

3.   The Descent of the Holy Spirit

4.   The Assumption of Mary

5.   The Coronation of Mary, Queen of Heaven and Earth

How to Pray the Rosary

Opening

1.   Begin on the crucifix and pray the Apostles' Creed.

2.   On the first bead, pray the Our Father.

3.   On each of the next three beads, pray the Hail Mary. (Some people meditate on the theological virtues of faith, hope, and charity on these beads.)

4.   On the fifth bead, pray the Glory Be.

5.   Pray the Fatima Prayer.

The Body

Each decade (set of ten beads) is organized as follows:

1.   On the large bead that comes before each set of ten, announce the mystery (see above), and pray one Our Father.

2.   On each of the ten smaller beads, recite one Hail Mary while meditating on the mystery.

3.   Pray one Glory Be at the end of the decade. (There is no bead for the Glory Be.)

Conclusion

Pray the following prayer at the end of the Rosary:

> *Hail, Holy Queen*
> Hail, holy Queen, Mother of Mercy,
> our life, our sweetness, and our hope.
> To thee do we cry,
> poor banished children of Eve.
> To thee do we send up our sighs,
> mourning and weeping in this valley of tears.
> Turn then, most gracious advocate,
> thine eyes of mercy toward us,
> and after this our exile,
> show unto us the blessed fruit of thy womb, Jesus.
> O clement, O loving, O sweet Virgin Mary.
>
> V. Pray for us, O holy Mother of God,
> R. That we may be made worthy of the promises of Christ.
> Amen.

The Stations of the Cross

The Stations of the Cross is a meditative prayer based on the Passion of Christ. This devotion developed in the Middle Ages as a way to allow the faithful to retrace the last steps of Jesus on his way to Calvary without making the journey to the Holy Land. Most Catholic churches have images or symbols of the Stations depicted on side walls to help Catholics imagine the sufferings of Jesus and focus on the meaning of the Paschal Mystery. Praying the Stations means meditating on each of the following scenes:

1. Jesus is condemned to death.

2. Jesus takes up his Cross.

3. Jesus falls the first time.

4. Jesus meets his mother.

5. Simon of Cyrene helps Jesus carry his Cross.

6. Veronica wipes the face of Jesus.

7. Jesus falls the second time.

8. Jesus consoles the women of Jerusalem.

9. Jesus falls the third time.

10. Jesus is stripped of his garments.

11. Jesus is nailed to the Cross.

12. Jesus dies on the Cross.

13. Jesus is taken down from the Cross.

14. Jesus is laid in the tomb.

Some churches also include a fifteenth Station, the Resurrection of the Lord.

How to Pray the Divine Mercy Chaplet

You can use rosary beads or a special Divine Mercy Chaplet to pray the Divine Mercy Chaplet.

Opening

1. Make the Sign of the Cross.

2. Pray the Optional Opening Prayer:

St. Faustina's Prayer for Sinners

> O Jesus, eternal Truth, our Life, I call upon you and I beg your mercy for poor sinners. O sweetest Heart of my Lord, full of pity and unfathomable mercy, I plead with you for poor sinners. O Most Sacred Heart, Fount of Mercy from which gush forth rays of inconceivable graces upon the entire human race, I beg of you light for poor sinners. O Jesus, be mindful of your own bitter Passion and do not permit the loss of souls redeemed at so dear a price of your most precious Blood. O Jesus, when I consider the great price of your Blood, I rejoice at its immensity, for one drop alone would have been enough for the salvation of all sinners. Although sin is an abyss of wickedness and ingratitude, the price paid for us can never be equaled. Therefore, let every soul trust in the Passion of the Lord, and place its hope in his mercy. God will not deny his mercy to anyone. Heaven and earth may change, but God's mercy will never be exhausted. Oh, what immense joy burns in my heart when I contemplate your incomprehensible goodness, O Jesus! I

desire to bring all sinners to your feet that they may glorify your mercy throughout endless ages. (*Diary of Saint Maria Faustina Kowalska*, 72)

You expired, Jesus, but the source of life gushed forth for souls, and the ocean of mercy opened up for the whole world. O Fount of Life, unfathomable Divine Mercy, envelop the whole world and empty yourself out upon us.

O Blood and Water, which gushed forth from the Heart of Jesus as a fount of mercy for us, I trust in you! (*Repeat three times.*)

3. Pray the Our Father.

4. Pray the Hail Mary.

5. Pray the Apostles' Creed.

Body

6. On a large bead pray the Eternal Father:

Eternal Father, I offer you the Body and Blood, Soul and Divinity, of your dearly beloved Son, Our Lord Jesus Christ, in atonement for our sins and those of the whole world.

7. On the ten small beads of each decade say:

For the sake of his sorrowful Passion, have mercy on us and on the whole world. (*Repeat for the remaining four decades.*)

Concluding Prayer

8. Pray the Holy God:

Holy God, Holy Mighty One, Holy Immortal One, have mercy on us and on the whole world. *(Repeat three times.)*

9. Pray the Closing Prayers:

Eternal God, in whom mercy is endless and the treasury of compassion—inexhaustible, look kindly upon us and increase your mercy in us, that in difficult moments we might not despair nor become despondent, but with great confidence submit ourselves to your holy will, which is Love and Mercy itself.

O greatly merciful God, Infinite Goodness, today all mankind calls out from the abyss of its misery to your mercy—to your compassion, O God; and it is with its mighty voice of misery that it cries out. Gracious God, do not reject the prayer of this earth's exiles! O Lord, Goodness beyond our understanding, who are acquainted with our misery through and through, and know that by our own power we cannot ascend to you, we implore you: anticipate us with your grace and keep on increasing your mercy in us, that we may faithfully do your holy will all through our life and at death's hour. Let the omnipotence of your mercy shield us from the darts of our salvation's enemies, that we may with confidence, as your children, await your [Son's] final coming—that day known to you alone. And we expect to obtain everything promised us by Jesus in spite of all our wretchedness. For Jesus is our Hope: through his merciful Heart, as through an open gate, we pass through to heaven. (*Diary*, 1570)

CHALLENGE QUESTIONS

In considering the mystery of Jesus Christ, who is both God and man, there are many related questions to ponder and study. Here are some additional questions and information related to topics central to this course.

Are the Writings in the Bible True?

Yes, the Bible conveys God's truth. The Bible teaches "firmly, faithfully, and without error that truth which God, for the sake of our salvation, wished to see confided to the Sacred Scriptures" (*Dei Verbum*, 11).

But if this question refers to whether everything in the Bible is scientifically or historically true, the answer is no. Think of the Bible as a library of books with many different literary forms. These include poetry, allegories, fables, speeches, short stories, census lists, and historical accounts. To discover the religious truth of the Bible, we must first identify which type of literature is being examined. Then we must ask what the biblical writer meant to communicate about God and salvation by using that particular literary form.

Take, for example, the parable of the prodigal son (Lk 15:11–32). Was there historically a younger son like the one Jesus described in his story, one who squandered his inheritance? Most likely there was no real, historical person behind the passage. Jesus told this vivid short story to reveal in a graphic way God's forgiving love for sinners.

The historical accuracy of whether Jesus told the parable is clearer. The Gospels and many other elements of the Bible (for example, the chronicles of the Israelite kingdom and the missionary travels of St. Paul) are reliable and verifiable historical records.

The Bible must always be read under the guidance of the Holy Spirit, by whose inspiration it was written. Further, to understand the truth of the Bible, we must be attentive to both the content and the unity of the whole Scripture. For example, we can understand more clearly the meaning of the Old Testament passages in light of what Jesus accomplished in the New Testament. Also, the Bible should always be read within the living Tradition of the Church, meaning that we should be attentive to the Church's interpretation of Scripture. Finally, those who interpret Scripture must be attentive to the analogy of faith—that is, how the various truths of faith are related among themselves and to God's whole plan of salvation (see *CCC*, 112–114).

It always takes prayerful reflection to understand the truth of the Bible. Furthermore, it is helpful to refer to a good biblical commentary for further insight. Finally, Catholics should look to the Church's Magisterium for help to understand the controversial passages, since Jesus entrusted the pope and bishops to interpret authentically the Word of God. This is what it means to read the Bible within the living Tradition of the Church.

Further Research

Catholics understand the Bible as the "book of the Church," while some non-Catholic Christians describe membership in a "church of the Book." What do these descriptions mean? How are they different? See the *Catechism of the Catholic Church*, paragraph 108.

How Can You Be Sure That What the Catholic Church Teaches Comes from God?

The truth about God revealed by Jesus was entrusted to St. Peter and the Apostles. The Catholic Church—the Church in union with the pope, the successor of St. Peter—bases her teachings on the understanding of Revelation that has developed through history. Her claim to teach the truth about God is based on the consistent witness of every generation of the faithful.

Many ecclesial communities with roots in the Protestant Reformation base their teachings on Scripture, on the reformers' interpretation of Scripture, and on modern theology. They feel no particular obligation to maintain a connection with the understanding of Revelation in other periods of history.

The Catholic Church, on the other hand, is never free to disregard those things that have been declared truths of faith by the Church in earlier generations. The Catholic Church places a strong emphasis on the presence of the Holy Spirit guiding the Church in all generations. The Catholic Church does not ignore the faith of any of the generations of the Church because all of the generations are part of the whole.

Further Research

Read paragraphs 74–79 of the *Catechism of the Catholic Church*. How is God's Revelation transmitted through the Apostolic Tradition of the Church?

What Did Jesus Teach about the End of the World?

In the Nicene Creed, Catholics profess that Jesus "will come again to judge the living and the dead" (see the subsection "The Father Assigns Judgment to the Son" in Chapter 2, Section 3). Whereas your particular judgment occurs at the moment of your death, the Last or General Judgment is reserved for the end of the world. People of every generation have wondered when this will be.

When the disciples asked, "When will this happen?" (Mt 24:3), Jesus told them, "But of that day and hour no one knows, neither the angels of heaven, nor the Son, but the Father alone" (Mt 24:36). Nevertheless, it is clear from the record of the early Church in the Acts of the Apostles that many early Christians believed that Jesus's Second Coming would occur in their lifetimes. The Second Coming is the name for the final judgment of all humanity when Christ returns to earth. It is also known by its Greek name, *Parousia*, which means "arrival."

Though the day and hour of Christ's return and the end of the world are unknown, Jesus emphasized the need to always be prepared. He reminded the disciples that in the days before Noah entered the ark, people were living their lives without any sense that a great flood was coming. Jesus reminded his audience, and people of every generation, "Stay awake! For you do not know on which day your Lord will come" (Mt 24:42).

Further Research

What will occur at the end of time when God establishes the "new heaven and new earth"? See the *Catechism of the Catholic Church*, paragraphs 1042–1047.

Can God Be Thought of as "Mother"?

The Church teaches that God is pure spirit and has no gender. Christ himself revealed God as Father. However, there are certainly attributes of both motherhood and fatherhood that can help us understand how God the Father takes care of his people.

Old Testament references to God's parental tenderness and love as maternal traits include the following:

- "As a mother comforts her child, so I will comfort you" (Is 66:13).

- "Can a mother forget her infant, be without tenderness for the child of her womb? Even should she forget, I will never forget you" (Is 49:15).

Jesus himself used feminine images when teaching about God's love. For example, he compared God to a woman who rejoiced when she found a lost coin (see Luke 15:8–10). On another occasion, he said his own desire to gather the people of Jerusalem was like that of a hen who gathered her young under her wings (see Matthew 23:37).

In 1999, Pope John Paul II, in his reflections on the parable of the prodigal son, said that the father in the parable had "all the characteristics of fatherhood *and* motherhood" and that when the father embraced the son, he seemed to show "the profile of a mother."

Further Research

Read the *Catechism of the Catholic Church*, paragraphs 355 and 369–370. What additional insight did can you add to the question "Can God be thought of as 'Mother'?"

Does God Love a Person No Matter What They Do?

Yes, God does love a person no matter what. God's nature is love. He cannot ever stop loving you—the person he made in his own image. He proved his love by sending his only Son, Jesus Christ, to suffer and die for your sins. Does this mean that you can do whatever you want and just assume God will forgive you? No, it doesn't. There are two reasons why this is so.

The first is that you may develop the attitude that you can sin and not worry about it because God will forgive you some time in the future. This attitude is the sin of presumption—that is, presuming that God will forgive you despite your disregard of his commandments.

The second danger with this attitude is that you would really be using God. And to use God in that way is to mock him. You would be daring God to forgive you because of his great compassion and love. However, don't forget this point: God can only forgive you if you are truly sorry for your sins. True sorrow or contrition for your sins means that you turn away from your sins and whatever leads you into sin. You must also have a "firm purpose of amendment"—that is, of not sinning again.

True, God's love is boundless and eternal. But your salvation does have a condition attached to it: you must freely respond to his love by turning away from your sins.

Further Research

The Bible teaches the immense love God has for each person. The Bible also teaches one condition of God's love: God does not love sin. List one example from the Old Testament and one example from the New Testament of the condition God places on humans to give up their sinfulness.

Given the Human Inclination to Sin, Can a Person Really Have Free Will?

The Church teaches that the Original Sin of Adam and Eve has been transmitted or passed down to all of their descendants. So, each person is born in a condition of sin. This condition can be removed through Baptism and the merits of Jesus Christ. Nonetheless, much of the pain and sorrow in the world is not due to Original Sin but to the continued and deliberate sins of individuals and groups. Unlike Original Sin, these are actual sins. They are offenses against God that people deliberately choose to commit. However, committing a sin is not inevitable. You are not programmed to say yes to the temptation to sin. You do have free will; you can say no.

God has honored you with the ability to choose because he knows that love needs freedom. In the First Letter to the Corinthians, St. Paul reminds the Church in Corinth that "God is faithful and will not let you be tried beyond your strength" (1 Cor 10:13). In this passage, St. Paul is also referring to grace. If a temptation is too strong for you, it is not too strong for God; he will strengthen you if you ask for help. God also gives you sufficient wisdom to choose to do the right thing.

Further Research

Read paragraph 1732 of the *Catechism of the Catholic Church*. Summarize this statement as an answer to the question posed above.

GLOSSARY

apocalypse A word meaning "revelation" or "unveiling" and often associated with the end times or the Second Coming of Christ. Also, *apocalyptic writing* is the name of the literary genre in the Bible that uses inspired, highly symbolic language to bolster faith by reassuring believers that the current age, subject to forces of evil, will end when God intervenes and establishes a divine rule of goodness and peace.

Arianism A heresy common in certain times and places during the early Church that denied that Jesus was truly God. It is named after Arius (AD 250–336), a priest and popular preacher from Alexandria, Egypt.

Assumption of Mary The dogmatic teaching of the Church that when the earthly life of Mary was completed, she was taken body and soul into the presence of God. Mary was granted this grace because she is the sinless Mother of God.

Benediction A service in which Christ is adored in the Sacred Host exposed on the altar and in which the priest blesses the faithful with the Sacred Host. The liturgy may include the singing of Latin hymns written by St. Thomas Aquinas, and it concludes with recitation of the Divine Praises.

Church Fathers Bishops, theologians, teachers, and scholars whose writings have greatly contributed to Church doctrine and practice. In both the Western Church and the Eastern Church, four Fathers are most prominent. In the Western Church, they are St. Ambrose (AD 340–397), St. Jerome (AD 347–420), St. Augustine (AD 354–430), and St. Gregory the Great (AD 540–604). In the Eastern Church, they are St. Basil (ca. AD 329–379), St. Athanasius (ca. AD 296–373), St. Gregory of Nazianzus (AD 329–ca. 398), and St. John Chrysostom (AD 347–407).

Communion of Saints The unity among members of Christ's Body, living and deceased, made possible by Baptism. The Communion of Saints is the Church on earth, in heaven, and in Purgatory.

concupiscence The disordered nature of human appetites or desires, one of the temporal consequences of Original Sin. The state of concupiscence remains even after Baptism and produces an inclination to sin.

Deposit of Faith The body of saving truths and core beliefs of Catholicism that are contained in Sacred Scripture and Sacred Tradition and are faithfully preserved and handed on by the Magisterium. The Deposit of Faith contains the fullness of God's Revelation.

divine providence God's loving and watchful guidance over his creatures on their way to their final goal and perfection.

Docetism A first-century heresy that taught that Jesus only "seemed" to be human. Docetism comes from a Greek word meaning "to seem."

domestic church A name for the Christian family. In the family, parents and children exercise their priesthood of the baptized by worshipping God, receiving the sacraments, and witnessing to Christ and the Church by living as faithful disciples.

evangelization The bringing of the Good News of Jesus Christ to others through words and actions.

Exsultet The first words in Latin of the proclamation sung at the Easter Vigil. The opening words in English are, "Now let the angelic host of heaven exult, exult the mysteries divine; and for the victory of so great a King, sound the trumpet of salvation." The Exsultet was originally credited to St. Augustine in the fifth century, but it was probably composed later.

First Saturday A devotion requested by Mary of the children of Fatima for the reparation of sins. To complete the First Saturday devotion, Catholics must do all of the following on the First Saturday of the month for five consecutive months: (1) go to Confession (may be eight days before or after First Saturday); (2) receive Holy Communion (can be at a Saturday evening vigil Mass); (3) pray five decades of the Rosary; (4) keep Our Lady company for fifteen minutes. This can be done by meditating on one or more of the mysteries of the Rosary.

free will The capacity to choose among alternatives. Free will is "the power, rooted in reason and will . . . to perform deliberate actions on one's own responsibility" (*CCC*, 1731).

idolatry The worship of idols. Idolatry is an offense against the First Commandment, in which God says that we are to have "no other gods besides me." A form of idolatry prevalent today is secularism, in which people claim to be free to create their own destiny. Idolatry is always a grave sin.

Immaculate Conception The belief that Mary was conceived in her mother's womb without the stain of Original Sin that all other human beings inherit. This teaching was declared infallible by Pope Pius IX in 1854.

Last (or General) Judgment Jesus Christ's judgment of the living and the dead on the last day, when he will come again to fully establish God's Kingdom.

metanoia A change of heart from sin to the practice of virtue. Literally, "repentance" or "penance."

Monophysitism From the Greek words *monos*, which means "one" or "alone," and *physis*, which means "nature"; a fifth-century heresy that promoted the error that Jesus had only one nature, a divine nature. In response, the Church taught that Christ has two natures, divine and human.

monstrance A sacred vessel that holds the Blessed Sacrament when it is exposed for veneration. The word *monstrance* comes from the Latin word for "show."

original holiness and original justice The state of man and woman in paradise before sin. The grace of original holiness was to share in the divine life (see *CCC*, 375). "The inner harmony of the human person, the harmony between man and woman, and finally the harmony between the first couple and all creation, comprised the state called 'original justice'" (*CCC*, 376). "From [Adam and Eve's] friendship with God flowed the happiness of their existence in paradise" (*CCC*, 384).

Original Sin Refers to the personal sin of the first two people, called Adam and Eve, which, in an analogous way, describes the fallen state of human nature into which all generations are born. Adam and Eve transmitted Original Sin to their descendants. Jesus came to save the world from Original Sin and all personal sin.

particular judgment The individual judgment of every person right after death, when Christ will rule on one's eternal destiny in heaven (after purification in Purgatory, if needed) or in hell.

precepts of the Church Basic obligations all Catholics are called to follow to help them become good and moral people. The precepts include attending Mass on Sundays and holy days of obligation, confessing one's sins at least once a year, receiving Holy Communion as a minimum requirement during the Easter season, observing days of fasting and abstinence, and providing for the needs of the Church.

Protoevangelium A term that means "the first gospel," which is found in Genesis 3:15, where God reveals that he will send a Savior to redeem the world from its sins.

redemption The name for Christ's sacrificial Death on the Cross that paid the price to free us from the slavery of sin.

religion A set of beliefs and practices followed by those committed to the service and worship of God (*CCC*, Glossary).

Sh'ma The Hebrew name for "hear." It is the first word of the most important Jewish prayer, which is recited daily in the morning and at night: "Hear, O Israel, the Lord is our God, the Lord is one. And as for you, you shall love the Lord your God with all your heart, with all your soul, and with all your strength."

Targums The name for Aramaic paraphrases or translations of the Jewish Bible that came into prominence in the first century when Hebrew was declining as the spoken language in and around Palestine.

theological virtues Three foundational virtues that are infused by God into the souls of the faithful: faith (belief in and personal knowledge of God), hope (trust in God's salvation and his bestowal of the graces needed to attain it), and charity (love of God and love of neighbor as oneself).

tongues Private speech directed toward God in inarticulate terms. Needs interpretation to be understood by others.

NOTES

1. Jesus Is the Way, the Truth, and the Life

1. John Paul II, *Crossing the Threshold of Hope* (New York: Knopf, 1994).

2. Paraphrased from Fr. Dwight Longenecker, "Evidence for the Resurrection," *Catholic Digest*, May 4, 2020.

3. Michael Joseph Carzon, "Historical Evidence for the Resurrection of Jesus," *Missio Dei*, October 3, 2022.

2. Jesus Reveals What God Is Like

1. John Paul II, *Crossing the Threshold of Hope*.

2. Pope John Paul II, *Crossing the Threshold of Hope*.

3. John Paul II, *Crossing the Threshold of Hope*, 62.

4. John Paul II, *Crossing the Threshold of Hope*, 66.

3. Jesus Reveals More about God in Three Persons

1. Quoted from St. Maximilian Kolbe, *Final Sketch*, in H. M. Manteau-Bonamy, *Immaculate Conception and the Holy Spirit: The Marian Teachings of St. Maximilian Kolbe*, trans. Richard Arnandez (Kenosha, WI: Prow Books, 1977).

2. Peter Kreeft, "What Catholics Believe," in *God*, Part I (New Haven, CT: Knights of Columbus, 2000).

4. Jesus's Own Life Reveals More about the Nature of God

1. *Koine* is pronounced "KOY-nay."

2. St. Justin, Apol. 1, 65–67: PG 6, 428–29, quoted in *CCC*, 1345.

3. John Paul II, *Crossing the Threshold of Hope*.

5. Jesus's Own Mother Leads Us to Him

1. Paraphrased from Raymond J. de Souza, "Is Mary the Mother of God . . . or Only the Mother of Jesus?" *Missio Immaculatae*, January 13, 2017.

2. Paraphrased from Raymond J. de Souza, "Is Mary the Mother of God . . . or Only the Mother of Jesus?" *Missio Immaculatae*, January 13, 2017.

3. *The Works of Luther*, Weimar edition.

4. Irenaeus, *Against Heresies*.

5. Cyril of Alexandria, *Against the Emperor Julian*, 8.

6. *Against Heresies*, III, Ch. 2, 4

7. Pope John Paul II, "Mary, the New Eve, Freely Obeyed God," quoted from EWTN, 1999.

8. *On Luke* 2.6–7.

9. *Angelus* address, October 28, 1978.

10. Pope Francis, *Video Message to the Bishop of Gozo*, 3.

6. Jesus Calls Us to Faith

1. St. Alphonsus Liguori, *Glories of Mary*.

2. *Brothers Karamazov*, quoted in Michel Bettigole and James D. Childs, *The Catholic Spirit: An Anthology for Discovering Faith through Literature, Art, Film, and Music* (Note Dame, IN: Ave Maria Press, 2010).

3. Much of this information is from "St. José Sánchez del Río: Teenage Martyr for the Faith," *Catholic News Herald*, February 5, 2022.

4. Interview with St. Josemaría Escrivá, "The Virtue of Poverty," published in *Conversations with Saint Josemaría Escrivá* (Princeton, NJ: Scepter, 2002), and online at https://stjosemaria.org/category/blog/homilies/.

5. "How Are Schools Preventing Bullying?," 2023, report provided by study.com.

6. Basically, those who do not display autistic or atypical thoughts or behaviors.

7. Denis Grasska, "Catholic Teen with Special Needs Heads to High School," *Southern Cross*, September 6, 2020.

8. Fr. Goyo Hidalgo's book about his return to the practice of the Catholic faith is called *From Prodigal to Priest: A Journey Home to Family, Faith, and the Father's Embrace* (Notre Dame, IN: Ave Maria Press, 2023).

9. Hidalgo, *From Prodigal to Priest*

10. *Adv. haeres.* 1, 10, 1–2: PG 7/1, 549–52, quoted in *CCC*, 173.

11. The talks took place from February 6 to April 5, 1980.

12. Brian Porter, "Catholic Church in Poland," Making the History of 1989 (website), https://chnm.gmu.edu/1989/exhibits/roman-catholic-church/introduction.html.

13. Quoted from *Today's Catholic*, December 21, 2021.

14. Julie Asher, "First National Prayer Vigil for Life Post-Roe Calls Catholics to Bring God's Love into 'Empty Spaces,'" *Catholic Review*, January 20, 2023.

7. Jesus Calls Disciples

1. Information from a 2018 Pew Research Study.

2. "'I Want the Church to Go into the Streets'—Pope Addresses Fellow Argentines," *Salt and Light Media*, July 26, 2013.

3. "Prayer Has the Power to Change Lives, Hearts, Pope Says," Catholic News Service, January 9, 2019.

4. General Audience, February 3, 2021.

8. Jesus Calls You

1. Scarlett Thompson, "Radiant Light: Elizabeth Wang," Bridgeman Images, August 23, 2021, and Radiant Light website (www.radiantlight.org/uk).

2. Sarah J. Pedrozo, "The Bridge of St. Catherine of Siena," April 30, 2022, Catholic365.com.

3. Opening Address by Pope Francis, World Youth Day, 2013.

4. Sermon 73, 4: PL 54, 396, quoted in *CCC*, 412.

5. Cindy Wooden, "Adore Jesus' Real Presence in the Eucharist, Pope Tells U.S. Catholics," Catholic News Service, June 19, 2023.

SUBJECT INDEX

PHOTO CREDITS

Adobe Stock
page 109

Alamy
pages 4, 7, 8, 11, 16, 17, 26, 37, 41, 60, 80, 81, 88, 101, 119, 120, 122, 130, 135, 160, 179, 180, 198, 227, 228, 230, 231, 265, 276

AP Newsroom
page 277

Ave Maria Press
page 286

Bridgeman Images
pages 77, 115, 125, 136, 352

Catholic Relief Services
page 285

Conrad Schmitt Studios, Inc.
page 232

Getty
pages 2, 5, 8, 13, 15, 19, 24, 25, 28, 29, 31, 32, 33, 34, 35, 36, 38, 40, 42, 44, 46, 48, 56, 62, 63, 64, 65, 67, 68, 70, 73, 74, 77, 83, 85, 86, 87, 90, 91, 92, 106, 108, 109, 111, 112, 113, 118, 119, 124, 126, 131, 139, 142, 148, 158, 161, 162, 164, 168, 170, 172, 174, 176, 177, 178, 180, 184, 185, 187, 200, 204, 206, 207, 208, 209, 211, 214, 216, 218, 219, 220, 223, 224, 235, 237, 239, 242, 245, 246, 247, 258, 264, 267, 269, 270, 271, 275, 278, 282, 283, 289, 290, 292, 294, 302, 306, 308, 309, 310, 314, 315, 316, 319, 320, 321, 323, 326, 328, 329, 331, 333, 335, 336, 354, 355, 357, 358, 360, 361, 362, 366, 367, 369, 371, 372, 376, 377, 379, 380, 381, 391

Granger
page 43

Militia of the Immaculata
page 139

Reuters
pages 192, 240, 348

TheCatholicKid.com
page 115

Vanderbilt University Divinity Library
page 134

Wikimedia Commons
pages 153, 198, 262